CALIFORNIA

McDougal Littell Science

Interactive
Reader

FOCUS ON PHYSICAL SCIENCES

Focus on Physical Sciences
Interactive Reader

Table of Contents

To the Student

The Interactive Reader makes reading science exciting. As you read, you can interact with this book. You can write in the book to help you remember what you have read.

Before each chapter, The Big Idea helps you understand what the chapter will be about. You can review ideas and words that you learned earlier. Use the preview activities to help you learn new words.

As you read each chapter:

- Instant Replay questions quickly check your understanding of what you read. You can write your answers on the page.

- Mark It Up boxes are near some of the pictures. These will help you draw a reminder about the concepts you have just learned.

- Activity reminders refer to activities and labs in the student text. They give you a fun way to do science.

- Academic Vocabulary words are defined at the bottom of some pages. These words occur in all subject areas.

- Sample Calculations show you how to use scientific formulas. You can follow the steps needed to solve a problem.

- Visual Connections refer to helpful pictures in your student text.

- ClassZone.com boxes tell you about more activities on the Internet.

At the end of each chapter, review what you have learned. Answer the questions about vocabulary and key concepts. Practice using your math skills. The Big Idea question reminds you about the main focus of each chapter. Test Practice questions help you become comfortable with multiple-choice science questions.

The Interactive Reader makes science fun and easier to understand!

CHAPTER

1 Motion

the BIG idea

The motion of an object can be described and predicted.

Getting Ready to Learn

Review Concepts

- Objects can move at different speeds and in different directions.

- Pushing or pulling on an object will change how it moves.

Activity

Rolling Along
See student text, page 7.

Review Vocabulary

Draw a line to connect each word with its definition.

horizontal	a unit of time equal to $\frac{1}{60}$ of a minute
meter	straight up and down from a level surface
second	level, parallel to the ground
vertical	a unit of length equal to 39.37 inches

Preview Key Vocabulary

Following are some key terms you will see in this chapter. As you read the chapter, note how different terms are related. Use the diagrams to explain the relationship between each pair of terms.

position ——————— motion

speed ——————— velocity

velocity ——————— acceleration

Student text pages
8–15

How can you describe where something is?

Where is your science reading workbook? Most likely, it is right in front of you. When you say your book is right in front of you, you are describing the position of your book. The **position** of an object* or place is the location of that object or place. Often you describe where something is by comparing its position to where you are.

What is the position of an object?

_____

Highlight the sentence that gives the definition.

Activity

Location
See student text,
page 9.

Use a Reference Point

When you say that your book is in front of you, you are describing the book's position using a reference point. In this case, the reference point is you. Any object or place can be a reference point. A **reference point** is a location to which you can compare another location. How could you describe the position of the bus in the picture? What reference point would you use? Here is one way:

The bus is in front of the school.

| the object | the reference point |

*Academic Vocabulary: An **object** is a thing. You can see and touch objects.

Use a Reference Direction

A reference point is one thing you need to describe the position of an object or a place. The other thing you need is a reference direction. Suppose someone tells you that a bird is ten meters above a house. The *house* is the reference point. The reference direction is *above*. To find the bird, you would look up ten meters over the house. The reference direction tells which way the object is from the reference point. The bird is ten meters *above* the *house*.

We use different sets of reference directions to talk about places. *In front of, behind, above,* and so on, tell about the position of something that is close to the reference point. To locate things farther away, we use the directions north, south, east, and west. We can also use combinations of directions. These include northeast, northwest, southeast, and southwest.

Using a Reference Point and a Reference Direction

Suppose you want to describe the position of a city. First you need a reference point. This could be another city that many people know. For example, Brasília is a large city in Brazil. Someone living in Brazil might use Brasília as a reference point. Find Santiago, Chile, on the map. Where is Santiago compared with the reference point of Brasília? You need a reference direction. Use the compass rose to help you. Santiago is southwest of Brasília.

A reference direction, however, is not enough to locate Santiago. You also need to know how far away Santiago is from Brazília. The distance is 3000 kilometers (km). Your full description of the position would include the reference point, the reference direction, and the distance. Santiago is 3000 kilometers southwest of Brazília.

To tell the position of an object or place, what three things do you need?

_____   _____   _____

What is Motion?

The picture shows a girl making a long jump. If you could watch her jump, you would see her moving. We say that she is in motion. **Motion** is a change of position over time.

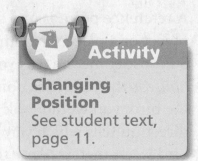

Activity

Changing Position
See student text, page 11.

Vertical

Horizontal

As the girl jumps, she moves forward. We say that her horizontal position changes. As the girl jumps, she also goes up. Then she comes down. We say that her vertical position changes.

If you did not see the girl jump, you could still tell that she had moved. That is because first she is in one place. A few seconds later, she is in another place. The change in position tells you that motion occurred.

How do you know if something has moved?

_____

SECTION 1.1	
SUMMARIZE	**VOCABULARY**
1. Pick an object in the room you are in. Describe its position. Label the reference point or reference points you used. Circle each reference direction you used. _____ _____ _____	Circle the word that makes each sentence correct. 2. The **position / reference point** of a place or object is the location of that place or object. 3. A **reference direction / reference point** is a location you use to compare other locations. 4. A change in **position / reference point** shows that motion has occurred.

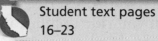

Student text pages 16–23

What is speed?

When you ride a bicycle, you might pass people who are walking. You are going at a faster speed than the walkers. In science, **speed** is a measure of how fast something moves, or the distance an object covers in a set time. Speed can be calculated from measures of distance and time.

Activity

Speed
See student text, page 16.

Understanding Speed

The girl on the bicycle goes from point 1 to point 2. The distance is 4 meters. The clock shows that it took her 1 second. The girl went 4 meters in 1 second.

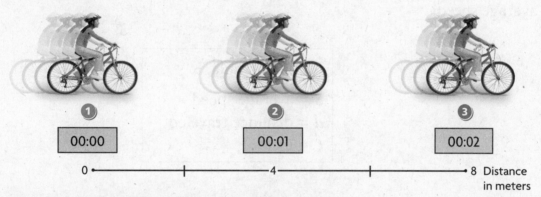

① 00:00   ② 00:01   ③ 00:02

0 ———————— 4 ———————— 8 Distance in meters

Measuring Distance and Time

To figure out the speed of something, you need to know two things—the distance the object went and the time it took to go that distance.

1. **Distance** The distance an object moves is the amount of space, measured along a line, between the starting and ending points. You can measure distance in many different units. Scientists often use meters or kilometers to measure distance.

2. **Time** The time an object takes to move a distance is usually measured in seconds, minutes, or hours.

What two things do you use to measure speed?

_____   _____

What is average speed?

When you ride a bicycle, you probably change your speed often. You go slower when you ride uphill. You go faster when you ride downhill. It is hard to figure out your speed at each second. Your average speed is the speed at which you would have gone if you'd made the same trip at a constant speed. Your average speed will be between your slowest and fastest speeds.

Calculating Average Speed

The average speed is the total distance an object moved divided by the time it took to move that distance. You can calculate average speed using this formula:

$$\text{Average speed} = \frac{\text{total distance traveled}}{\text{total time elapsed}} \qquad S = \frac{d}{t}$$

SAMPLE CALCULATION A girl rides her bicycle 8 meters in 2 seconds. What is her average speed?

$$S = \frac{d}{t}$$

$$S = \frac{8 \text{ m}}{2 \text{ s}}$$

$$S = \frac{4 \text{ m}}{\text{s}}$$

> In this formula,
>
> S = average speed
> d = distance traveled
> t = time

The girl's average speed on her bicycle is 4 meters per second, or 4 m/s.

 In the formula $S = \frac{d}{t}$, what do the three letters stand for?

_____ _____ _____

What does a distance-time graph show?

A good way to show how the speed of an object changes is by using a distance-time graph.

Look at the graph to the right. In a distance-time graph, time is on the horizontal axis. Distance is on the vertical axis.

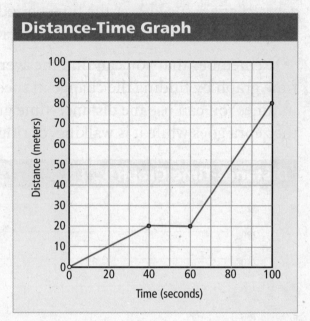

Distance-Time Graph

1 As an object moves, the distance it travels increases with time. This can be seen as a rising line on the graph.

2 A flat, or horizontal, line shows a period of time when the distance does not change. This means that the object is not moving. Its speed is 0 meters per second.

3 A steeper line shows a time period when the speed is greater than at other times when the line is less steep.

Fill in the blanks: In a distance-time graph,

_____

is on the horizontal axis and distance is on the

_____ axis.

Slope and Speed

On a distance-time graph, the slope of the line gives the speed of the object. The slope of a line is the rise divided by the run. On a distance-time graph, the slope of the line is the change in the distance divided by the change in the time for that particular time period. Notice that this is the same as the formula for calculating speed: distance divided by time.

Mark It Up

Circle the part of the distance-time graph that shows the highest speed.

When the line is steep, the slope is large, and the speed is high. When the line is less steep, the slope is smaller, and the speed is lower. When the line is flat, the slope is 0, and the object is not moving.

Calculating Average Speed Using a Distance-Time Graph

The graph below is a distance-time graph for a zebra. It shows how the zebra changes speed over the time period of a minute. The zebra walks, then stops to graze. As the zebra grazes, it senses a lion, and starts to run.

Remember that you can find the average speed using a distance-time graph by finding the change in speed and dividing by the change in time. You can use the distance-time graph to find the average speed the zebra goes while it is walking, during the first 20 seconds.

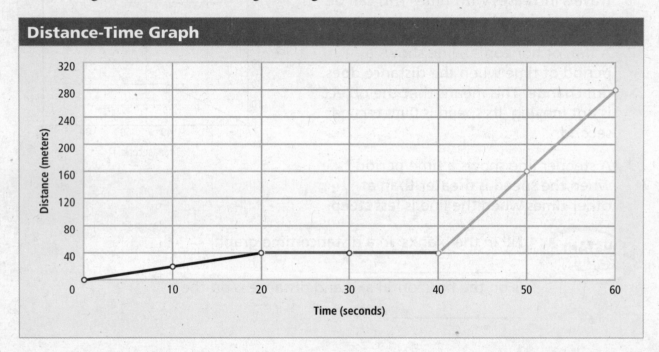

Distance-Time Graph

- The graph shows the change in distance is from 0 meters to 40 meters. Subtracting (40 m − 0 m), you find the change in distance is 40 m.

- The graph shows the change in time is from 0 seconds to 20 seconds. Subtracting (20 s − 0 s), you find the change in time is 20 s.

- To find the average speed, you divide change in distance by change in time. Dividing (40 m / 20 s), you find the average speed is 2 m/s.

Visual Connection
See distance-time graph in student text, page 21.

INSTANT REPLAY How can you find the zebra's speed as it runs from the lion?

_____

_____

_____

What is velocity?

Velocity is speed in a specific direction. Say you walk to school. You might walk at a speed of 4 kilometers per hour. Say your school is south of your home. When you walk to school, the direction you walk is south. On your walk to school, your velocity is southward at 4 kilometers per hour.

Velocity is an example of a vector. A **vector** is a quantity that has both size and direction. For velocity, the size is the speed. The direction is the direction of motion. Speed alone is not a vector because it does not have direction.

Arrows can show vector quantities. The length of the arrow shows the speed. The way the arrow points shows the direction.

  same speed, same direction

 same speed, different direction

 different speed, same direction

different speed, different direction

Mark It Up

Draw two arrows that show two velocities with the same speed but opposite directions.

What two things does a vector show?

_____ _____

SECTION 1.2

SUMMARIZE	VOCABULARY
1. How does speed differ from velocity? _____ _____ _____ _____ _____ _____	Fill in each blank with the correct word from the list. speed slope vector **2.** To find average _____, you need to divide change in distance by change in time. **3.** A _____ has both size and direction. **4.** The _____ shows speed on a distance-time graph.

Student text pages
25–31

How can velocity change?

Imagine you throw a ball high in the air. Say the ball starts with a velocity of 10 meters per second upward. As the ball rises, it slows down. At the top of its arc, the ball comes to a stop for just a moment. Then, it begins to fall to the ground. It speeds up as it falls. By the time you catch it, its velocity would be about 10 meters per second downward.

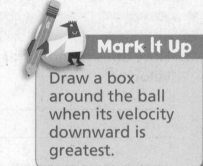

Defining Changes in Velocity

The example of the ball shows that the velocity of an object can change over time. A change in velocity is called **acceleration.** People often use the word *accelerate* to mean "speed up," or go faster and faster. In science, accelerate has a wider meaning. Acceleration occurs when something:

- speeds up
- slows down
- changes direction
- speeds up or slows down and also changes direction

Mark It Up

Draw a box around the ball when its velocity downward is greatest.

INSTANT REPLAY Define acceleration. _____
Underline the sentence that gives the definition.

Examples of Acceleration

A moving car can accelerate in different ways. In each of the following situations, the velocity of the car changes.

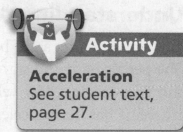

Activity

Acceleration
See student text, page 27.

Speeding Up A driver can accelerate a car by pushing on the gas pedal. This will cause the car to speed up.

Slowing Down The driver can also accelerate the car by pushing on the brake pedal. This will cause the car to slow down.

 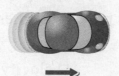

Changing Direction The driver can accelerate the car by turning the steering wheel. This will cause the car to change direction.

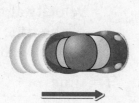 

Changing Speed and Direction The driver can accelerate the car in two different ways at the same time. The driver can turn the steering wheel and push on either the gas pedal or the brake pedal. This will cause the car to change both speed and direction.

Mark It Up

Circle the three examples of cars accelerating that involve a change in speed.

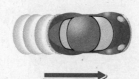 

 Tell how a driver can use both the steering wheel and the brake pedal at the same time to accelerate.

_____

_____

Understanding Acceleration

You are watching a girl bike along a street. She moves slowly at first. She pedals hard and starts to move faster. When she passes you, she is moving very fast. Her velocity has been changing for the entire bike ride. She has been accelerating.

Acceleration is a change in velocity. To find the acceleration of an object, you need to know three things.

- the velocity of the object at the beginning of a time period
- the velocity of the object at the end of the time period
- the length of the time period

The formula* below shows how to use these three quantities to find acceleration.

$$\text{Acceleration} = \frac{\text{velocity at the end} - \text{velocity at the beginning}}{\text{time}}$$

$$a = \frac{v_{final} - v_{initial}}{t}$$

a = acceleration

v_{final} = velocity at the end of the time period (final velocity)

$v_{initial}$ = velocity at the start of the time period (initial velocity)

t = time

As the cheetah jumps, he accelerates because he is changing direction.

*Academic Vocabulary: A **formula** is a kind of statement with an equal sign in the middle. It shows how different quantities are related to each other.

To find acceleration, you have to do two things in order.

Step 1 Subtract the starting velocity from the ending velocity.

Step 2 Divide the results from step 1 by the length of the time period.

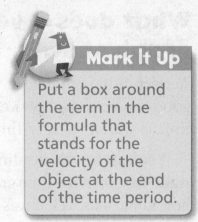

Mark It Up

Put a box around the term in the formula that stands for the velocity of the object at the end of the time period.

To find acceleration, first you have to

_____

Next you have to _____

Units of Acceleration

In science, velocity is often measured in meters per second (m/s). The unit of acceleration is the unit of velocity divided by the unit of time. The division gives you units of meters per second per second (m/s/s).

We can use math to make the units simpler. Meters per second per second (m/s/s) is the same thing as meters per second squared (m/s^2). You will usually see the units of acceleration written as m/s^2.

What do the units mean? Think about a girl riding a bike down a big hill. She might accelerate at 4 meters per second squared. This means that every second, her velocity is 4 m/s faster. Suppose she starts with zero velocity. After one second, she is going 4 m/s. After two seconds, she is going 8 m/s. After three seconds, she is going 12 m/s. After each second, her velocity increases by 4 m/s. That is what it means when you say the girl's acceleration is 4 meters per second squared (m/s^2).

Fill in the chart to compare velocity, acceleration, and their units.

Term	Definition	Units in word	Abbreviation
Velocity	the distance an object covers in a set time and the direction it moves in		m/s
Acceleration		meters per second per second -or- meters per second squared	

What does a velocity-time graph show?

Acceleration is change in velocity over time. A good way to show how velocity changes over time is with a velocity-time graph.

Look at the velocity-time graph to the right. In a velocity-time graph, time is on the horizontal axis. Velocity is on the vertical axis. This graph shows how the velocity of a student on a scooter changes over time.

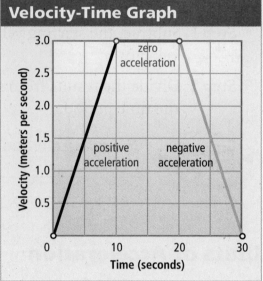

Velocity-Time Graph

1. The student's velocity increases with time. This can be seen as a rising line on the graph. We say that his acceleration is positive.

2. The student coasts at the same velocity for a while. His velocity does not change. His acceleration is 0. This can be seen as a flat, or horizontal, line on the graph.

3. The student's velocity decreases. This can be seen as a falling line on the graph. We say that his acceleration is negative.

On a velocity-time graph, what does a flat line mean?

_____

Distance-Time Graphs and Acceleration

Velocity can involve a change in speed. In Section 1.2, you learned to find speed by looking at the slope of the line on a distance-time graph. The speed is related to the steepness of the line on a line graph.

Look at the distance-time graph to the right. This graph is related to the velocity-time graph above. It shows how the student's distance changes over time during his scooter ride.

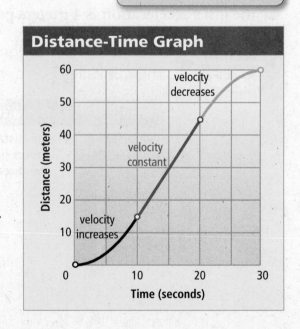

Distance-Time Graph

1 The student's distance from the starting point increases faster and faster. The distance-time graph shows a curved line that gets steeper over time. The slope of this line gets larger. This means that the student's velocity is increasing. The student is accelerating.

2 The student coasts at a constant velocity. His distance from his starting point increases at a steady rate. The distance-time graph shows a straight line. The slope of this line is constant. His acceleration is 0 meters per second squared.

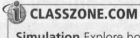

CLASSZONE.COM

Simulation Explore how changing the acceleration of an object changes its motion.

3 The student slows down. His distance from his starting point increases more slowly. The distance-time graph shows a curved line that gets less steep over time. The slope of this line gets smaller as the student's velocity decreases. Again, he is accelerating.

What are two times when the line on a distance-time graph is curved?

_____   _____

Linear and Nonlinear Relationships

When the line on a graph is straight, it shows a linear relationship. When the line on a graph curves, it shows a nonlinear relationship.

The relationship between distance and time is linear when velocity is constant. On a distance-time graph, the line is straight. The relationship between distance and time is nonlinear when velocity is changing. On a distance-time graph, the line curves.

Activity

Acceleration and Slope
See student text, page 32–33.

SECTION 1.3	
SUMMARIZE	**VOCABULARY**
1. Two students are racing. One student speeds up, passes the other student, and slows down. The other student runs at a steady pace. Is either student accelerating? Explain. _____ _____	Draw a line to connect each term with the phrase it best matches. 2. acceleration a. curving line on a graph 3. nonlinear relationship b. straight line on a graph 4. linear relationship c. change in velocity

Vocabulary Complete the chart by filling in the blanks.

Term	Description
1	speed in a specific direction
2 speed	
3 reference point	
4	a change in velocity over time

Math in Science Use the graph to answer questions 5–7.

5 Juanita ran 50 meters in 8 seconds. What was her average speed?

_____

6 How long did it take Angela to finish the race? _____

7 Which runner ran the fastest? How do you know?

_____

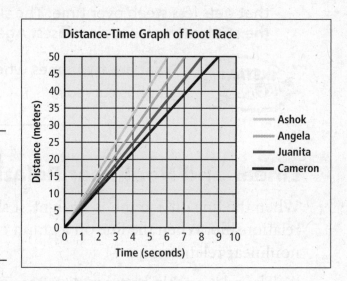

Distance-Time Graph of Foot Race

Ashok
Angela
Juanita
Cameron

the **BIG** idea

8 Describe how your motion changes during one jump on a trampoline.

_____

_____

Test Practice

9 In a bike race, one racer goes 75 miles in 3 hours. What is the racer's average speed?

A 3 miles per hour
B 25 miles per hour
C 75 miles per hour
D 225 miles per hour

10 Mary and Keisha walk with the same speed in opposite directions. They have

A the same position
B different accelerations
C different times
D different velocities

CHAPTER

2 Forces

the BIG idea

Forces change the motion of objects in predictable ways.

Getting Ready to Learn

Review Concepts

- An object's motion is described by position, direction, speed, and acceleration.
- Velocity and acceleration can be measured.

Activity

Popping Ping-Pong Balls
See student text, page 39.

Review Vocabulary

Fill each blank with the correct word from the list.

acceleration   mass   vector   velocity

A quantity that has size and direction is a _____.

_____ is a change in speed or a change in direction or both.

_____ is how much matter there is in an object.

Speed in a certain direction is known as _____.

Preview Key Vocabulary

Define the word in the central circle. For each of the terms outside the central circle, tell how the word in the central circle relates to it.

net force: _____

inertia: _____

force:

reaction force: _____

Newton's second law: _____

Student text pages
41–47

What is a Force?

A **force** is a push or a pull. You use a force to push a
window open. You use a force to pull a door closed.

Any time you make something move, you push it or
pull it in some way. Any time you change the direction of
something that is already moving, you have to push at it
or pull on it. Any time you slow or stop something that is moving, you
pull or push on it. Any time you change the motion of something, you
are using a force.

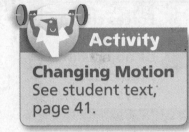

Activity

Changing Motion
See student text,
page 41.

What is a force? _____

Examples of Forces

Here are a few everyday examples of using forces:

- picking up or putting down a backpack
- throwing, catching, hitting, kicking, or stopping a ball
- typing on a keyboard
- turning a key
- writing with a pen or pencil

Size and Direction of Forces

Force is a vector. As you saw in Chapter 1, a vector is a quantity that has
both size and direction. We use arrows to show vectors. The length of
the arrow gives the size. The arrow points in the direction of the vector.

Different forces can have different sizes.
Think about a person walking a dog on a leash.
When the dog pulls on the leash, the person is
pulled by the force. If the dog pulls hard, the
force is large. If the dog pulls more gently, the
force is smaller.

The direction of a force is also important. If a dog on a leash pulls straight ahead, the force on the person acts straight ahead. If a dog pulls to the right, the force on the person acts to the right. Whatever direction the dog pulls in is the direction of the force.

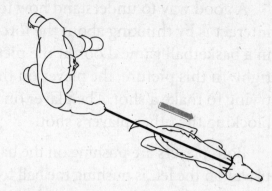

How Do Forces Combine?

Most of the time, more than one force acts on an object. Think about a person skateboarding. The main forces acting on him are listed here.

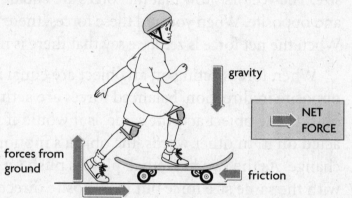

- Gravity pulls down on him.
- The ground pushes up on him.
- As he uses his foot to push on the ground, the ground pushes back on his foot. This helps move him and his skateboard forward. A force from the ground also pushes up on the skateboarder.
- The force of friction between the skateboard wheels and the ground pushes in the direction opposite to the direction the skateboard moves.

All of these forces combine. This results in a net* force. The **net force** is the overall force acting on an object. The arrow to the right of the skateboarder shows the net force acting on him.

Balanced Forces

Sometimes the net force acting on an object is zero. This does not mean that there are no forces acting on the object. Instead it means all the forces in all directions balance each other. When the forces are added together, the sum is zero.

*Academic vocabulary: *Net* is an adjective related to the amount remaining after all the adding and subtracting has been done.

A good way to understand how forces can interact is by thinking about the forces on a ball in a basketball game. Look at the picture to the right. In this picture, the player on the left is trying to make a shot. The player on the right is blocking the other player's shot.

Both players are pushing on the ball. The player on the left is pushing the ball to the right with some force. The player on the right is pushing the ball to the left with a force of equal size. The vectors show that the forces are equal and opposite. When you add these forces, there is a net force of zero. When the net force is zero, we say that there is no net force.

When forces acting on an object are equal in size but opposite in direction, balanced forces are acting on the object. The object acts the same as it would if no forces acted on it. In other words, the object's motion does not change. As the two basketball players push on the ball with the same size force but in opposite directions, the ball does not move.

Mark It Up

Draw two arrows that show balanced forces.

Unbalanced Forces

Suppose the player on the right starts pushing with more force. The forces are now unbalanced. Then, the ball begins to move. It moves in the direction that the player on the right is pushing.

Unbalanced forces result in a net force. Here, the net force is in the direction of the larger force. The size of the net force is the difference between the larger force and the smaller force. When a net force acts on an object, the motion of that object changes.

What happens to a ball's motion when unbalanced forces act on the ball?

_____

How do forces affect the velocity of objects?

Remember that velocity is one way to describe an object's motion. Velocity is a vector. It includes both speed and direction.

Balanced Forces and Motion

If balanced forces act on an object, the motion of the object does not change. This means that if the object is not moving, it will remain still. If the object is moving, it will continue going at the same speed. It will also continue going in the same direction.

Mark It Up

Make a label to show a force that would slow down the biker.

Unbalanced Forces and Changes of Velocity

Remember that when there is a net force on an object, the forces on the object are unbalanced. Here are the three ways unbalanced forces on an object can change the velocity of the object.

1. **Speeding up** Unbalanced forces can cause an object to speed up. For instance, if you pedal hard on a bicycle, you exert more force to make the wheels turn faster. This extra force speeds up your bike.

2. **Slowing down** Unbalanced forces can cause an object to slow down. For instance, if you squeeze your bicycle brakes, the brake pads rub against the wheels. There is a lot of friction, and the wheels turn slower. The extra friction slows your bike.

3. **Changing direction** Unbalanced forces can cause an object to change direction. For instance, if you turn your handlebars, a force pulls your bike at an angle from your direction of motion. This force makes your bike turn into a new direction.

What are three ways unbalanced forces can change the motion of an object?

_____ _____ _____

_____

What is Newton's first law of motion?

In the 1600s, English scientist Sir Isaac Newton studied how forces affect objects. He came up with three laws. These laws describe how and why things move. We still use Newton's laws today.

Newton's first law of motion summarizes what you just read on page 21. It tells about forces and changes in motion. Newton's first law states: **Objects at rest remain at rest, and objects in motion remain in motion with the same velocity, unless they are acted upon by unbalanced forces.**

Visual Connection
See Newton's First Law in the student text, page 45.

Restate Newton's first law of motion in your own words.

_____

Forces and an Object at Rest

A referee puts a soccer ball on the ground. The ball is not moving. Balanced forces are acting on the ball. There is no net force on the ball. The ball remains at rest, as Newton's first law predicts.

Then a player runs up and kicks the ball. During the kick, the forces on the ball become unbalanced. Now the second part of Newton's law applies. There is a net force on the ball. That is why the ball goes into motion. It flies into the air.

Mark It Up

Add to the picture to show unbalanced forces on the ball. Use an arrow to show the size and direction of the net force.

Forces and an Object in Motion

A soccer ball is rolling on the ground. Balanced forces are acting on the ball. There is no net force on it. The ball keeps moving at a constant speed. It also keeps moving in the same direction.

The ball is moving toward the goal. The goalie reaches out her hands. She grabs the ball. When she grabs the ball, the forces on the ball become unbalanced. Now the second part of Newton's law applies. There is a net force on the ball. That is why the ball changes direction or stops moving. The goalie has applied a force that changes the ball's motion.

What is inertia?

Inertia (ih-NUR-shuh) is the resistance of an object to a change in motion. It is easy to kick a soccer ball and send it flying. It is much harder to make a bowling ball move. That is because a soccer ball and a bowling ball have different inertias. The bowling ball has more inertia than the soccer ball.

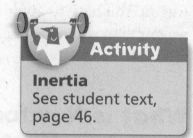

Activity

Inertia
See student text, page 46.

Suppose you have an object with a lot of inertia. If the object is still, it is hard to start it moving. If the object is moving fast, it is hard to slow it down. If the object is moving slowly, it is hard to speed it up. It is also hard to make the object change direction.

Inertia is related to mass. Mass is the amount of matter in an object. An object with a larger mass has more inertia than an object with a smaller mass.

SECTION 2.1	
SUMMARIZE	**VOCABULARY**
1. According to Newton's first law, when will objects change their velocity? _____ _____ _____ _____ _____	Draw a line to connect each term with its definition. **2.** force a. the resistance of an object to change its motion **3.** friction b. a push or a pull **4.** inertia c. the force in the opposite direction of an object's motion **5.** net force d. the result of combining all forces on an object

SECTION
2.2
Key Concept
Forces and mass determine acceleration.

Student text pages 49–55

What do you know about applying forces?

Suppose you have an empty wagon and a wagon full of sand. Which is easier to pull? The empty wagon, of course. The wagon full of sand has much more mass than the empty wagon. You have to apply more force to accelerate the full wagon than you do to accelerate an empty wagon the same amount.

small force

acceleration

What is Newton's second law of motion?

Newton's second law of motion states that: **The acceleration of an object increases with increased force, decreases with increased mass, and is in the same direction as the force.**

The second law of motion relates these three things:

- the size of a force
- the mass of the object the force acts on
- the acceleration that the object has as a result of the force

Acceleration is a change in velocity. An object that is accelerating can change its speed, direction, or both.

larger force

acceleration

INSTANT REPLAY

What three things does Newton's second law connect?

_____ _____ _____

The Three Parts of Newton's Second Law

Newton's second law includes three statements.

1. The acceleration of an object increases with increased force.

This means the harder you push on the handle of a grocery cart, the faster the speed or direction of the cart will change.

2. If you apply the same force to an object with more mass, the object will not accelerate as much. The speed or direction of the object will change more slowly.

Suppose you fill up an empty grocery cart with bags of food. In this way, you increase the mass of the cart. You push the full cart with the same force you applied to the empty cart. The full cart will speed up more slowly. This means its acceleration is lower.

3. When you apply a force on an object, the acceleration is in the same direction that the force acts.

Remember that force and acceleration are both vectors. Each has size and direction. You apply a force to a grocery cart when you push it forward. The acceleration vector points forward, in the same direction as the force. If you pull it backward, the acceleration vector points backward.

small mass

acceleration

larger mass

acceleration

 **INSTANT REPLAY** Fill in the blanks: The acceleration of an object increases with _____ force, decreases with increased mass, and is in the same _____ as the force.

Mark It Up

Circle the symbol used to show a large mass. Underline the vectors that show acceleration.

How can you use math to find force?

Newton's second law can be written as a simple formula. It is:

Force = mass × acceleration
$$F = ma$$

In this formula,

F = force m = mass a = acceleration

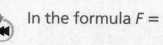 **INSTANT REPLAY** In the formula $F = ma$, what do the three letters stand for?

_____ _____ _____

Units of Force

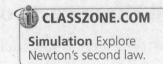

CLASSZONE.COM

Simulation Explore
Newton's second law.

In the formula $F = ma$

- mass is measured in kilograms (kg)
- acceleration is measured in meters per second squared (m/s^2)

The unit for measuring force combines these two units into another unit called the newton (N). The newton is named after Isaac Newton.

A newton is defined as the amount of force needed to accelerate 1 kilogram (1 kg) at a rate of one meter per second squared (m/s^2). So 1 N is equal to 1 kg-m/s^2.

What unit is used to measure force?

_____

Calculating Force

Suppose you know the mass of an object. Suppose you also know the acceleration of the object. Then you can use the formula from Newton's second law to figure out how large a force is acting on the object.

SAMPLE CALCULATION A book has a mass of 2 kilograms. It is falling at a rate of 10 m/s^2. What is the force on the book?

$$F = ma$$
$$F = 2 \text{ kg} \times 10 \text{ m/s}^2$$
$$F = 20 \text{ kg-m/s}^2 \text{ or } 20 \text{ N.}$$

The force on the book is 20 newtons.

Mark It Up

Underline the units of measurement that make up the newton.

What two things do you need to know to figure out the size of a force acting on an object?

_____   _____

What kind of force makes objects move in a circle?

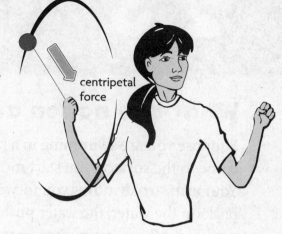

centripetal force

A force can accelerate an object by changing its speed. A force can also accelerate an object by changing the direction that the object moves. For example, a force can make an object move in a circle. When an object moves in a circle, its direction of motion changes from moment to moment. A **centripetal force** is a steady force that keeps an object moving in a circle.

Suppose you are whirling a ball on a string. You are using centripetal force. You pull on the string to make the ball move in a circle. To make the ball spin faster, you pull harder on the string. You are increasing the centripetal force on the ball. As the diagram shows, the force points toward the center of the circle.

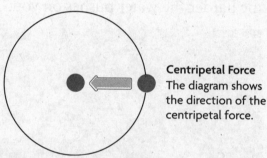

Centripetal Force
The diagram shows the direction of the centripetal force.

What happens if you let go of the string? The ball stops moving in a circle. Instead, the ball and the string fly off in a straight line. They move in the direction they were headed the moment you let go. There is no longer any force causing them to change direction. That is why the ball and string move in a straight line.

Activity

Motion and Force
See student text, page 54.

INSTANT REPLAY

What kind of force makes an object move in a circle?

_____

_____

SECTION 2.2	
SUMMARIZE	**VOCABULARY**
Circle the words that give a correct restatement of Newton's second law. The acceleration of an object 1. **increases/decreases** with increased force, 2. **increases/decreases** with increased mass, and 3. is in the **same/opposite** direction as the force.	Write the terms that answer the riddles. **acceleration centripetal force mass** 4. what you need to apply to keep something circling around you _____ 5. what you need to know to calculate force _____

Student text pages 57–61

What are action and reaction forces?

Suppose you are swimming in a race. You dive into the water. As you come to the surface, you start moving your arms as quickly as you can. Your arm stroke moves you forward. Why does this happen? As you push back on the water, the water pushes forward on you. The harder you push, the harder the water pushes on you. That is what makes you go forward.

Mark It Up

Draw and label an arrow to show the reaction force from the water pushing on the swimmer.

Forces always act in pairs. Any time something exerts* a force on an object, the object applies a force back. One force is called the action force. The other force is called the reaction force. The force you apply to the water is an action force. The force of the water pushing back on you is a reaction force. Action and reaction forces are equal in size but opposite in direction. Newton's third law states: **When one object exerts a force on another object, the second object exerts an equal and opposite force on the first object.**

How do forces work in pairs?

_____

*Academic Vocabulary: In physics, to **exert** means to bring something into action, or to apply something.

What is Newton's third law of motion?

The idea of forces acting in pairs is the main idea of Newton's third law. This law states every time an object exerts a force on another object, the second object exerts a force that is equal in size and opposite in direction on the first object.

Suppose you are paddling in a canoe. When you push the water with the paddle, the water pushes back on the paddle. The water pushes the canoe forward.

Action and reaction forces do not always result in motion. Both forces can be present even when there is little or no motion. What happens if you bang your foot on the leg of a table? Your foot hits the table leg with a certain force. The table leg exerts the same amount of force back on your foot. That force is what makes your foot hurt.

INSTANT REPLAY Fill in the blanks: If you exert a force on an object, the object exerts a _____ on you that is _____ in size to your force.

Understanding Newton's Third Law

Action and reaction forces happen naturally. The reaction force occurs at the same time as the action force. You cannot have a force without also having the reaction force. If you push on something, it will push back on you.

Activity

Newton's Third Law
See student text, page 58.

Look at the pictures of the skaters. In the first picture, both skaters are standing still. The girl pushes the boy's back. As you might expect, the boy moves forward because of the girl's push. This push is the action force.

Whenever there is a force, there has to be a reaction force. The action force is the push the girl gives to the boy's back. The reaction force is the boy's back pushing on the girl's hands. The boy does nothing to try to push the girl. The reaction force happens naturally, the moment the girl makes contact with the boy's back.

As you have read, the action force that the girl exerts causes the boy to move forward. The reaction force of the boy's back on the girl's hands causes the girl to move, as well. She rolls backward, away from the boy. The action and reaction forces are in opposite directions. This explains why the skaters move as they do.

Mark It Up

Draw arrows on the picture to the right to show how each skater is moving.

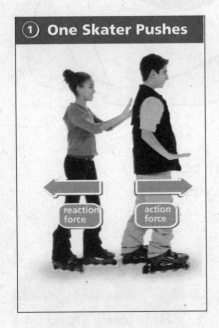

① One Skater Pushes

reaction force   action force

② Both Skaters Move

Why does the girl in the picture move backwards?

_____

How can you apply Newton's three laws of motion?

Newton's three laws of motion are summarized in this chart.

Newton's Laws of Motion	Summary
First law	An object at rest or moving at a constant velocity will only change its motion if a force is applied to it.
Second law	The acceleration of an object increases if the force on the object is increased. The acceleration of an object decreases if mass is added to the object. The acceleration of an object is always in the same direction as the force.
Third law	When an object exerts a force on another object, the second object exerts an equal and opposite force on the first object.

Suppose you are in a canoe race. You might pick your canoe based on Newton's second law. You can accelerate more easily in a lighter canoe. At the beginning of the race, you have to apply Newton's first law. You need to exert a force to start the canoe moving. You also need to continue exerting a force to keep accelerating. This will help you go faster and faster. Why paddling helps you move is explained by Newton's third law. You push the canoe paddle back against the water. The water pushes the paddle and the canoe forward.

Visual Connection
See Newton's Three Laws of motion in the student text, page 60.

Which of Newton's laws explains the forward motion of a canoe?

_____

SECTION 2.3	
SUMMARIZE	**VOCABULARY**
1. Restate Newton's third law in your own words.	2. Fill in the blanks with the words below.
_____	**action force** **pairs** **reaction force**
_____	Forces act in _____. For example, if you push against a wall, the wall pushes back on you. The force you exert is the _____. The force the wall exerts is the _____.
_____	
_____	
_____	

Review
CHAPTER
2 Forces

CLASSZONE.COM

Go to ClassZone.com
for activities, links, and
more test practice.

Vocabulary Match the words with their definition.

1 centripetal force   a a push or a pull

2 force   b the result of adding and subtracting all
forces acting on an object

3 inertia   c causes an object to move in a circle

4 net force   d the resistance of an object to accelerate

Math in Science

5 You need to move a grocery cart with a mass of 40 kg. You need it
to accelerate at 0.5 m/s^2. How much force do you need to apply?

_____

6 A block of ice accelerates at 2 meters per second. The ice has a
mass of 2 kilograms. What size force is acting on it?

_____

7 John pushes a box to the right with a force of 5 newtons. Beth
pushes the opposite side of the box to the left with a force of
6 newtons. What is the size and direction of the force?

_____

the BIG idea

8 Describe what will happen if you push against a wall with a
force of 5 newtons.

_____

Test Practice

9 Newton's second law states that to
increase acceleration, you need to

A decrease force
B increase force
C increase mass
D increase inertia

10 A skateboarder moves at a constant velocity. All the forces on
the skateboarder are

A balanced
B unbalanced
C increasing
D decreasing

3 Gravity, Elastic Forces, and Friction

Newton's laws apply to all forces.

Getting Ready to Learn

Review Concepts

- The motion of an object will not change unless the object is acted upon by unbalanced forces.
- The acceleration of an object depends upon force and mass.
- For every action force, there is an equal and opposite reaction force.

Activity

Let it Slide
See student text, page 69.

Review Vocabulary

Draw a line to connect each word to its definition.

force	a change in speed or a change in direction or both
centripetal force	keeps an object moving in a circle
mass	a push or a pull
acceleration	the amount of matter an object has

Preview Key Vocabulary

For each word below, pick a word from the list to the right that is closely related to it. For each pair of words, tell why you put them together.

gravity and _____
are a pair because: _____

tension and _____
are a pair because: _____

friction and _____
are a pair because: _____

air resistance
compression
orbit
weight

Key Concept

Gravity is a force exerted by masses.

Student text pages
71–77

What is gravity?

When you drop most objects, they fall to the ground. Why? Earth exerts a force on objects that pulls them to the ground. That force is called gravity. **Gravity** is the force that an object exerts on another object because they both have mass.

What is gravity?

_____

Underline the sentence that gave you the answer.

A Universal Force

Gravity is a force of attraction. This means that gravity pulls objects toward one another. Gravity is a universal force. That means it acts between any two objects anywhere in the entire universe. There is a force of attraction between you and the planet you are standing on. There is a force of attraction between two dust specks in a cloud that is deep in space.

The strength of the force of gravity depends on two things—the mass of the objects and the distance between the objects.

Mass of the objects

Remember that mass is the amount of matter an object has. The more mass an object has, the greater the force of gravity between it and other objects. If the mass of the object doubles, the force of gravity doubles as well.

Mark It Up

Draw a pair of objects that would have a smaller force of gravity between them than the objects in the diagram.

Greater mass results in greater force.

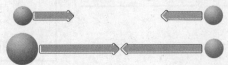

In the diagram, a larger circle means the object has more mass than a smaller circle. The arrows represent the force of gravity. The size of the arrow shows the size of the force.

Distance Between the Objects

The closer two objects are, the greater the force of gravity they exert on one another. The more distance between the objects, the smaller the force of gravity between them. If the distance between the objects doubles, the force of gravity decreases to a fourth of what it was.

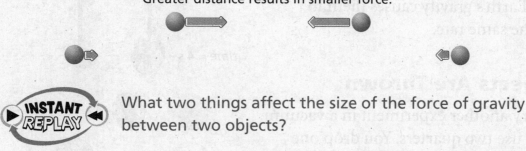

Greater distance results in smaller force.

INSTANT REPLAY What two things affect the size of the force of gravity between two objects?

_____

How do we experience gravity on Earth?

The force of gravity acts between any two objects. It acts between you and your pencil. It acts between you and your desk. However, the most massive thing near you is the planet Earth. Earth has many trillions of times more mass than any object on Earth. So the force of gravity between you and Earth is many times stronger than the force of gravity between you and anything else on Earth.

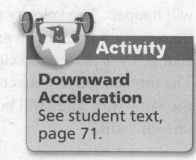

Activity

Downward Acceleration
See student text, page 71.

You do not notice the force of gravity attracting you to your pencil, your desk or other objects. Those forces are much, much smaller than most of the other forces that act on you. You do, however, notice the force of gravity attracting you to Earth. When you jump, gravity pulls you back down again.

When Objects Fall

Earth's gravity causes objects on Earth to fall toward Earth. The objects speed up as they fall. They accelerate because of the force of gravity. All objects have the same acceleration because of gravity. If there were no air on Earth, all objects would fall the same distance in the same amount of time. In real life, air causes most objects to fall more slowly.

CLASSZONE.COM

Visualization Explore how objects fall at the same rate in a vacuum.

A place that has no air is called a vacuum. Suppose you could set up an experiment to drop a quarter and a penny in a vacuum. The quarter has a greater mass than the penny. However, if the coins are dropped from the same height at the same time, they will reach the floor at the same instant. Earth's gravity causes them to accelerate at the same rate.

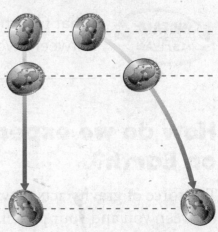

When Objects Are Thrown

Say that you try another experiment in a vacuum. This time you use two quarters. You drop one quarter and throw the other quarter, releasing both at the same time. The picture to the right shows what will happen. The velocity you gave the quarter you threw makes it fall in an arc, or curve. But it does not change the quarter's acceleration toward the ground. The force of gravity affects both quarters in exactly the same way. They will both hit the floor at the same instant.

What is the difference between mass and weight?

Mass and weight are similar. But they are not the same. Mass is a measure of how much matter an object has. Mass is measured in kilograms (kg). You use a balance to measure mass. You can measure the mass of an object anywhere in the universe. The object will always have the same mass.

Activity

Gravity and Speed
See student text, page 76.

Would the mass of an object change if you brought it to another planet? Explain.

_____

Weight is not the same thing as mass. **Weight** is a measure of the force of gravity on an object. Weight is measured in newtons (N).

Your weight on Earth is a measure of the force of Earth's gravity pulling on you. Suppose you went to the Moon. The Moon has much lower mass than Earth docs. So the Moon's gravity pulls with less force than Earth's gravity. If you could weigh yourself on the Moon, you would find that you weight is about one-sixth your weight on Earth.

On Earth:
Mass = 50 kg
Weight = 490 N

On the Moon:
Mass = 50 kg
Weight = 82 N

Mark It Up

Put a box around the place where the girl weighs less.

How does gravity affect the universe?

Gravity is an important force in the universe. In outer space, the force of gravity acts on huge clouds of dust and gas. Because of gravity, particles in the cloud attract one another. They stick together, so there is more mass in one place. The larger clumps have stronger gravity. More particles fall into the growing clumps. The cloud gets smaller and more compact. The particles and clumps of gas in the cloud get even closer together. With decreased distance, the force of gravity between the particles gets even stronger. Over time, gravity causes the cloud to collapse into a hot, glowing ball of gas. It has become a star.

INSTANT REPLAY

What force causes clouds of dust in outer space to form stars? _____

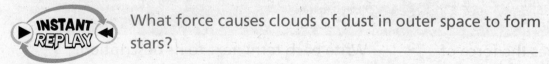

Gravity and the Planets

Many young stars have rings of dust and gas swirling around them. Gravity acts on these rings of gas and dust in the same way that it acted on the cloud that formed the star. The particles clump together, pulled by gravity. Over time, planets form from the dust rings.

Gravity and the Solar System

A solar system is a star with a set of planets moving around it. The Sun is the star at the center of our solar system. Gravity caused the solar system to form billions of years ago. Gravity is still an important force acting in the solar system today.

Find the Sun at the center of the diagram of the solar system. The Sun has a large mass. Its gravity pulls on all the planets in the solar system. The path a planet takes around the Sun is called an orbit. An **orbit** is an elliptical path one object takes around another object. An elliptical path is shaped like an ellipse. An ellipse looks like a flattened circle.

Orbits in The Solar System

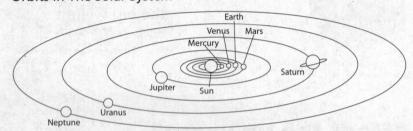

Mark It Up

Add an arrow to the picture to show how the force of gravity acts on the planet Saturn.

The force of gravity between the Sun and each planet keeps the planets moving in their orbits. Remember that a centripetal force is a force that keeps things turning in a circle. The Sun's gravity acts as a centripetal force on the planets, keeping them in their orbits.

What keeps the planets orbiting the Sun?

_____

SECTION 3.1	
SUMMARIZE	**VOCABULARY**
1. How does the force of gravity change with mass and distance? _____ _____ _____ _____	Write each term next to its description. **gravity**　　　**orbit** 2. the path an object takes around another object _____ 3. the force that any object exerts on other objects because of mass

Elastic forces resist stretching and pressing.

Student text pages 79–83

What are elastic forces?

You have to pull on a rubber band to stretch it. By pulling on the rubber band, you exert a force on it. At the same time, the rubber band pulls back on you. This is an example of Newton's third law. Stretching the rubber band is the action force. The force of the rubber band on your fingers is the reaction force.

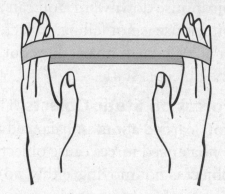

What allows rubber bands and other objects to exert reaction forces? The answer lies within the objects. All objects are made of particles. You may have learned that these particles are atoms or molecules. There are forces between the particles. These forces push or pull the particles to help the object keep its shape.

Mark It Up

Draw arrows to show the reaction force the rubber band exerts. Label your arrows.

The **elastic force** is the force an object exerts to resist being stretched or pressed. A stretched rubber band presses into your fingers because of the elastic force.

What is the elastic force?

_____

Underline the sentence that gave you the answer.

What situations involve elastic forces?

Objects exert elastic forces in two different situations.

1. **Tension** An object exerts an elastic force when forces act to pull on or stretch the object. When this happens we say that the object is under tension.

2. **Compression** An object exerts an elastic force when forces act to press or squeeze the object. When this happens, we say that the object is under compression.

Objects Under Tension

A birdhouse hangs from the branch of a tree. A string attaches the birdhouse to the tree branch. You know that the force of gravity is pulling the birdhouse downward. You can also see that the birdhouse is not falling. In fact, it is not moving at all. When an object does not move, we say that the object is static.

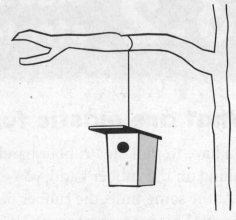

Forces on Static Objects Think back to what you learned about unbalanced and balanced forces. Unbalanced forces cause objects to accelerate. If an object is not moving, either no forces are acting on it or balanced forces are acting on it.

What can this tell you about the birdhouse? The force of gravity on the birdhouse is the weight of the birdhouse. This force acts downward. But the birdhouse isn't moving. That means another force must be acting on the birdhouse to balance the force of gravity. That force has to be equal to the weight of the bird house. It also has to be acting in the upward direction.

The string prevents the birdhouse from falling. There must be a force in the string that pulls upward on the birdhouse. The size of the force is the same size as the downward force, which is the birdhouse's weight.

> **Mark It Up**
>
> Two balanced forces act on the birdhouse. Add these force arrows to the drawing.

Understanding Tension The force of gravity pulls on the birdhouse, stretching the string downward. The stretching force is called **tension.** Gravity is not the only force that can produce tension. Think about pulling on a rubber band. When you stretch it sideways, you put the rubber band under tension. If a friend pulls on your arm, your friend's tug puts your arm under tension.

The elastic force in the string resists the tension. This force supplies the upward pull that keeps the birdhouse from falling. Sometimes the elastic force that resists tension is also called tension.

> **Activity**
>
> **Measuring Elastic Forces**
> See student text, pages 84–85.

INSTANT REPLAY When you pull on a rope, what type of force stretches the rope?

Objects under Compression

When you sit down on a couch, the couch cushion is pressed between you and the frame of the couch. The particles in the cushion are pushed closer together. A force that pushes particles in an object closer together is called **compression**.

Even through you are seated and not moving, the force of gravity still affects you. It pulls down on you with a force equal to your weight. What keeps you from falling through the couch to the floor? The elastic force in the couch cushion pushes up on you. This force is equal in size but opposite in direction to your weight.

Objects made of different materials respond differently to compression. For instance, it is difficult to compress wood. That is because the elastic forces among particles in the wood are very strong. Clay, on the other hand, is easy to compress. That is because the elastic forces among the clay particles are very weak. You can reshape a piece of clay over and over again.

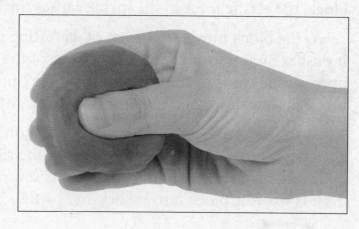

 What is compression?

_____

How can the elastic force cause back-and-forth motion?

Some springs can be stretched and compressed very easily. In such springs, the elastic force increases the more you stretch or compress the spring. This means that if you push the spring so it is a little shorter, you will feel the spring push back lightly on you. If you push on the spring so it is even shorter, you will feel the spring push back harder on you.

Activity

Elastic Forces
See student text, page 79.

A spring that stretches and compresses easily can be attached to a wooden block. The pictures show what will happen if you pull back on the block and let go. The block will move back and forth several times.

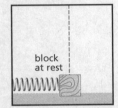  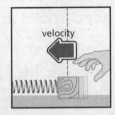 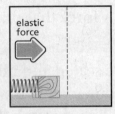 

You stretch the spring, pulling the block to the right. The elastic force in the spring opposes the tension you apply. When you let go of the block, the elastic force in the spring causes the block to move to the left.

As the block moves to the left of its resting position, it pushes on the spring. The elastic force of the spring opposes the compression. The elastic force causes the block to slow down and then move to the right.

As the block moves past its resting position, it stretches again. The elastic force pulls the block to the right. The cycle of tension and compression repeats several times. That is why the block moves back and forth.

 What force in the spring opposes both tension and compression?

_____

Mark It Up

Circle the drawing or drawings in which the spring is under tension.

CLASSZONE.COM

Simulation Explore elastic forces.

SECTION 3.2	
SUMMARIZE	**VOCABULARY**
1. A book is on a table. Gravity acts to pull the book downward. Why doesn't the book move? _____ _____ _____ _____ _____	Circle the word that makes each sentence correct. 3. An object is under **tension / compression** when a force pushes its particles close together. 2. An object is under **tension / compression** when a force stretches it. 4. Objects resist tension and compression because **the elastic force / gravity** acts to hold the particles in the object at a certain distance from each other.

Friction is a force that opposes motion.

Student text pages 86–90

What is Friction?

It is easier to push furniture across a wood floor than across a thick carpet. That is because of friction. **Friction** is a force that opposes* motion. Friction occurs when you try to slide an object on a surface. There is a lot of friction between the legs of the furniture and a thick carpet. That is because the carpet has a rough surface. There is less friction between the furniture legs and the wood. That is because the wood floor has a smoother surface.

What is friction?

_____

The Cause of Friction

Friction occurs when two objects or surfaces are in contact and forces act to slide the objects across each other. All substances are made up of particles that are too small to see. At the surface of any object, the particles form bumps and ridges. With very rough objects, you can see or feel bumps and ridges. However, even objects that look and feel very smooth have bumpy surfaces. The bumps and ridges are far too small to see, but they are still there.

When the surfaces of objects touch, the ridges on the surfaces bump against one another. If you try to move one of the touching objects past the other, the ridges have to slide over one another. Also, the bumps between two surfaces can get stuck together. This can happen even on very smooth surfaces. In order to slide the objects, you need to break the bumps apart. You feel the stickiness as a force working against your force. We call this force friction.

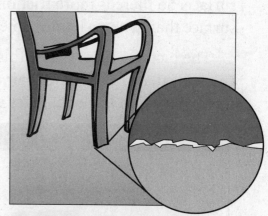

The bumps on the two surfaces stick together. This causes friction when you push on the chair.

Mark It Up

Label the part of this picture that shows where two surfaces are touching.

*Academic Vocabulary: **Oppose** means to go against something.

Factors Affecting Friction

Two main factors* affect the amount of friction between objects. One factor is the surface texture of each object. The other factor is the weight of the objects.

Activity

Friction
See student text, page 89.

Surface Texture You have probably had experiences with friction on different surfaces. Generally, if the surface is smooth, the force of friction is low. Think about how easy it is to slide on ice. That is because the friction between ice and the bottom of a shoe is very low. However, it is not easy to slide across a sidewalk. Friction between the bottom of a shoe and concrete is much higher than between the bottom of the shoe and ice.

Weight When an object is placed on a surface, the object presses down on the surface. The force the object presses down with is its weight. The larger the weight, the harder the object presses. The harder the object presses, the more friction there is between the object and the surface. So there is more friction when a heavier object slides over a surface than when a lighter object slides over the surface.

The pictures below show this. First, the student pushes an empty chair. Next, he pushes the chair after someone has sat down in it. The force of friction is much larger with the increased weight.

Less Weight

applied force

weight

friction

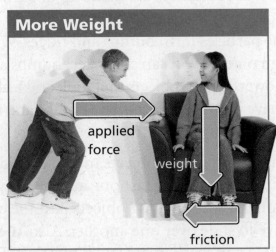

More Weight

applied force

weight

friction

When is there more friction, when a person pushes an empty chair, or when a person pushes a chair that has a person seated in it? Why?

_____

*Academic Vocabulary: Something that contributes to a particular result is called a **factor**.

How does friction affect nonmoving and moving objects?

Friction affects nonmoving and moving objects differently. There is more friction on nonmoving objects. The pictures below show this.

The student is trying to push the chair. He pushes hard, but the chair doesn't move. The force of friction prevents him from being able to move the chair. As he pushes, friction equals the force he applies. He keeps pushing harder and harder. Friction increases and balances his force, so the chair still does not move. Finally, he pushes so hard that his force is larger than the greatest force of friction that the chair and floor can produce. The chair suddenly moves forward.

Once the student has gotten the chair into motion, he doesn't have to push as hard to keep it moving. That is because the force of friction on a moving object is lower than the greatest force of friction on an object that is not moving.

 When is there more friction, just before an object moves, or just after the object starts moving?

_____

Before Object Moves

applied force

friction

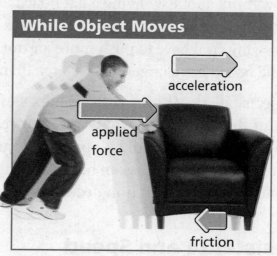

While Object Moves

acceleration

applied force

friction

What happens when objects move through air?

In a vacuum, objects fall to Earth with the same acceleration. Objects that fall from the same height hit the ground at the same time.

Air causes falling objects to fall more slowly. It also causes objects moving horizontally to have less acceleration. The air pushes on all sides of the moving object. This pushing is called resistance. The friction objects experience when they move through air is called **air resistance.**

 **INSTANT REPLAY** What is air resistance?

_____

Air resistance depends on how much air hits the object as it moves. Air resistance also depends on how fast the object is moving.

Air Resistance and Surface Area

Surface area is the area of the outside of an object. Think about swinging a stick. The thin stick has a small surface area. It moves through the air very easily. Now think about swinging a flat board. Even if the board has the same mass as the stick, it is harder to swing. You have to push more air out of the way because the board has a larger surface area than the stick.

As objects fall, they bump into air particles and push them out of the way. This is what causes air resistance. So increasing the surface area of an object will increase its air resistance. More air particles can bounce off the falling object. The object's acceleration decreases.

Mark It Up

Underline the object that has the smaller surface area. Circle the object that falls more slowly through air.

Air Resistance and Speed

How fast an object is moving also affects how much air resistance there is. An object moving at a high speed will bump against more air particles than an object moving at low speed. The faster an object moves, the more air resistance there is. Suppose an object falls so fast that the air resistance balances gravity. When this happens, the object stops accelerating. It falls at a constant speed.

What happens when an object moves through other fluids?

You have read that objects slow down when they move through air. Objects also slow down when they move through water. Air and water are both fluids. **Fluids** are substances that flow easily. All gases and liquids are fluids.

When an object moves through any fluid, the fluid presses against the object and slows it down. The larger the surface area of the object, the more the fluid will slow it down. The faster the object is moving through the fluid, the more the fluid will slow the object down.

► INSTANT REPLAY ◄◄

Fill in the blanks: The larger the _____ of the object, the more the fluid will slow the object down. The _____ the object is moving, the more the fluid will slow the object down.

SECTION 3.3

SUMMARIZE	VOCABULARY
1. You push hard on a big box to move it across the floor. It does not move. Explain why the box doesn't move using the idea of forces. _____ _____ _____ _____ _____	Fill in each blank with the correct word from the list. **air resistance** **fluid** **friction** 2. A substance that flows is called a _____. 3. A force that opposes the motion of objects through air is called _____. 4. The force that opposes motion when objects slide is called _____.

CHAPTER 3 Gravity, Elastic Forces, and Friction

CLASSZONE.COM
Go to ClassZone.com for activities, links, and more test practice.

Vocabulary Fill in each blank with the correct word.

1 _____ is the force that opposes the motion of an object.

2 _____ is the force that causes an object to resist stretching.

3 _____ is the force that objects exert on one another because of their masses.

compression
friction
gravity
tension

Reviewing Key Concepts

4 Why does the planet Venus orbit around the Sun?

_____

5 You pull on a block that is connected to a spring and then let go of the block. What happens?

_____

the BIG idea

6 You are sitting on a chair. Describe the forces acting on you. Tell how Newton's laws apply to those forces.

_____

Test Practice

7 You kick a box on a level sidewalk. It slides to a stop because

A there is no force on the box
B gravity slows the box down
C the forces on the box are balanced
D friction slows the box down

8 Suppose you jump down on a trampoline. Why do you then move up into the air?

A Gravity pushes you upward.
B Friction between your feet and the trampoline prevent you from moving downward.
C The elastic force of the trampoline pushes you upward.
D Air resistance pushes up on you.

4 Density and Buoyancy

the BIG idea

Forces act in fluids.

Getting Ready to Learn

Review Concepts

- The motion of an object does not change if the net force on the object is zero.
- Gravity is an attractive force between objects that depends on mass and distance.
- Weight is the force of gravity on an object.

Activity

Will It Float?
See student text, page 101.

Review Vocabulary

Write the correct term for each description.

force   mass   gravity   net force   fluid

Something that flows easily, like water _____

A push or a pull _____

Objects exert this force on each other. _____

How much matter there is in an object _____

All the forces on an object, combined _____

Preview Key Vocabulary

Following are some key terms you will see in this chapter. When you reach each one, sketch a picture in the box below to help you remember it.

Term	Definition	Sketch
volume	the space that an object takes up	
density	mass per unit volume	
pressure	a measure of how much force is acting on a certain area	
buoyant force	the upward force of objects in a fluid	

Student text pages
103–109

How can you describe density?

An object with a lot of matter in a small space is very dense. Most metals, such as gold, are very dense. An object with less matter in the same amount of space is less dense. A cotton ball is not very dense.

All objects have density. Some objects have a high density. Others have a lower density. Density depends on how much matter there is in an object.

What does density depend on?

_____

How can you calculate density?

To calculate density you need to know two things—volume and mass. You can measure both of these things.

1. **Volume** The **volume** of an object is the amount of space it takes up. A basketball has a greater volume than a baseball because it takes up more space.

2. **Mass** The mass of an object is the amount of matter in the object. Mass is harder to see than volume. A large ball and a small ball could have the same amount of matter in them.

What two things do you need to know to calculate density?

_____   _____

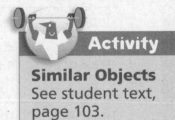

Activity

Similar Objects
See student text, page 103.

Measuring Mass

You measure mass using a balance*. You put the object on one end of a balance and known masses on the other end. Add or remove known masses until the balance is level. Then you can read the mass of the object. The mass of this bowling ball is 3000 grams.

Balance

 **What instrument do you use to measure mass?**

_____

Measuring Volume

You can measure volume in two ways.

1. Regular shapes For objects that are regular shapes, you use a formula. Regular shapes include cubes, spheres, and cylinders.

Sphere

The **formula** for the volume of a cube is

Volume = length • width • height

$$V = lwh$$

> In this formula,
> V = volume
> l = length
> w = width
> h = height

Cube

 **In the formula, what does _V_ stand for?**

_____

Cylinder

SAMPLE CALCULATION Suppose a solid cube is 8 cm on a side. That is, the length (l), the width (w), and the height (h) are all 8 cm. You would find the volume this way:

$$V = lwh$$

$$V = 8 \text{ cm} \times 8 \text{ cm} \times 8 \text{ cm}$$

$$V = 512 \text{ cm}^3$$

Mark It Up

Draw a cube and label the length, width, and height all 8cm.

*Academic Vocabulary: In everyday speech, the word **balance** refers to two sides being equal. In science it also means the instrument you use to measure mass.

2. Irregular shapes For objects that are irregular shapes, you use the displacement* method. You need a container of water large enough to put the object into. A graduated cylinder works well for small objects. You need to be able to measure how much water is in the container before and after you put the object in.

Irregular Shape

Step 1 Add water to the graduated cylinder. Note the volume of water (50 mL).

Step 2 Put the object into the water. Note the volume of water (55 mL).

Step 3 Subtract the volume of water without the object (from step 1) from the volume of water with the object (from step 2).
55 mL – 50 mL = 5 mL

5 mL of water was displaced by the object. Since 1 mL = 1 cm^3, the volume of the object is 5 cubic centimeters, or 5 cm^3.

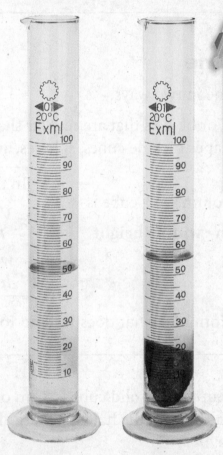

Mark It Up

The rock in the graduated cylinder is an irregular shape. Draw another irregular shape, such as a piece of popcorn.

What happens to the water level when you add the object?

_____

*Academic Vocabulary: If you put an object into water, some of the water will be moved out of the way, or **displaced**. When you use the **displacement** method to measure the mass of irregular objects, you measure the volume of water that is displaced.

Calculating Density

Once you know the mass and the volume of an object, you can figure out its density. You calculate the density of an object using this formula:

$$\text{Density} = \frac{\text{mass}}{\text{volume}}$$

$$D = \frac{m}{V}$$

In this formula,
D = density
m = mass
V = volume

SAMPLE CALCULATION A marble has a mass of 6 g and a volume of 3 cm^3. What is the density of this marble?

$$D = \frac{m}{V}$$

$$D = \frac{6g}{3cm^3}$$

$$D = \frac{2g}{cm^3} \text{ or } 2g/cm^3$$

"2 grams per centimeters cubed"

Mark It Up
Circle the final answer in the sample calculation. Underline the unit in the final answer.

The results of a density calculation will always be in a unit of mass over a unit of volume.

In the formula $D = m/V$, what do the three letters stand for?

_____   _____   _____

How do you define density?

The definition of density comes right out of the formula $D = m/V$.

Density is mass per unit volume.

the amount of matter in an object

"for every"

one of the units in which volume is expressed

Mass is often expressed in grams (g). If volume is expressed in centimeters cubed, unit volume is one cm^3. When mass is in grams, and volume is in centimeters cubed, the unit of density is g/cm^3. You can read this as grams "per centimeter cubed" or "per cubic centimeter."

How do you define density?

_____

How do the densities of various substances compare?

The density of a substance is a property of the substance. It is like color or texture. It does not depend on the amount of the substance you have. The density of a substance is the same no matter how much of the substance you have.

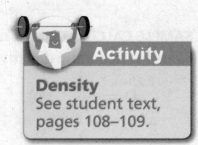

Activity

Density
See student text, pages 108–109.

If you know the densities of two substances, you can compare them.

- The density of lead is 11.34 g/cm^3. This means that if you have one cubic centimeter of lead, its mass is 11.34 grams.

- The density of aluminum is 2.70 g/cm^3. This means that if you have one cubic centimeter of aluminum, its mass is 2.70 grams.

- Since 11.34 grams is greater than 2.70 grams, the density of lead is greater than the density of aluminum.

Fill in the blank: The density of a substance is _____ no matter how much of the substance you have.

SECTION 4.1	
SUMMARIZE	**VOCABULARY**
1. Which has a greater density, a piece of bread or a piece of steel of the same size? Why? _____ _____ _____	Draw a line to connect each word with its definition. **2.** volume **a.** Mass per unit volume **3.** density **b.** The amount of space an object takes up **4.** mass **c.** The amount of matter in an object

Student text pages
110–114

How can you describe pressure?

Suppose you have a container filled with water. One end of the container is large, and the other end is small. You feel the weight of the water any way you hold the container. But you feel a greater pressure when you hold it with the small end down. Why is this?

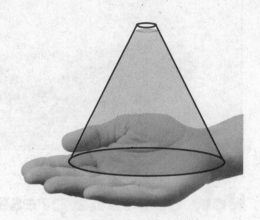

In both cases, the water exerts a pressure on your hand. But the pressure of the water on the smaller area is greater. That is because all of the weight of the water is concentrated on one spot. The pressure of the water on the larger area is lower. That is because the weight is spread out.

The weight of the water (that is, the force it exerts) is the same in both cases. But the pressure it exerts depends on the area. **Pressure** is defined as force per unit area.

INSTANT REPLAY

How is pressure defined?

_____

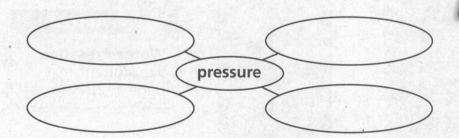

pressure

Vocabulary

In the ovals, write words or phrases that help explain the key term *pressure.*

CLASSZONE.COM

Visualization Explore how fluid produces pressure.

How does water apply pressure to a diver?

The water exerts pressure on the diver from all sides. It pushes up on the diver as well as down.

Mark It Up

Add arrows to the photograph to show how the water is pushing on the diver.

Visual Connection
See diver in student text, page 111.

How does the pressure of water on an object vary?

Suppose the diver goes deeper underwater. Will the pressure of the water on the diver be the same? No. The pressure of the water will be greater the deeper she goes. This is because when she goes deeper under water, there is more water pressing in from all sides. The added weight of the water above her makes the pressure greater all around.

In the picture on the left, the shorter arrows show less pressure on the object. The longer arrows on the right show more pressure on the object in deeper water. In general, pressure in fluids increases with depth.

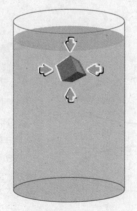
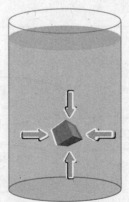

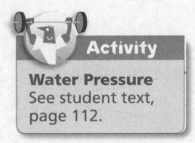

Activity

Water Pressure
See student text, page 112.

Where is water pressure greater, at the top or the bottom of a container?

How is air pressure like water pressure?

Both water and air are fluids. A **fluid** is a substance that flows. You can see water—and other liquids—flow. If you drop a leaf into a stream, you can watch it move down stream with the flowing water.

low pressure

high pressure

You cannot see air—and other gases—flow. But you can see how moving air affects things that are in it. The leaves on a tree move as air flows through the tree. Wind can carry a leaf away just as moving water can.

Like water, air presses on objects that are in it. Air does not have to be moving to press on the objects in it. Air is pressing on this hiker from all directions.

Air pressure is like water pressure in another way. The deeper you go, the higher the pressure. Standing on Earth's surface, however, you are already at the bottom of the layer of air. When you climb higher, air pressure gets lower.

Where is air pressure greater, at the top or the top of a mountain or the bottom?

_____

SECTION 4.2

SUMMARIZE

1. One fish is swimming near the sea floor. Another is swimming near the surface of the water. On which fish is the water pressure greater? Why?

   _____

   _____

   _____

   _____

   _____

VOCABULARY

Fill each blank with the correct word from the list.

area   fluid   deeper

1. A _____ can be a liquid or a gas.

2. The _____ you go underwater, the higher the water pressure.

3. Pressure is defined as force per unit _____.

Student text pages 116–122

What is the buoyant force?

Gravity is the force that pulls objects toward Earth. A fluid—such as air or water—exerts forces on an object from all directions. Some of the fluid's force is from underneath the object. It pushes up on the object. It works in the opposite direction of gravity. This upward force is called the **buoyant force.**

What causes the buoyant force on an object in water?

This picture shows a water-filled balloon under water in a beaker. The arrows show the pressure of the water on the balloon. The pressure on the bottom of the balloon is greater than the pressure on the top of the balloon. The difference in pressure creates the upward force on the balloon.

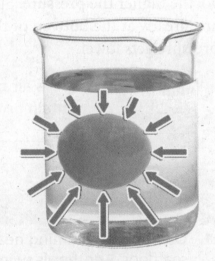

When you put the balloon into the water, the water level rises. This is because the balloon pushes some of the water out of the way. The size of the buoyant force depends on how much water the balloon displaces, or pushes aside.

INSTANT REPLAY

Is there more water pressure pushing up on the balloon or down on the balloon?

_____

Activity

Forces in Liquid
See student text, page 116.

How does the buoyant force depend on the displaced fluid?

The buoyant force is equal to the weight of the displaced fluid. If you put the balloon in water, it would displace a certain amount of water. The weight of this water equals the buoyant force on the balloon. Like water, air exerts a buoyant force. A balloon in air displaces some of the air. In this case, the buoyant force is equal to the weight of the displaced air.

When will an object float?

When you put an object into a fluid, it might sink or it might float. What makes the difference? Whether an object sinks or floats depends on two things:

- The weight of the object
- The buoyant force on the object

The weight of the object is the force of gravity pulling down on it. The buoyant force on an object is equal to the weight of the fluid that is displaced. If you know these two amounts, you can predict whether an object will sink or float.

 To predict whether an object will float, what two things do you need to know?

_____ _____

Comparing Weight and Buoyant Force

One way to predict whether an object will sink or float is to compare its weight with the buoyant force. If you place an object into a fluid (in the middle) here's what happens:

If the object's weight is greater than the buoyant force, the object moves downward, or sinks.

If the object's weight is less than the buoyant force, the object moves upward and floats.

What if the buoyant force on the object is the same as the object's weight? The object will neither sink nor rise. It will remain where you place it.

Comparing the Densities of the Fluid and the Object

Mark It Up

Label each ball with the number of the statement that describes it.

Another way to predict whether an object will float in a fluid is to compare the density of the object with the density of the fluid.

(1) If the object is denser than the fluid, the object will sink.

(2) If the object is less dense than the fluid, the object will float.

(3) If the object and the fluid are the same density, the object will not rise or fall in the fluid. It will remain where it is placed. It will be suspended.*

 When an object and the fluid it is in have the same density, what will happen to the object?

_____

How does the density of a fluid affect the buoyant force?

The density of a fluid, like the density of a solid object, is mass per unit volume. Here are some densities of common fluids.

Fluid	Density (g/cm³)
Corn syrup	1.36
Whole milk	1.03
Water	1.00
Gasoline	0.73

Water is less dense than milk, and gasoline is less dense than water.

Activity

Buoyancy
See student text, page 118.

*Academic Vocabulary: An object is **suspended** when it does not move up or down but hangs or floats in one place.

The amount of the buoyant force depends on the density of the fluid the object is in. The buoyant force that water exerts is greater than the buoyant force that air exerts. Corn syrup is denser than water. The buoyant force that corn syrup exerts is greater than the buoyant force that water exerts. This is because the greater the density, the greater the weight of the displaced fluid.

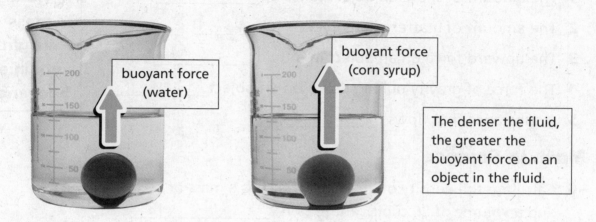

buoyant force (water)

buoyant force (corn syrup)

The denser the fluid, the greater the buoyant force on an object in the fluid.

INSTANT REPLAY

Which fluid will exert a greater buoyant force on a 6-gram marble, a denser fluid or a less dense fluid?

_____

SECTION 4.3	
SUMMARIZE	**VOCABULARY**
1. Suppose you drop a lump of clay into a glass of milk. The density of the milk is 1.03 g/cm^3. The density of the clay is 1.83 g/cm^3. Would the clay sink or float? _____ _____ _____ _____	Circle the word that makes each sentence correct. 2. An object's **weight / buoyancy** is the force of gravity pulling down on the object. 3. The buoyant force is the force pushing **up / down** on an object in a fluid. 4. An object will **float / sink** if it is more dense than the fluid it is in.

4 Density and Buoyancy

Vocabulary Write the term that matches each definition.

| fluid |
| mass |
| weight |
| volume |
| buoyancy |

1 The amount of space an object takes up _____

2 The amount of matter in an object _____

3 The upward force on an object in a fluid _____

4 The force of gravity pulling down on an object _____

5 A substance that flows _____

Math in Science

6 Calculate the density of an object that has a mass of 10 grams and a volume of 20 cubic centimeters. _____

7 What is the density of an object that has a mass of 40 grams and a volume of 200 cubic centimeters? _____

8 You find that 2mL of a liquid has a mass of 2 grams. What is the density of the liquid? _____

the BIG idea

9 Describe how the buoyant force affects a beach ball floating on a pool.

_____

Test Practice

10 When you place an object in a fluid, the object will float if it has

A a higher density than the fluid
B a lower density than the fluid
C a smaller volume than the fluid
D more mass per unit volume than the fluid

11 The density of an object is found by dividing the mass of the object by the

A volume of the object
B weight of the object
C unit volume of the object
D unit weight of the object

5 Properties of Matter

Getting Ready to Learn

Review Concepts

- Matter has mass and volume.
- Each element is made up of one kind of atom.

Activity

Internet Activity: Size of an Atom
See student text, page 135.

Review Vocabulary

Write the correct term for each description.

density   mass   matter   particle   volume

What is the measure of the amount of matter an object has?

_____

What is a small piece of matter? _____

What is a measure of the amount of space an object takes up?

_____

What is mass per unit of volume of a material? _____

What is anything that has mass and volume? _____

Preview Key Vocabulary

Following are some key terms you will see in this chapter. As you read the chapter, note how different terms are related. Use the diagrams to explain the relationship between each pair of terms.

(atom)————————————(molecule)

(element)————————————(compound)

(physical change)————————————(chemical change)

SECTION
5.1

Key Concept
Matter is made of atoms.

Student text pages
137–141

What is an atom?

Suppose you are looking at a brick wall. You can see the individual bricks that form the wall. You take one brick and hit it with a hammer. You can see the clay dust that forms the brick. Say you could take this dust and break it into the smallest pieces possible. You would have a pile of atoms. An **atom** is the smallest basic unit* of matter.

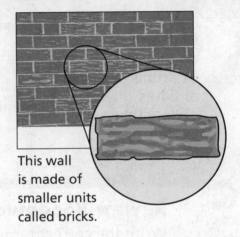
This wall is made of smaller units called bricks.

INSTANT REPLAY

What is an atom?

_____

Underline the sentence that gives the definition.

You cannot see atoms. They are too small. Even if you looked at a material under a microscope, you could not see any atoms.

The Size of Atoms

Atoms are so small that billions of atoms form the dot on top of this *i*. A teaspoon of water is made of about 500,000,000,000,000,000,000,000 atoms. So there are millions of times more atoms in a teaspoon of water than there are people in the entire world.

INSTANT REPLAY

Why can't you see atoms? _____

The Mass of Atoms

Atoms are very, very small. But they still have mass. Scientists measure the mass of atoms by measuring the mass of many atoms together. Then they divide this measurement by the number of atoms they have.

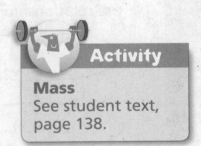
Activity

Mass
See student text, page 138.

*Academic Vocabulary: A **unit** is a single building block which can be combined with others to form a larger whole.

What is a molecule?

Two or more atoms can bond together. When atoms combine like this, they form a new particle. This kind of particle is called a molecule. A **molecule** is a particle of matter that is made up of two or more atoms bonded together.

 Fill in the blanks: A _____ is a particle of matter that is made up of two or more _____ bonded together.

Molecules as Units of Matter

Some substances are made of molecules, not of individual atoms. The molecule is the smallest unit of these substances. For instance, water is made up of molecules. Each water molecule is made of two atoms of hydrogen and one atom of oxygen. Suppose you split a water molecule into its atoms. You would get hydrogen and oxygen atoms. Hydrogen and oxygen are different from water. At room temperature, water is a liquid. But at room temperature, hydrogen and oxygen are gases. Hydrogen and oxygen can both catch on fire easily. Water, on the other hand, will put out a fire.

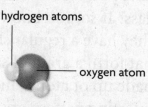

hydrogen atoms

oxygen atom

Water molecule

How Molecules Can Vary

Water is an example of a molecule that is made up of different kinds of atoms. Some molecules, however, are made up of two or more atoms of the same kind. For example, a molecule of oxygen gas is made of two atoms of oxygen.

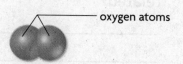

oxygen atoms

Molecule of oxygen gas

   The number of atoms in a molecule can also vary. For example, many molecules are made of only a few atoms. Molecules of hydrogen gas, oxygen gas, and water are each made of two or three atoms. However, molecules of some substances are made of a large number of atoms. For example, a molecule of vitamin E is made of 81 atoms.

Some molecules are made of many atoms strung together in a long chain. We call these long-chain molecules **polymers.** Nylon is a polymer. The molecules that form nylon are long chains. They stretch and bend when you pull a piece of nylon.

What do we call molecules made of long chains of atoms?

_____

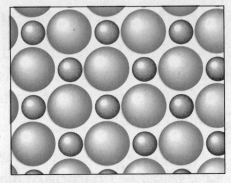

Salt is a crystal. The units that form it repeat in a pattern.

What is a crystal?

Have you ever looked at a grain of salt with a magnifying glass? If so, you know that grains of salt are tiny cubes. They have a regular shape. That is because the units that form a grain of salt repeat in a clear pattern. Solids made up of atoms, molecules, or other units that have a repeating pattern are called **crystals.** Salt is a crystal. Ice is also a crystal. Many other solids also form crystals.

Mark It Up

The units that make up this salt crystal form a regular repeating pattern. Use a highlighter to outline the pattern.

SECTION 5.1	
SUMMARIZE	**VOCABULARY**
1. How are atoms and molecules related? _____ _____ _____	Circle the word that makes each sentence correct. **2.** A molecule made of a long chain of atoms is called a **polymer / crystal.** **3.** A solid with a regular shape formed of a repeating pattern of atoms, molecules or other units is called a **polymer / crystal.**

5.2 Matter combines to form different substances.

Student text pages
143–147

What is an element?

You have learned that matter is made up of particles called atoms. There are different kinds of atoms. Hydrogen atoms and oxygen atoms are two kinds of atoms. Gold atoms and aluminum atoms are two more kinds of atoms. Altogether, there are more than 100 different kinds of atoms.

Some substances are made of a single type of atom. Such substances are called elements. An **element** is a substance formed of only one kind of atom. Hydrogen, oxygen, gold, and aluminum are each elements. There are as many elements as there are kinds of atoms. So there are more than 100 elements.

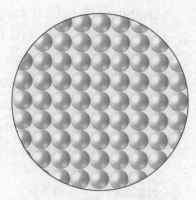

Aluminum is an element. Only aluminum atoms are found in aluminum foil.

Complete the sentence: An element is a substance formed of _____

What is a compound?

You've seen that atoms of different kinds sometimes form bonds. For example, hydrogen atoms and oxygen atoms bond to form water molecules. Substances formed of two or more kinds of atoms bonded together are called **compounds.** Water is a compound. It is formed of hydrogen atoms and oxygen atoms bonded together.

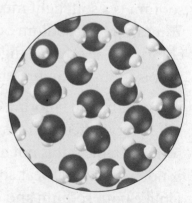

Water is a compound. It is formed of molecules made up of hydrogen and oxygen atoms bonded together.

What is a compound?

_____

Underline the sentence that gives the definition.

Forming Compounds

For any compound, the kinds of elements that form the compound are always the same. For example, water is always formed of the elements hydrogen and oxygen. Water is never formed of any other elements.

The elements that form a compound always combine in specific numbers. For example, a molecule of water always has two hydrogen atoms for every oxygen atom. There are never four hydrogen atoms in a molecule of water. There are never two oxygen atoms in a molecule of water. The number and kinds of atoms that form each unit of a compound is always the same.

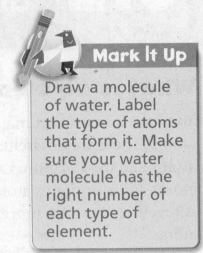

Mark It Up

Draw a molecule of water. Label the type of atoms that form it. Make sure your water molecule has the right number of each type of element.

Suppose you have two molecules of the same compound. How do the two molecules compare?

_____

Properties of Compounds Compared to Their Elements

Compounds almost always have different properties* from the elements that form them. For example, table salt is a compound of two elements, sodium and chlorine. By itself, sodium is a soft, light metal. It explodes if it comes near water. You cannot eat sodium because it is poisonous. By itself, chlorine is also very dangerous. It is a greenish-yellow gas. It is poisonous if you breathe it.

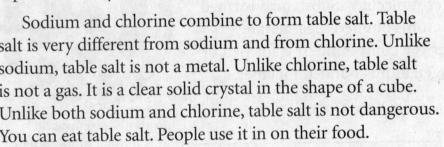

Sodium and chlorine combine to form table salt. Table salt is very different from sodium and from chlorine. Unlike sodium, table salt is not a metal. Unlike chlorine, table salt is not a gas. It is a clear solid crystal in the shape of a cube. Unlike both sodium and chlorine, table salt is not dangerous. You can eat table salt. People use it in on their food.

Circle the word or phrase that makes the sentence correct: Compounds usually have **the same properties as / different properties from** the elements that form them.

*Academic Vocabulary: A **property** is an important feature of an object or substance. A property helps you define the object or substance. It helps you distinguish the object or substance from all others.

What are pure substances?

A pure substance is made up of only one type of atom or molecule. A bar of gold is a pure substance. It is formed of atoms of only one type—gold atoms. Water that has been filtered, boiled, and treated very carefully might be a pure substance. It is formed of molecules of only one type—water molecules.

A pure substance is either an element or a compound. Pure substances are not very common. Most things that you see around you are made up of a mixture of substances. For example, your drinking water probably looks like pure water. However, drinking water has minerals in it. It also usually has chemicals added to it. These chemicals help kill germs in water that could make you sick.

What is a mixture?

Two or more substances are combined in a mixture. A **mixture** is a combination of substances. A mixture has these features:

- The substances in a mixture keep their individual properties.

- You can put different amounts of the substances into a mixture and still have the mixture be recognizable.

- The substances in a mixture can be separated from each other physically.

 Underline the key words in the list describing the three features of a mixture.

An Example of a Mixture

A salad is a good example of a mixture. To make a salad, you cut different kinds of vegetables into small pieces. Then you mix the pieces together.

If you serve yourself some salad, you will be able to recognize the different vegetables. The carrot slices still look and taste like carrots. The lettuce pieces still look and taste like lettuce. In this way, substances that make up the salad mixture keep their individual properties.

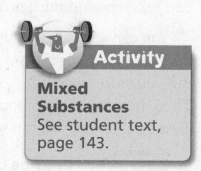

Activity

Mixed Substances
See student text, page 143.

After tasting the salad, you might decide that it needs more carrot. The mixture will still be a salad, even if you add an extra carrot. You can also add any amount of any of the vegetables, and the mixture will be recognizable as a salad.

If you stir a spoonful of sugar into a glass of water, you have a mixture. This mixture is sugar water. As a mixture, sugar water differs from salad. That is because you cannot see the parts that make up the mixture. The sugar dissolves in the water. Then you can no longer see it.

Even though you can't see the sugar in the sugar water, you still can identify it in the mixture. You can taste the sugar mixed in the water. So both the sugar and the water keep their properties after they are mixed together.

Mark It Up

Label the different substances that are in the salad mixture shown here.

You can make sugar water by mixing a teaspoon of sugar in a glass of water. You can make sugar water by mixing several teaspoons of sugar in the water. You can make sugar water by mixing a half a cup of sugar in the water. Just about any amount of sugar added to water will make sugar water. The mixture will be recognizable no matter the amount of sugar you add.

Separating Mixtures

One property of a mixture is that you can physically separate the different substances in the mixture. If the salad has a vegetable you don't like, you can pick out the pieces of this vegetable. In this way, you can separate substances in the salad from one another.

You can separate the sugar from the sugar water as well. It is not as easy to remove sugar from sugar water as picking vegetables out of salad. But you still can do it. You have to heat up the water or let it sit in sunlight. Then the water will evaporate. The sugar will remain on the bottom of the glass. In this way, you can separate the parts that make up the mixture.

Describe one way to separate a mixture.

_____

How do compounds and mixtures differ?

Compounds and mixtures both have different substances combined in them. However, compounds and mixtures differ in important ways. The chart summarizes the differences.

Activity

Mixtures and Compound See student text, page 146.

Compounds	Mixtures
When the substances combine, they bond. This causes a new substance (the compound) to form. The compound has different properties from the original substances.	The substances combine by mixing together. The individual parts keep their original properties.
To make the compound, you have to combine specific substances in set numbers. Otherwise the compound will not form.	To make the mixture, you can combine the substances in any amount. You don't need set amounts of each substance to make the mixture.
You can't use physical means to get the original substances back. You would have to use chemical means to break the bonds between the atoms.	You can remove the original substances by physical means.

Circle the correct answer: When two different substances combine by making chemical bonds, the result is

a compound   a mixture   either a compound or a mixture

SECTION 5.2

SUMMARIZE	VOCABULARY
1. Is sugar water a pure substance? Explain your answer. _____ _____ _____ _____ _____ _____	Draw a line to connect each word with its definition. 2. compound — made of substances that are combined but not chemically bonded 3. element — made of only one kind of atom 4. mixture — made of two or more different kinds of atoms bonded together

Student text pages
149–155

What are physical properties of matter?

Suppose you want to describe the chair you sit in during science class. You might describe its size and shape. You might describe its color and texture. You might describe whether it is hard or soft. All of these characteristics* are physical properties. A **physical property** is any characteristic of a substance you can observe without changing the identity of the substance.

Fill in the blank: A physical property is any characteristic of a substance you can observe

_____

of the substance.

Observing Physical Properties

You use your five senses to observe the properties of substances.

- You use your sense of sight to observe color, size, and shape.

- You use your sense of touch to observe texture, hardness, softness, and stretchiness.

- You use your sense of smell or taste to observe sweetness and sourness.

- You can use your sense of hearing to find out if an object is solid or hollow.

These are few examples of physical properties you can easily observe.

Observing a physical property of an object doesn't change the identity of the object. Think about a rubber band, for example. You can pull on a rubber band and observe how it stretches. But stretching a rubber band doesn't change the rubber band into something else. It is still a rubber band.

*Academic Vocabulary: A **characteristic** is something that helps you identify, describe, or recognize an object.

Changing Physical Properties of Objects

Sometimes you can change a physical property of an object without changing the object. For example, you can change the color of a wooden chair. You can paint it. Even though the chair is a different color, it is still a wooden chair.

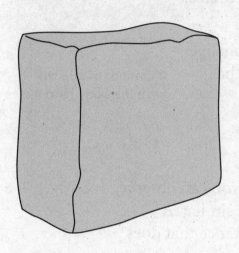

Block of clay

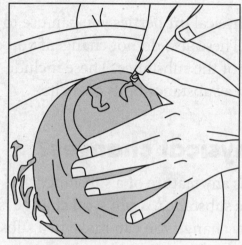

Shaped clay

Another example is clay. You can cut a block of clay in half. Now the clay block has a different shape, a different mass, and a different volume. But it is still clay. You can mold it into a bowl and it is still clay. You are changing some physical properties of the block of clay. But you still have the same substance. The clay is still clay.

Activity

Physical Properties
See student text, page 149.

Which physical properties help you to identify substances?

There are some physical properties of substances that you cannot change. One of these properties is density. You read in Chapter 4 that density is the mass of an object divided by its volume.

Suppose you cut a block of clay in half to make a bowl. The new block of clay has half the mass and half the volume of the original block. The density is the same as the original block of clay.

What is one physical property you can use to help identify a substance?

Density is not the only physical property of a substance you can use to identify the substance. Hardness can also help you identify many substances. Many rocks and minerals can be identified by their hardness. For example, diamonds are very hard. They are difficult to scratch or dent. The size and shape of the diamond doesn't matter. All diamonds are hard.

There are other physical properties you can use to identify a substance. These also do not change if you change the shape or amount of the substance. These include the temperature at which a substance boils or melts.

Diamonds of all sizes have the same hardness.

What are physical changes?

A physical property is any feature of a substance that you can observe without changing the substance. A **physical change** is similar. A physical change is any change you can make in a substance that does not change the substance into something else.

What is a physical change? _____

Underline the sentence that gives the definition.

Everyday Examples of Physical Changes

Stretching a rubber band is a physical change. When you stretch a rubber band, the rubber band changes size. Its color may look a little lighter, too. But stretching the rubber band does not change the material the rubber band is made of. The rubber band is still made of rubber.

Visual Connection
See the sweater-making process in the student text, page 153.

Painting a chair is also a physical change. The chair looks different but it is still made of wood. Cutting and shaping a block of clay are physical changes, as well. The size and shape of the block change, but the material has not changed. It is still clay. Other examples of physical changes include ripping paper, tearing cloth, and chopping food. There are many other examples. In each example, the change alters what the object looks like. But the substance the object is made of does not change.

Physical Changes and States of Matter

Matter exists in different states. The most familiar states of matter are solids, liquids, and gases. Think about water. Water in its solid form is ice.

Suppose an ice cube melts. It becomes a small puddle of liquid water. Is an ice cube melting a physical change? The size and shape of the material both changed. But has the material changed? Ice and liquid water are both water. Both are formed of water molecules. So melting an ice cube doesn't change the material the ice cube is made of. That means melting ice is a physical change.

Any other change in state of matter is a physical change, as well. Liquid water can evaporate and become a gas. You see this gas when you look at clouds. A liquid changing into a gas is a change in state. It is a physical change. A gas changing into a liquid is also a change in state. You see this happen when you see rain falling from a cloud. A gas changing into a liquid is a physical change.

Mark It Up

Label the physical change that is shown in this picture.

Why is melting an ice cube a physical change?

_____

_____

What are chemical properties of matter?

Suppose you are sitting with your friends around a campfire. As time passes, the fire begins to burn down. You want to keep the fire burning. You add more wood to the fire. Wood is what people burn in campfires. That is because of one the chemical properties of wood is that it burns easily. This property is called combustibility. Wood is combustible. This means that wood burns well.

A **chemical property** describes an ability of a substance to form new substances. When wood burns, it changes dramatically. Think about a wooden log you might put in the fire. Before you burn the wood, it is a dense brown cylinder. After you burn the wood, it is a pile of gray, flaky ashes. Wood can form new substances by burning. The ability to burn is a chemical property of wood. As you read on page 75, this chemical property is called combustibility.

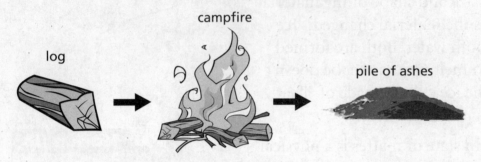

log   campfire   pile of ashes

Wood is not the only substance that has the chemical property of combustibility. Paper also has this chemical property. So does sugar. When sugar burns, it changes from a pile of small white crystals into a hard black solid mass.

Other materials have other chemical properties. For example, iron has the chemical property of being able to rust. Silver and copper have the chemical property of being able to tarnish.

What are chemical changes?

When a substance changes into another substance, a **chemical change** has occurred. Burning, rusting, and tarnishing are all chemical changes.

 What happens to a substance when it undergoes a chemical change?

Mark It Up

In the drawing, label the original substance and the new substance.

An Example of a Chemical Change

Think about a piece of iron. When iron is in contact with air, rust often forms on its surface. Rust is not pure iron. It is iron combined with oxygen. Rust forms due to the chemical change of iron atoms and oxygen atoms bonding to one another.

 CLASSZONE.COM

Simulation Explore some physical and chemical changes.

Signs of Chemical Changes

It is not always easy to tell if a chemical change has occurred. Here are some signs of a chemical change. If you notice two or more of them as a substance changes, you probably are observing a chemical change.

Mark It Up

Draw a small sketch to go along with each of the five signs of chemical change.

A new smell is produced. You can smell smoke from a campfire. The smoke includes gases the wood releases when it burns.

The temperature changes. When wood burns, it give off heat.

The color changes. When iron rusts, it turns orange. When silver tarnishes, it turns black. When copper tarnishes, it turns bluish-green.

Bubbles form. If you bake bread, bubbles form in the loaf. The bubbles are places where the dough released gases during chemical changes that occur in baking.

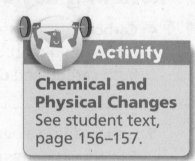

Activity

Chemical and Physical Changes
See student text, page 156–157.

A solid forms. When some liquids are mixed, a new solid substance settles at the bottom of the container. If a new solid forms, a chemical change has occurred.

INSTANT REPLAY List three signs that a chemical change could have occurred.

_____ _____ _____

SECTION 5.3	
SUMMARIZE	**VOCABULARY**
1. You have an object that changes color. Can you tell if a physical change or a chemical change has occurred? Explain. _____ _____ _____ _____ _____ _____	Fill in each blank with the correct term. **physical property** **chemical property** **physical change** **chemical change** 2. You change a substance and produce a new substance. You have caused a _____. 3. The size of an object is a _____. 4. You change the appearance of an object, but what the object is made of does not change. You have caused a _____.

Review

CHAPTER

5 Properties of Matter

ClASSZONE.COM

Go to ClassZone.com
for activities, links, and
more test practice.

Vocabulary Match the words with their definitions.

1 atom — occurs when substances change into new substances

2 chemical change — occurs when substances change in some way but they keep their identity

3 physical change — the smallest basic unit of matter

Reviewing Key Concepts

4 Carbon dioxide is a compound formed of carbon and oxygen. Do you think carbon dioxide would have features similar to both carbon and oxygen? Explain your answer.

_____

5 Is sharpening a pencil a physical change or a chemical change? Explain your answer.

_____

the **BIG** idea

6 What happens to atoms and molecules when a chemical change occurs?

_____

_____

Test Practice

7 Breaking a water molecule apart

   A makes a smaller amount of water

   B is impossible because water is a compound

   C is impossible because water is a mixture

   D gives hydrogen and oxygen

8 Density is an example of

   A a chemical property

   B a physical property

   C a chemical change

   D a physical change

6 States of Matter

the BIG idea

Particles of matter are in constant motion.

Getting Ready to Learn

Review Concepts

- Atoms combine to form molecules.
- Atoms and molecules are in constant motion.

Activity

Moving Colors
See student text, page 163.

Review Vocabulary

Write the word on the line that answers each question.

matter   **particle**   **volume**

What is a very small piece of matter, such as an atom?

_____

What is the amount of space an object takes up?

_____

What is anything that takes up space and has mass?

_____

Preview Key Vocabulary

For each set of terms, explain what they have in common. Then, tell how they are different.

solid   **liquid**   **gas**

Similar: _____

Different: _____

melting point   **freezing point**   **boiling point**

Similar: _____

Different: _____

Matter exists in different physical states.

 Student text pages
165–171

What are the states of matter?

Have you seen ice cubes floating in a cold drink? Have you felt water coming out of the faucet? Have you felt the stickiness of a hot, humid day? If so, then you have experienced water in three different states of matter. Ice cubes are solid water. The water flowing from the faucet is liquid water. There is a lot of water vapor on a hot, humid day. Water vapor is water in the form of a gas. You can't see water vapor, but you can feel its effects.

The **states of matter** are the different forms in which matter can exist. You are probably familiar with three states of matter. They are solid, liquid, and gas. Another state of matter is plasma, which is an electrically charged gas. The matter in the Sun is an example of a plasma.

Ice is water in its solid form.

 List three states of matter.

_____ _____ _____

How do the states of matter differ?

Remember that matter is made up of very, very small particles called atoms and molecules. Liquid water, ice, and water vapor are all made up of the same type of molecules. They each are made up only of water molecules. The main difference between the different states of matter is how the particles move and how they are arranged. Look at the differences between solids, liquids, and gases.

Activity

Solids and Liquids
See student text,
page 165.

Solid The particles in a solid are close together. They stay in one place. But they do move a little bit. They vibrate back and forth in place.	
Liquid The particles in a liquid are close together. But they are not as close together as particles in a solid. The particles in a liquid move freely. They slide past one another.	
Gas The particles in a gas are far apart compared to particles in solids and liquids. The particles in a gas can move freely in any direction.	

 In which state of matter do the particles vibrate back and forth?

_____

The particles in a solid are arranged like the people sitting in a theater. They are close together. They stay in one place. But they can shift forward or lean back. They can move from side to side.

The particles in a liquid are like the people in a crowd. They can move past one another. But the surrounding people limit how far they can move. They also limit how fast they can move.

The particles in a gas are like people walking by themselves outside. There are just a few particles moving in a large area. They all move freely and independently of each other. There is plenty of space between them.

Mark It Up

Circle the drawing in the table that is most like people sitting in a theater.

How do we define solids?

A piece of ice, a block of wood, and a drinking glass are solids. A **solid** is defined as something that has these properties:

- a definite shape

- a definite volume

Snowflakes are made of ice crystals.

This means that the shape of a particular solid object will not change. The volume of the solid object also will not change.

Many solids have particles that are arranged in a regular pattern called crystals. Ice is a solid formed of crystals. Crystals of ice have six sides. Snowflakes have six-sided shapes because of the ice crystals that form them.

What two properties do all solids have?

_____   _____

How do we define liquids?

Water, milk, and oil are liquids. A **liquid** is defined as something that has these properties:

- a definite volume

- no definite shape

Activity

Liquids
See student text, page 169.

The same amount of a liquid will always have the same volume. But the liquid doesn't always keep the same shape as a solid does. The liquid will take the shape of any container it fits into.

For example, you can pour a liquid into a tall, thin container. Then the liquid will have a tall, thin shape. You can pour the liquid into a short, wide container. Then the liquid will have a short, wide shape. The shape of the liquid is not definite. It depends on the shape of the container it is in.

What two properties do all liquids have?

_____   _____

How do we define gases?

The air all around you is a gas. Helium in a party balloon is a gas. Neon in neon lights is also a gas. A **gas** is a substance that has these properties:

- no definite shape

- no definite volume

Visual Connection
See Gas and Volume in the student text, page 170.

Like a liquid, a gas doesn't have a definite shape. It will take the shape of any container that it is put in.

However, unlike liquids, gases do not have a definite volume. It doesn't matter what size container you put a gas into. The gas can fill a container of any size. Suppose the container is small. Then the particles that form the gas will move closer together to fit in the small space. Suppose the container is large. Then the particles that form the gas will spread out. They will move to every part of the container.

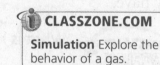
CLASSZONE.COM
Simulation Explore the behavior of a gas.

Fill in the blanks: A gas is like a liquid because both have no definite _____. A gas is different from a liquid because a gas has no definite

_____.

SECTION 6.1	
SUMMARIZE	**VOCABULARY**
1. Compare how the particles in solids, liquids, and gases move. _____ _____ _____ _____	Match each word with the properties that define it. Each word should be matched to two properties. gas liquid solid 2. definite shape _____ 3. definite volume _____ 4. no definite shape _____ 5. no deifinite volume _____

Key Concept
Temperature depends on particle movement.

 Student text pages 173–178

What is kinetic energy?

An object that moves in any way has kinetic energy. **Kinetic energy** is the energy of motion. You walk down a hall in your school. Another student moves quickly past you on the way to class. Outside, a school bus drives by. You, other students, and the bus all have kinetic energy.

Even objects that are too small for you to see have kinetic energy. Atoms and molecules have kinetic energy because they move constantly. The faster the particles move, the more kinetic energy they have.

 What is kinetic energy?

_____

Underline the sentence that gives the definition.

The Kinetic Theory of Matter

The kinetic theory* of matter explains many things that happen with matter. The **kinetic theory of matter** states that all particles that form matter are in motion. The kinetic theory of matter helps explain the differences between solids, liquids, and gases.

1. Solids The particles in a solid are not free to move from place to place. They are held close together by strong bonds. However, the particles in a solid do move. They vibrate back and forth in place.

2. Liquids The particles in a liquid have more kinetic energy than they would have in the solid state. The particles do not stay in one place. They move around a lot. They slide past each another. They tumble over one another. They are close together.

*Academic Vocabulary: In science, a **theory** is something that explains a set of related observations. Theories are supported by a lot of evidence, and are widely accepted by scientists.

3. Gases The particles in a gas move around at high speeds. Sometimes they collide with one another. The particles have much more kinetic energy than they would have in the solid state. They also have more kinetic energy than they would have in the liquid state.

gas
(water vapor)

liquid
(water)

solid
(ice)

In the picture above, make an X next to the state of matter in which the water molecules tend to have the most kinetic energy. Make an O next to the state of matter in which the water molecules tend to have the least kinetic energy.

Kinetic Energy and Temperature

You cannot measure the kinetic energy of each particle in a substance. But you can find the average kinetic energy of the particles. Remember that an average is a typical amount.

You can find the average kinetic energy of the particles in an object easily. You just need to find the temperature of the object. **Temperature** is a measure of the average kinetic energy of all the particles in an object.

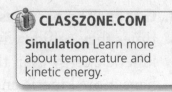

CLASSZONE.COM

Simulation Learn more about temperature and kinetic energy.

Suppose you have a cup of hot chocolate. The cup feels quite warm. It has a high temperature. This means that the particles that form the drink are moving very fast. Fast-moving particles have a lot of kinetic energy. The high temperature is a sign that the average kinetic energy of the particles in the hot chocolate is high.

Suppose you have another drink. It is a fruit smoothie. It is cold. A cold drink has a low temperature. This means that the particles that form the drink are moving more slowly. Slower particles have less kinetic energy than faster particles do. The lower temperature means that the average kinetic energy of the particles in a cold drink is lower than in a hot drink.

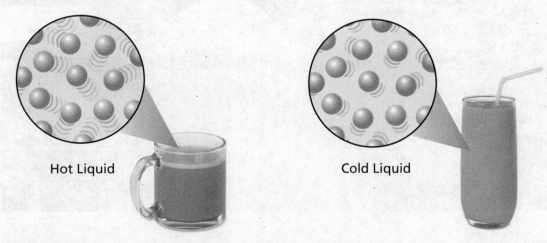

Hot Liquid   Cold Liquid

What does temperature measure?

_____

How can you measure temperature?

Think of a time when you needed to find out a temperature. Perhaps you were doing a lab in science class. Perhaps you were sick and had a fever. Perhaps you just wanted to see if you needed to wear a jacket outside. In each case, you could find out the temperature using a **thermometer.** A thermometer is a device for measuring temperature.

Activity

Temperature
See student text, page 173.

A thermometer has lines and numbers on it. The lines and numbers are a temperature scale. To read the thermometer you use the scale.

There are two common temperature scales. One scale is the Fahrenheit (FAR-uhn-HYT) scale. This is the scale we use most often in the United States. On the Fahrenheit scale, temperature is measured in degrees Fahrenheit ($^{\circ}$F). Water freezes at 32°F. Water boils at 212°F. Room temperature is about 70°F.

The other scale is the Celsius (SEHL-see-uhs) scale. This is the scale scientists use. Most people outside the United States use the Celsius scale, as well. On the Celsius scale, temperature is measured in degrees Celsius ($^{\circ}$C). Water freezes at 0°C. Water boils at 100°C. Room temperature is about 21°C.

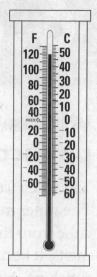

Thermometer

What device do you use to measure temperature?

_____

Activity

Temperature Measurements
See student text, page 177.

SECTION 6.2

SUMMARIZE	VOCABULARY
1. You see a frozen puddle. Do the particles in the ice have kinetic energy? Explain. _____ _____ _____ _____ _____ _____	Draw a line to connect each word with its definition. **2.** kinetic energy **a.** a quantity that is a measure of the average energy of motion of particles **3.** temperature **b.** a device used to measure the average energy of motion of particles **4.** thermometer **c.** energy of motion

6.3 Changes of state are physical changes.

Student text pages
180–185

Why is a change in state of matter a physical change?

You fill an ice-cube tray with water and put it in the freezer. The water freezes. You have solid ice cubes. You take an ice cube from the freezer and put it on a plate. The ice cube melts. It becomes liquid water. You leave the plate out in the sunshine. After a while, the water on the plate disappears. The liquid water has become a gas. It has become water vapor.

When the water changes state, it undergoes a physical change. As water freezes, for example, you can picture the water molecules slowing down and coming together in crystals. Once the ice has formed, the molecules are locked into the rigid structure where they can only move in place. Both frozen water and liquid water are the same substance, made of the same molecules. They have not undergone a chemical change. The only difference between water and ice is how easily the molecules can move from place to place, and how much kinetic energy they have.

Why is a change in state of matter a physical change?

_____

How does matter change during changes of state?

Remember that matter is made up of particles. The particles are always moving. How much energy they have depends on the temperature. When heat is added, the temperature and the energy of the particles increases.

Think about a solid. The particles in the solid are close together. They move back and forth in place. Suppose you heat up the solid. Heating gives the particles more energy. They vibrate faster and faster. Some start to break away from the particle next to them. They start to tumble and slide over the other particles. When this happens, the solid changes. It becomes a liquid.

If you continue heating the liquid, the particles gain even more energy. They start to move around rapidly. Soon, some of the particles have enough energy to form bubbles of vapor inside the liquid. The liquid is changing. It is becoming a gas. If enough energy is added, all the particles move fast enough to become a gas.

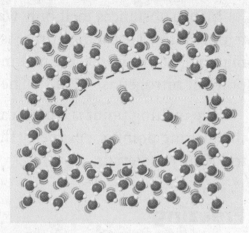

Bubbles of vapor form inside the boiling liquid.

 You heat a substance so that it changes state. How do the particles in the substance change?

_____

How does matter change from solid to liquid and back?

When a substance changes from a solid to a liquid, we say that it melts. When a substance changes from a solid to a liquid, we say that it freezes.

Melting

Melting is the process by which a solid becomes a liquid. Pure substances melt at a specific temperature. For example, ice melts at 0°C (32°F). A freezer is just a little colder than 0°C so ice stays frozen. A refrigerator is warmer than 0°C. Ice will melt if you put it in the refrigerator.

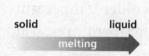

solid   liquid
melting

Other solids melt at temperatures that are much colder than the coldest temperature you've felt. Nitrogen melts at a very low temperature, at about -210°C (-320°F). Nitrogen is a gas at the temperatures you normally encounter.

Many other solids melt at temperatures that are much higher than those you come across every day. For example, iron is an important metal used in building and household items. Iron melts at 1535°C (2821°F). It takes a very hot fire to melt iron.

Visual Connection
See Melting a Solid on student text page 181.

 Fill in the blanks: Melting is the process by which a _____ becomes a _____.

Many substances melt only when they are at a particular temperature. That temperature is called the **melting point** of the material. For example, the melting point of ice is 0°C. The melting point of nitrogen is −210°C. The melting point of iron is 1535°C.

The melting point is a physical property of substances. Like density, the melting point is a property that cannot be changed. You can use it to identify materials.

Freezing

Freezing is the opposite of melting. **Freezing** is the process by which a liquid becomes a solid. You probably think something is cold if you hear it is frozen. But many things are frozen at room temperature. Anything you see around you that is solid is frozen at room temperature. Your desk is frozen. Your book is frozen. The walls of the room you are in frozen.

solid   liquid
freezing

Some materials freeze at a particular temperature. That temperature is called the **freezing point.** The freezing point of a material is the same temperature as the melting point. For example, the freezing point of water is 0°C. At 0°C, water can be a solid (ice) or a liquid. At colder temperatures liquid water becomes solid. At higher temperatures, solid water becomes liquid.

Activity

Freezing Point
See student text,
pages 186–187.

Water begins to melt at 0°C. At what temperature does it begin to freeze?

_____

How does matter change from liquid to a gas and back?

As you've read, the molecules of a substance are closer together in the liquid form of the substance than they are in the gas form. So when a substance turns from a liquid into a gas, you can expect the molecules to move farther apart. It is harder to see the change from liquid water to water vapor than it is to see water freezing or melting. This is because water vapor is invisible. It is mixed into the air.

You learned that water vapor is in air when it turns back into liquid again. This happens, for example, when hot air comes out of a tea kettle and turns into steam. Steam is tiny droplets of liquid water. It also happens when liquid water drops form on the outside of a cold glass in hot weather.

There are two different ways that a liquid can change into a gas—these are called boiling and evaporating.

 **Why don't we see water vapor? How do we know it is there?**

_____

_____

Boiling

When a liquid reaches a certain temperature and changes into a gas, the liquid is **boiling.** Boiling water makes bubbles. The bubbles contain water vapor. They contain water that has turned into a gas. The bubbles rise to the surface of the liquid. The gas escapes from the liquid.

Liquids boil at a particular temperature. That temperature is called the **boiling point.** The boiling point of water is 100°C (212°F). The boiling point of nitrogen is about −196°C (−295°F). The boiling point of iron is 2750°C (5008°F).

Like the melting point, the boiling point is an important physical property of some liquids. It is a property that cannot be changed. So you can use it to identify liquids.

 **What is the boiling point of a liquid?**

_____

Underline the sentence that gives the answer.

liquid   gas

◀ condensation

Evaporating

You probably have noticed that puddles can disappear on a sunny day. The puddles disappear because the liquid water changes to a gas. The gas is water vapor. The water vapor floats into the air.

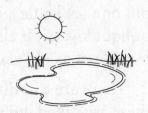

A puddle evaporates in the sunshine.

But puddles do not boil away. The water temperature is too low for the water to boil. Instead, water molecules on the surface of the puddle escape from the liquid. The process is called evaporation*. **Evaporation** is the process by which a liquid changes to a gas at temperatures lower than the boiling point.

Evaporation can occur at any temperature. Liquids evaporate faster at higher temperatures. But even at a very low temperature a liquid will evaporate.

How does evaporation differ from boiling?

_____

Condensation

Have you ever seen beads of water form on the side of a glass holding a cold drink? The water droplets don't come from inside the glass. Instead, they come from outside the glass. The drops of water come from the air. They form when the warm, moist air hits the cold surface of the glass. The water vapor in the air cools off. When it cools off, it changes state. It changes from a gas to a liquid. The liquid shows up as water droplets on the side of the glass.

condensation

*Academic Vocabulary: The root of a word can help you remember what it means. The root of the word *evaporation* is *vapor*. Remember that water vapor is a gas. Evaporation occurs when a liquid changes to a gas.

Mark It Up

Label the source of the water drops on the outside of the glass.

The process by which a gas changes into a liquid is called **condensation.** Condensation can occur at any temperature. The cooler the temperature, the faster condensation occurs. Your breath contains a lot of water vapor. When you breath out on a cold day, that water vapor condenses because it comes into contact with the cold air. This is why you can sometimes see your breath. You see the water droplets.

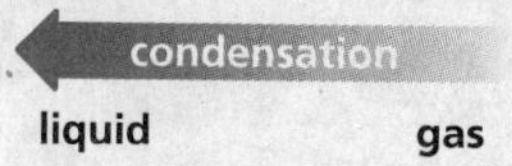

condensation

liquid   gas

INSTANT REPLAY Fill in the blanks: In the process of condensation, a _____ changes into a _____.

SECTION 6.3	
SUMMARIZE	**VOCABULARY**
1. List three ways matter can change from one state to another. _____ _____ _____ _____ _____ _____ _____ _____	Circle the word that makes each sentence correct. 2. The set temperature at which a substance changes from a liquid to a gas is called the **melting point / boiling point.** 3. The set temperature at which a substance changes from a liquid to a solid is the **condensation point / freezing point.** 4. If the water in a bowl disappears into the air, **evaporation / condensation** has occurred.

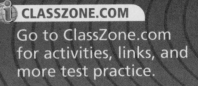
Vocabulary Complete the chart by filling in the blanks.

TERM	DESCRIPTION
1	state of matter with no definite shape and no definite volume
2	state of matter in which the particles of a substance have the lowest kinetic energy
3	a measure of the average kinetic energy of particles

Reviewing Key Concepts

4 How is a solid similar to people sitting in a movie theatre?

_____

5 You have a cup of hot water and a cup of cold water. In which cup do the particles move faster? Explain.

_____

the BIG idea

6 Compare the motion of particles in ice, liquid water, and water vapor.

_____

_____

Test Practice

7 Which has a definite volume but does not have a definite shape?

   A a solid
   B a liquid
   C a gas
   D a particle

8 Two processes by which a liquid can become a gas are

   A evaporation and boiling
   B melting and boiling
   C boiling and condensation
   D evaporation and condensation

7 Atomic Structure and the Periodic Table

the BIG idea

A substance's atomic structure determines its physical and chemical properties.

Getting Ready to Learn

Review Concepts

- Matter is made of particles called atoms that are too small to see with the eyes alone.
- Matter can be an element, a compound, or a mixture.
- Matter can undergo chemical and physical changes.

Activity

That's Far!
See student text, page 197.

Review Vocabulary

Match each word to with its definition.

_____ **atom**   a. mass per unit of volume

_____ **density**   b. something that describes how a substance can form new substances

_____ **element**   c. the smallest basic unit of matter

_____ **chemical property**   d. something that can be observed about a substance without changing its identity

_____ **physical property**   e. a substance that is formed of only one kind of atom

Preview Key Vocabulary

Use the frames to write important details about each of the terms.

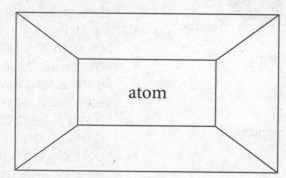

atom

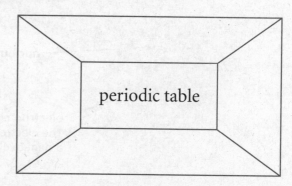

periodic table

Atoms are the smallest form of elements.

Student text pages
199–205

What makes up an atom?

In Chapter 5, you learned that atoms are the smallest basic units of a substance. Atoms themselves are made up of three smaller particles called protons, neutrons, and electrons. All the atoms of all the elements are some combination of these three particles.

- **Protons** are particles with a positive electric charge.
- **Neutrons** are particles that do not have any charge.
- **Electrons** are particles with negative electric charge.

What are the three particles that form atoms?

_____ _____ _____

> **Activity**
>
> **The Size of Atoms**
> See student text, page 199.

Particles in the Nucleus

The picture shows where protons, neutrons, and electrons are located in an atom. The protons and neutrons cluster together in the middle of the atom. They form the atomic nucleus. The **nucleus** is the central structure of the atom.

Atoms are made of protons, neutrons, and electrons.

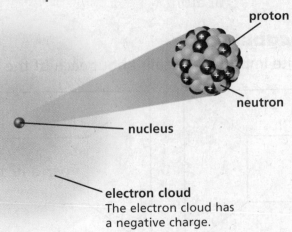

proton

neutron

nucleus

electron cloud
The electron cloud has a negative charge.

> **Mark It Up**
>
> Put a + next to the label of the particle with a positive electric charge. Put a – next to the label of the particle with a negative electric charge. Put a *0* next to the label of the particle with no electric charge.

The Electron Cloud

The electrons in an atom move around the nucleus at high speeds. We cannot tell exactly where any electron is at a given time. The electron cloud represents the area where the electrons might be. The electron cloud is very, very large compared to the nucleus. For example, suppose the nucleus were the same size as a nickel. Then the electron cloud would be bigger than your classroom!

Each electron in the electron cloud has a certain amount of energy. Electrons with similar amounts of energy move in a particular area called an energy shell. Each shell in the electron cloud can only hold a certain number of electrons.

 **What is the electron cloud?**

_____

Mass and Charge

The chart to the right shows the mass and charge of particles in an atom. Protons and neutrons have about the same mass. Together, they make up most of the mass of an atom. Electrons are much smaller than protons and neutrons. Electrons contribute very little mass to the atom.

Particle Charges and Mass		
Particle	**Relative Mass**	**Relative Charge**
Electron	1	−1
Proton	2000	+1
Neutron	2000	0

> **CLASSZONE.COM**
> **Simulation** Build a model of an atom.

The chart shows that each proton has a positive charge and each electron has a negative charge. Particles that have the same type of charge repel* each other. Electrons all have a negative charge. So electrons repel each other. That is why they stay spread out around the nucleus.

Particles that have unlike charges attract each other. The nucleus of an atom has a positive charge because it contains protons. Electrons move around the nucleus because they have an electrical attraction to the protons.

 **Which two atomic particles have opposite charges?**

_____   _____

*Academic Vocabulary: To **repel** something means to push the thing away.

How do atoms differ?

Remember that elements are the basic substances that form all matter. There are about 100 elements. The atoms that form a single element are all the same. For instance, gold atoms are all alike. Atoms that form different elements differ from one another. For example, gold atoms differ from silver atoms. They also differ from iron atoms and carbon atoms. They differ from atoms of all other elements.

Each element has a specific number of protons in its atoms. This number is different for each element. The number of protons in the nucleus of an atom is called the **atomic number** of that element. For example, a hydrogen atom has one proton in its nucleus. So hydrogen has the atomic number of 1. A gold atom has 79 protons in its nucleus. Gold has the atomic number of 79. Silver has 47 protons in its nucleus, so it has the atomic number of 47.

Fill in the blanks: The atomic number of an element is the number of _____ in the nucleus of an atom of that element.

What are symbols for elements?

Scientists have given each element its own chemical symbol. The symbols are letters. For many elements, the symbol is the first letter of the element's name. The elements below are examples. The symbol is in parentheses.

Mark It Up

Circle the chemical symbols for the different elements on this page and on page 99.

   hydrogen (H)   **sulfur (S)**   **carbon (C)**

Other elements have a symbol with two letters. The first letter is often the first letter of the element's name. The second letter is usually another letter in the name. Notice that the first letter is capitalized but the second letter is not.

   aluminum (Al)   **platinum (Pt)**   **zinc (Zn)**

The chemical symbols for some elements do not come from words in English. They come from the names of the elements in other languages. For instance, the symbol for gold is Au. This symbol comes from the Latin name for gold—*Aurum*.

 Write chemical symbols for two different elements. Give the name of each element next to its symbol.

_____ _____   _____ _____

What are isotopes?

Elements are identified by the number of protons in the nucleus of an atom of that element. Remember that this number is called the atomic number.

Neutrons are also in the nucleus of an atom. The number of neutrons in an atom of an element can vary. For instance, some atoms of the element carbon have 6 neutrons. Other atoms of the element carbon have 8 neutrons. Atoms of the same element that have different numbers of neutrons are called **isotopes.** The carbon atom with 6 neutrons and the carbon atom with 8 neutrons are different isotopes.

Isotopes and Atomic Mass Number

Isotopes of elements are identified by their masses. A proton and a neutron have about the same mass. So you can find the mass of an atom by adding the number of protons and the number of neutrons in the nucleus. The total number of protons and neutrons in an atom's nucleus is called the **atomic mass number.**

 What two things do you need to add to find an atom's atomic mass number?

_____   _____

Identifying Isotopes

Let's look at two isotopes of the element chlorine. Chlorine has an atomic number of 17. This means that chlorine always has 17 protons in its nucleus. One isotope of chlorine has 18 neutrons. You add the protons and neutrons in an isotope to find the atomic mass number of the isotope. So for this isotope of chlorine, you add 17 protons and 18 neutrons to find the atomic mass number of 35. So this isotope of chlorine is called chlorine-35.

Another isotope of chlorine has 20 neutrons. To name this isotope you first need to find its atomic mass number. You add the number of protons (17) to the number of neutrons (20) to get the atomic mass number of 37. This isotope of chlorine is called chlorine-37.

 How does chlorine-35 differ from chlorine-37?

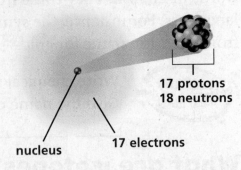

Chlorine-35
atomic mass number = 35

17 protons
18 neutrons

nucleus   17 electrons

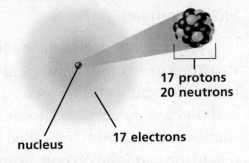

Chlorine-37
atomic mass number = 37

17 protons
20 neutrons

nucleus   17 electrons

What are ions?

A neutral atom has no net charge. This means for every positive charge, the atom also has a negative charge. So a neutral atom has equal numbers of protons and electrons.

Look at the isotopes of chlorine in the pictures above. The pictures show that chlorine has 17 protons and 17 electrons. That means that the isotopes of chlorine in the picture are both neutral.

Atoms are not always neutral. Atoms can lose electrons. When a neutral atom loses an electron, it has more protons than electrons. Therefore it has a net positive charge. Atoms can also gain electrons. When a neutral atom gains an electron, it has more electrons than protons. Therefore it has a net negative charge. Atoms that have either a positive or a negative charge are called **ions.** Atoms that have a positive charge are called positive ions. Atoms that have a negative charge are called negative ions.

How a Positive Ion Forms

The element sodium (Na) has the atomic number 11. This means it has 11 protons in its nucleus. A neutral sodium atom has 11 electrons moving around the nucleus. A sodium atom can lose an electron. Then it has 10 electrons. But it still has 11 protons. So it has a positive charge. The sodium atom has become a positive sodium ion.

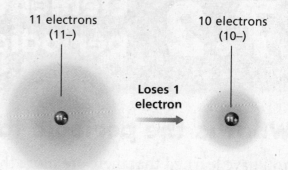

11 electrons (11–)

Loses 1 electron

10 electrons (10–)

Sodium Atom (Na)   **Sodium Ion (Na⁺)**

How a Negative Ion Forms

The element chlorine (Cl) has the atomic number 17. This means it has 17 protons in its nucleus. A neutral chlorine atom has 17 electrons orbiting the nucleus. A chlorine atom can gain an electron. Then it has 18 electrons, but it still has only 17 protons. So it has a negative charge. The chlorine atom has become a negative chloride ion.

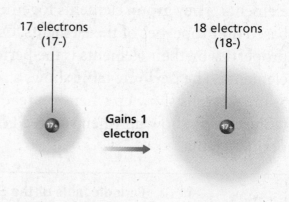

17 electrons (17-)

Gains 1 electron

18 electrons (18-)

Chlorine Atom (Cl)   **Chloride Ion (Cl⁻)**

How does an atom become a negative ion?

_____

SECTION 7.1

SUMMARIZE	VOCABULARY
1. The element carbon has the atomic number of 6. Two isotopes of carbon are carbon-12 and carbon-14. How do these isotopes differ? _____ _____ _____	Circle the word that makes each sentence correct. 2. A **neutron / proton** is a particle in an atom with a positive charge. 3. A(n) **electron / nucleus** is a particle in an atom with a negative charge. 4. Atoms of an element with different numbers of neutrons in the nucleus are called **ions / isotopes.**

Elements make up the periodic table.

Student text pages
207–213

What is the periodic table?

You have learned that there are more than 100 different elements. Each element is unique. But some elements share similar physical properties. Some share similar chemical properties.

Activity

Similarities and Differences among Objects See student text, page 207.

Scientists have studied the properties of different elements. They group elements together in different ways based on properties of the elements. One way to organize properties by their elements is the periodic table of elements. The **periodic table** shows a repeating pattern of properties. Some patterns show up when you read across the rows of the periodic table. Others show up when you read down the columns of the periodic table.

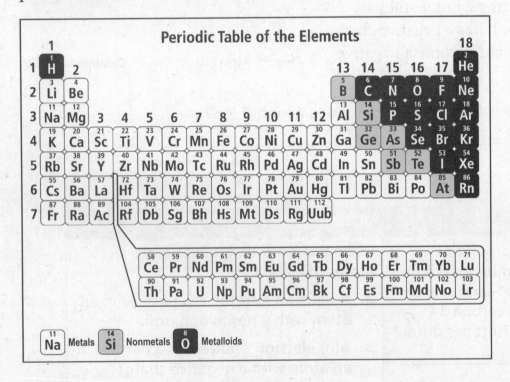

Visual Connection
See the periodic table of the elements on pages 210–211 of the student text.

Fill in the blank: The periodic table shows a _____ pattern of properties among groups of elements.

What does each square of the periodic table show?

Each element has its own square on the periodic table. The square gives key information about the element. Most periodic tables give all the information shown in the square below. What can you learn about the elements by looking at the periodic table?

1 The letter in the middle of the square is the symbol for the element. The name of the element is right below the symbol. Some elements have three-letter symbols. These elements do not have names yet. The three-letter symbol is used until an element gets an official name.

2 The number at the top of the square is the atomic number. Remember that the atomic number is the number of protons in an atom of the element. Scientists use the atomic number to identify each element. The element hydrogen has one proton in its nucleus.

3 The number below the name of the element is the atomic mass of the element. The atomic mass relates to the isotopes of an element. Remember that isotopes are atoms of an element that have different numbers of neutrons in the nucleus. The **atomic mass** is the average mass of all the element's isotopes.

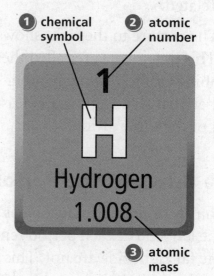

1 chemical symbol   **2** atomic number

3 atomic mass

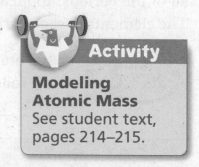

Activity

Modeling Atomic Mass See student text, pages 214–215.

INSTANT REPLAY

What is the number at the top of a square in the periodic table?

_____

What do the columns and rows of the periodic table show?

When you read a table, you can read down the columns or across the rows. The periodic table is big. But you read the periodic table the same way you read other tables. Elements can be grouped by which column or row they are in.

The Columns of the Periodic Table

The elements in a column of the periodic table are called a group. The number at the top of the column is the number of the **group.** The elements in each group share similarities. They have similar chemical properties. They often have similar physical properties. These elements are related.

The picture to the right shows the elements in Group 17. These elements are called the halogens. Halogens combine easily with many other elements. That is one property the halogens share. It is one reason they are all part of the same group.

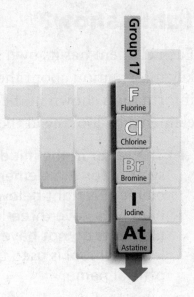

The Rows of the Periodic Table

Each row of the periodic table is called a **period.** Elements at the left side of each period tend to be metals. Elements at the far right side are not. This pattern is true for almost all of the periods. You read the periods from left to right. The elements in each period change in a predictable way.

Mark It Up

Circle the chemical symbols for the elements in the halogen group.

INSTANT REPLAY

What are the rows in the periodic table called?

_____

SECTION 7.2	
SUMMARIZE	**VOCABULARY**
1. List three things that each square of the periodic table tells you about an element. _____ _____ _____ _____	2. In the space below, sketch a simple picture of the periodic table. Label a group and a period.

7.3 The periodic table is a map of the elements.

Student text pages 216–222

How is the periodic table like a map?

You can tell a lot about a place by where it is on the map. A place in the mountains is different than a place in the desert or along a coast. In a similar way, you can tell a lot about an element by where it appears in the periodic table. The periodic table has three main regions. The largest one, on the left, is the metals. The nonmetals are on the right. And the narrow zigzag line between the two is the metalloids. You can see these regions in the diagram of the periodic table.

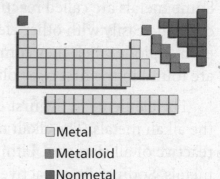

☐ Metal
■ Metalloid
■ Nonmetal

The Three Main Areas of the Periodic Table

What different kinds of elements are in the three main areas of the periodic table?

_____ _____ _____

As you read, the periodic table groups elements by their properties. One important property is how reactive an element is. An element that is likely to undergo a chemical change is **reactive.** A reactive element can easily combine with other elements. Very reactive elements are in groups 1 and 17. The elements in group 18, on the other hand, are almost completely unreactive.

Visual Connection
See the periodic table of the elements on pages 210–211 of the student text.

What are some groups of metal elements?

The area of the periodic table that contains metals is very large. That is because most of the elements are metals. **Metals** are elements that have these properties:

- They conduct electricity well.
- They are easy to shape.
- They are usually solid at room temperature.
- They conduct heat well.
- They are usually shiny.

Within the very large group of metals, there are several smaller groups. The elements in these smaller groups appear together on the table.

The Reactive Metals

Some metals are called reactive metals. These metals combine easily with other elements. Sometimes they even explode when they combine. The reactive metals are found in the first two columns of the periodic table.

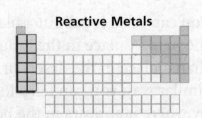

Reactive Metals

The elements in the first column, Group 1, are called the alkali metals. The alkali metals are some of the most reactive of all elements. Lithium and sodium are alkali metals. Sodium is so reactive, it will explode if it is put in water.

The elements in the second column, Group 2, are called the alkaline earth metals. They are not quite as reactive as the alkali metals. But they are still very reactive. Calcium and magnesium are alkaline earth metals.

Mark It Up

Use numbers to label the groups of elements that form the reactive metals and the transition metals.

What are the names of the two groups of reactive metals?

_____

The Transition Metals

The transition metals are much less reactive than the reactive metals. In fact, most transition metals are not very reactive at all. The transition metals include many familiar metals. Gold, silver, and copper are transition metals.

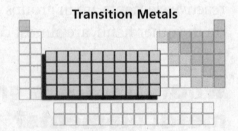

Transition Metals

There are many transition metals. The transition metals make up Groups 3–12 on the periodic table.

Give two examples of transition metals.

_____

_____

Rare Earth Elements

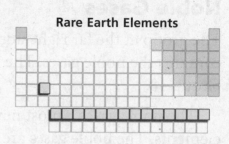

Rare Earth Elements

At one time, scientists thought the elements in this group were very rare. They could find only tiny amounts of them in the ground. Now we know that rare earth elements are not rare. They are fairly common. But it is very hard to find the rare earth elements in pure form. Neodymium, which is used to make very strong magnets, is a rare earth element.

The rare earth elements are usually shown below the periodic table. If they were put in the periodic table itself, the table would become very wide. Look at the picture that shows the rare earth elements. There are two rows of elements below the periodic table. The top row is made up of the rare earth elements.

Visual Connection
See the periodic table of the elements on pages 210–211 of the student text.

What are nonmetals?

The far right side of the periodic table is the area of the nonmetals. Find this area in the picture. Nonmetals tend to have the opposite properties of metals. **Nonmetals** are elements that have these properties:

Nonmetals

- They do not conduct electricity well.

- They do not conduct heat well.

- Most are gases at room temperature.

- Solid nonmetals are dull and are not easy to shape.

The two main groups of nonmetals are noble gases and halogens.

INSTANT REPLAY

List three properties of nonmetals.

_____

_____

_____

Noble Gases

The group at the far right side of the periodic table contains the noble gases. The noble gases form Group 18.

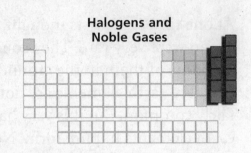

Halogens and
Noble Gases

The noble gases almost never react with other elements. The noble gases are sometimes called inert gases. *Inert* means "not able to move or act."

Helium, neon, and argon are noble gases. There are small amounts of some noble gases in the atmosphere.

Halogens

The column to the left of the noble gases contains the halogens. The halogens form Group 17. Unlike the noble gases, halogens are very reactive. For this reason, they are good at killing germs. The halogen chlorine (Cl) is used to kill germs in drinking water and swimming pools. The halogen iodine (I) is used to kill germs on skin.

 Name one noble gas. _____ Name one halogen. _____

What are metalloids?

Metalloids are found between the metals and the nonmetals on the periodic table. **Metalloids** are elements with properties of both metals and nonmetals. Silicon (Si), which is used to make computer chips, is a metalloid.

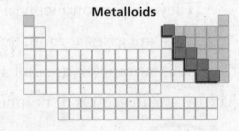

Metalloids

 What are metalloids?

_____

Underline the sentence that gives the definition.

What are radioactive elements?

Some elements are not stable*. When the nucleus of an element is unstable, it gives off particles. Sometimes it gives off protons and neutrons. Sometimes it gives off electrons. When a nucleus gives of particles, it also gives off energy. The particles and energy from an unstable atom are called **radioactivity.**

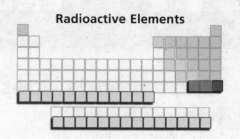
Radioactive Elements

Unstable elements are called radioactive elements. Over time, they can change into other elements. The radioactive elements are all elements with high atomic numbers and high atomic masses. Uranium (U) is an example of a radioactive element.

To be stable, an atom needs a balance of protons and neutrons it its nucleus. If an atom has too few neutrons, it will not be stable. If it has too many neutrons, it will not be stable. Radioactive elements do not have a balance of protons and neutrons in their nuclei. That is why they are unstable.

Activity

Radioactivity
See student text, page 221.

SECTION 7.3	
SUMMARIZE	**VOCABULARY**
1. What are the three main areas of the periodic table? _____ _____ _____ _____	Draw a line to connect each word with its definition. **2.** radioactive **a.** said of an element that combines easily with other elements **3.** reactive **b.** said of an element that has an unstable nucleus

*Academic Vocabulary: Something that is **stable** does not change easily.

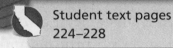
Student text pages
224–228

What trends does the periodic table show?

The periodic table shows some trends down the columns and across the rows. Elements in a column of the periodic table are called a group. A row of the periodic table is called a period.

Size of Atoms

Atoms of different elements vary in size. The size of an atom depends on the size of the atom's electron cloud. The size of the electron cloud depends partly on how many electrons it holds. It depends more on how the electrons are arranged in the energy shells in the cloud.

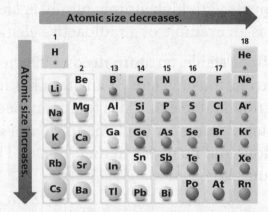

Groups 3 to 12 are not shown here.

The atom size in every group gets larger as you move down the group. The atom size gets smaller as you go from left to right across one period. The smallest atoms are in the top right corner of the periodic table. The largest atoms are in the bottom left corner of the periodic table.

Do atoms get bigger or smaller as you read down the periodic table? _____

Density and Hardness

Density describes how much matter is packed in a space. As you read down the columns of the periodic table, the elements get denser. The densest elements are at the center of the periods. At the right and left edges of the periodic table, the elements are less dense.

The densest elements are usually hard. Hard materials are difficult to scratch and dent. Dense elements are mixed into softer elements to make the softer elements harder.

Conducting Heat and Electricity

The ability to conduct heat is called **thermal conductivity.**
The ability to conduct electric current is called **electrical
conductivity.**

Activity

**Heat
Conductivity**
See student text,
page 227.

Some elements are good conductors of heat. They
usually conduct electricity well, too. The best conductors
are metals. They are on the left side and in the middle of the
periodic table. The worst conductors are nonmetals. They
are on the right side of the periodic table.

Melting Points and Boiling Points

The melting point of a material is a physical property. It is the
temperature at which the material changes from a solid to a liquid.
The boiling point of a substance is also a physical property. It is the
temperature at which the substance changes from a liquid to a gas.

Substances that have low melting points tend to have low boiling
points. Nonmetals tend to have lower melting and boiling points than
metals. On the left side of the periodic table, melting and boiling points
drop as you read down the groups. On the right side, melting and
boiling points rise as you read down the groups.

 Which kind of elements have the lowest melting and
boiling points? _____

SECTION 7.4	
SUMMARIZE	**VOCABULARY**
1. Look at a copy of the periodic table. Which do you think is larger, an atom of beryllium (Be) or an atom of neon (Ne)? What helped you decide the answer? _____ _____ _____	Answer the questions to define each term. 2. What is electrical conductivity? _____ 3. What is thermal conductivity? _____

Review

CHAPTER 7
Atomic Structure and the Periodic Table

CLASSZONE.COM
Go to ClassZone.com for activities, links, and more test practice.

Vocabulary Write the term that matches each definition.

electron
nonmetal
neutron
proton
thermal conductivity

1 A positively-charged particle in an atom
_____

2 The ability to conduct heat _____

3 A negatively-charged particle in an atom
_____

4 A kind of element that does not conduct heat well
_____

Reviewing Key Concepts

5 What do we call the Group 18 elements? _____

6 Which element would you expect to have a higher melting point, lithium (Li) or helium (He)? Why?

_____
_____

Period			Group						
	1								18
1	1 H	2		13	14	15	16	17	2 He
2	3 Li	4 Be		5 B	6 C	7 N	8 O	9 F	10 Ne
3	11 Na	12 Mg		13 Al	14 Si	15 P	16 S	17 Cl	18 Ar
4	19 K	20 Ca		31 Ga	32 Ge	33 As	34 Se	35 Br	36 Kr

the BIG idea

7 Explain how the structure of an atom determines its place in the periodic table. _____

Test Practice

8 The central part of an atom is called the

  A electron cloud
  B halogen
  C ion
  D nucleus

9 Isotopes are atoms of an element that

  A have different numbers of protons
  B have different numbers of neutrons
  C have an electrical charge
  D are electrically neutral

8 Chemical Bonds and Compounds

the BIG idea

The properties of compounds depend on their atoms and chemical bonds.

Getting Ready to Learn

Review Concepts

- Electrons occupy a cloud around an atom's nucleus.
- Atoms form ions by losing or gaining electrons.

Activity

The Shape of Things
See student text, page 241.

Review Vocabulary

Write the correct term for each description.

compound   electron   element

A material formed of only one kind of atom   _____

A substance formed of two or more different kinds of atoms joined by chemical bonds   _____

A particle in an atom that moves around the nucleus at high speeds   _____

Preview Key Vocabulary

Following are some key terms you will see in this chapter. When you reach each one, write its definition. Then sketch a picture in the space provided to help you remember the term and the definition.

Term	Definition	Sketch
ionic bond		
covalent bond		
metallic bond		

How do compounds differ from elements?

In Chapter 5, you learned that elements are formed of only one kind of atom, and that compounds are formed of two or more kinds of atoms. There are about 100 elements, but there are millions of compounds because elements can combine in many different ways.

Atoms form bonds when they combine to make a compound. These bonds between atoms are called **chemical bonds.** A compound's properties depend on these three things:

- the type of chemical bonds holding it together
- the elements in the compound
- the number of each kind of atom in the compound

What three things determine what a compound is like?

_____   _____   _____

Natural gas is a compound made of carbon and hydrogen atoms.

Kinds and Numbers of Atoms in a Compound

The same few atoms can make many different compunds. For instance, atoms of carbon and hydrogen form hundreds of different compounds. Plastics are compounds made of carbon and hydrogen, but natural gas and candle wax are also compounds formed of those two elements. These compounds differ because:

(1) They have different numbers of carbon and hydrogen atoms.

(2) The atoms are arranged differently in each compound.

Candle wax is a compound made of carbon and hydrogen atoms.

Activity

Compounds
See student text, page 243.

Properties of Compounds and the Elements that Make Them

The elements that form compounds often have very different properties from the compounds they form. For example, calcium and chlorine can combine to form calcium chloride, a white salt used on icy roads and sidewalks. Calcium by itself is a soft, silvery metal, and chlorine is a poisonous green gas. Calcium chloride is not like calcium or chlorine because it is a salt, not a metal or a poisonous gas. It has very different properties from the elements that form it.

Fill in the blank: Compounds usually have properties that are _____ the properties of elements that form them.

How do elements combine in a compound?

For any compound, the elements that form it are always the same. For example, ammonia is always made of nitrogen atoms and hydrogen atoms. These atoms always combine in a specific way. There are always three hydrogen atoms for every nitrogen atom. A comparison of quantities like this is called a ratio. We say that ammonia has a 3-to-1 ratio of hydrogen atoms to nitrogen atoms.

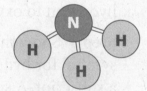
Ammonia is formed of hydrogen and nitrogen atoms in a 3-to-1 ratio.

There are two different ways to write a ratio. One way is with words. Water has a 2-to-1 ratio of hydrogen atoms to oxygen atoms. The other way is with numbers divided by a colon. Water has a 2:1 ratio of hydrogen atoms to oxygen atoms. Both ways of writing a ratio mean the same thing.

There are other compounds made of hydrogen atoms and nitrogen atoms, but these compounds have different ratios of the atoms. Only ammonia has a 3:1 ratio of hydrogen atoms to nitrogen atoms.

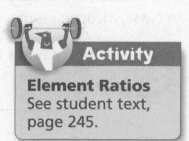
Activity
Element Ratios
See student text, page 245.

What makes ammonia different from other compounds formed from hydrogen atoms and nitrogen atoms?

_____

Writing a Chemical Formula

Have you ever heard of water being called "H-two-O"? This letter and number combination is actually the chemical formula for water. A **chemical formula** uses the chemical symbols for the elements to show the ratio of the atoms that are in a compound. This ratio can be shown with or without numbers.

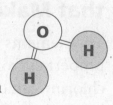

For example, water is formed of two elements—hydrogen and oxygen. For every oxygen atom, water has two hydrogen atoms. Here is how to write the chemical formula for water.

Step 1 Look at a periodic table. Find the chemical symbols for the elements in your compound. For water, you need to find the symbols for hydrogen (H) and oxygen (O).

Step 2 Look at the ratio of the different elements in water. The paragraph above tells you that there are 2 hydrogen atoms for each oxygen atom. So the ratio of hydrogen to oxygen is 2-to-1.

Step 3 Show the ratio by writing a small 2 next to the symbol for hydrogen (H). The 2 should be written as a subscript. A subscript is written to the right of a chemical symbol and slightly below it.

The ratio also tells you that there is 1 oxygen molecule, but the subscript *1* is never used. You do not need to write a subscript for the oxygen.

Step 4 Write the two symbols and their subscripts side by side. What you write should look like this: **H_2O.**

The chemical formula shows that water has one oxygen atom bonded to two hydrogen atoms.

What is the chemical formula for water and what does it show?

_____

Comparing Chemical Formulas

The chart below shows the chemical formulas of several compounds. Methane and propane are both made of carbon atoms and hydrogen atoms, but the ratio of the carbon and hydrogen atoms is different. Methane has a 1-to-4 ratio of carbon atoms to hydrogen atoms, and propane has a 3-to-8 ratio of carbon atoms to hydrogen atoms.

 What is the ratio of hydrogen atoms to chlorine atoms in hydrogen chloride?

_____

Chemical Formulas

Compound Name	Atoms	Atomic Ratio	Chemical Formula
Hydrogen chloride	H Cl	1:1	HCl
Water	H H O	2:1	H_2O
Ammonia	N H H H	1:3	NH_3
Methane	C H H H H	1:4	CH_4
Propane	C C C H H H H H H H H	3:8	C_3H_8

Same Elements, Different Compounds

Another example of how the same elements can combine to form different compounds is water and hydrogen peroxide. Water has two hydrogen atoms for every oxygen atom (H_2O). Hydrogen peroxide has two hydrogen atoms for every two oxygen atoms (H_2O_2).

Water and hydrogen peroxide have different properties. Hydrogen peroxide is a common compound you can buy in a drugstore. People use hydrogen peroxide mixed with water for first-aid to kill germs on skin. When hydrogen peroxide isn't mixed with water, it is a thick liquid like syrup and can be burned for fuel.

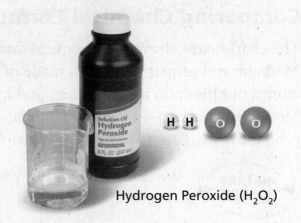

Hydrogen Peroxide (H_2O_2)

You can burn hydrogen peroxide, but you use water to put out a fire! You need to drink water to stay healthy, but drinking hydrogen peroxide would be harmful.

Water and hydrogen peroxide are both compounds made up of the same elements: hydrogen and oxygen. The only difference is that hydrogen peroxide has two oxygen atoms for every two hydrogen atoms. Water, on the other hand, has only one oxygen atom for every two hydrogen atoms. There is a difference of only one oxygen atom. What a difference one atom can make!

How does the chemical formula of water differ from the chemical formula of hydrogen peroxide?

_____

SECTION 8.1

SUMMARIZE

1. How are the properties of the elements likely to compare with the properties of a compound made with those two elements?

_____

_____

_____

_____

_____

VOCABULARY

Draw a line to connect each word with its definition.

2. chemical bond

   a. a number written next to and below a chemical symbol to indicate the number of atoms of that element in a compound

3. chemical formula

   b. a combination of chemical symbols and numbers that gives the ratio of atoms in a compound

4. subscript

   c. what holds atoms together in a compound

What holds atoms in compounds together?

If you are building a model, you might attach pieces of wood to one another. To hold the pieces of wood together, you could use glue, nails, or screws. You have several choices of how to connect the pieces of your model.

Chemical bonds hold elements together in a compound. Just as there are different ways to hold pieces of wood together in a model, there are also different kinds of chemical bonds that hold elements together.

All chemical bonds depend on electrons. Electrons move in an electron cloud that surrounds an atom's nucleus. Chemical bonds form when the electron cloud of one atom interacts* with the electron cloud of another atom. The kind of chemical bond that forms depends on how the electron clouds interact.

nucleus

electron
cloud

What do all chemical bonds have in common?

_____

How do atoms form bonds by gaining and losing electrons?

Ions form when atoms gain or lose electrons. A negative ion forms when an atom gains one or more electrons, and a positive ion forms when an atom loses one or more electrons.

*Academic Vocabulary: When two things **interact**, they affect each other in specific ways.

Pairs of Ions

An atom can lose one or more electrons to another atom. When this happens, both atoms become ions. The atom that loses the electrons becomes a positive ion, and the atom that gains the electrons becomes a negative ion.

Certain elements are more likely to form ions than others. Metals tend to lose electrons, so they form positive ions. Nonmetals tend to gain electrons, so they form negative ions.

The periodic table shows a pattern of which atoms become ions. Remember that a group is a set of elements in one column of the periodic table. Metals in Groups 1 and 2 often form positive ions. Nonmetals in Groups 16 and 17 often form negative ions.

Sodium (Na) is a metal from Group 1, so an atom of sodium tends to lose one electron. Chlorine (Cl) is a nonmetal from Group 17, so an atom of chlorine tends to gain one electron. When sodium and chlorine are near each other, an electron from the sodium atom moves toward the chlorine atom. The sodium atom becomes a positive ion, and the chlorine atom becomes a negative ion.

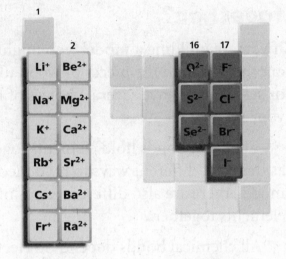

Metals form positive ions.

Nonmetals form negative ions.

Fill in the blank: Nonmetals tend to _____ electrons.

Nonmetals tend to form _____ ions.

Ionic Bonds

The top picture shows an electron from a sodium atom moving toward a chlorine atom. The bottom picture shows that the sodium atom lost an electron and became a positive ion (Na^+). The chlorine atom gained an electron, and became a negative ion (Cl^-).

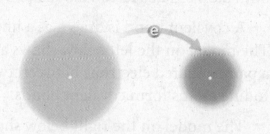

Sodium Atom (Na)   Chlorine Atom (Cl)

The sodium ion and the chloride ion have opposite charges. Because particles with opposite charges attract one another, the positive and negative ions are attracted to each other. They form a bond. The attraction between ions of opposite charges is called an **ionic bond.**

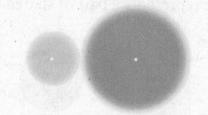

Sodium Ion (Na^+)   Chloride Ion (Cl^-)

Substances held together by ionic bonds are called **ionic compounds.** The compound formed by sodium and chloride ions is sodium chloride, or table salt.

What is an ionic bond?

_____

Mark It Up

Put a plus sign next to the positive ion. Put a minus sign next to the negative ion. Use lines to show the force of attraction between the ions.

How do atoms form bonds by sharing electrons?

Some atoms do not form ionic bonds. Instead, they bond by sharing electrons. Nonmetals usually bond by sharing electrons.

How a Covalent Bond Forms

A **covalent bond** forms when two atoms share a pair of electrons. Atoms always share pairs of electrons—they never share a single electron. A group of atoms held together by one or more covalent bonds is called a **molecule.**

What is a molecule?

_____

The shared electrons are attracted to the nuclei of both atoms. The electon clouds of both atoms overlap.

A covalent bond is drawn as a line between atoms. The model on the left below shows a line representing a pair of shared electrons between two iodine atoms. Iodine atoms form covalent bonds.

Overlapping Electron Clouds

The model on the right below shows a molecule of methane. Methane has four hydrogen atoms and one carbon atom. Each hydrogen atom shares a pair of electrons with the carbon atom. Each line represents a pair of shared electrons that makes the covalent bond.

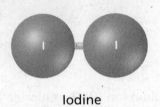

Iodine

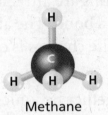

Methane

An atom may form more than one bond with another atom. For example, in carbon dioxide, one carbon atom bonds with two oxygen atoms. The carbon atom forms a double bond with each oxygen atom. A double bond occurs when atoms share two pairs of electrons. Two lines between atoms represent a double bond.

Some atoms form triple bonds with other atoms. An atom that forms a triple bond shares three pairs of electrons. When nitrogen atoms bond to each other, they form triple bonds. Three lines between the atoms show a triple bond.

Carbon Dioxide (CO_2)
Double Bond

Nitrogen (N_2)
Triple Bond

Two atoms form a triple bond. How many pairs of electrons do they share?

_____

How do ionic bonds help give compounds certain shapes?

Ionic compounds are held together by ionic bonds. In an ionic bond, ions of opposite charges pull on each other in every direction. Each positive ion bonds with the negative ions on all sides, and each negative ion bonds with the positive ions on all sides.

The picture shows how ionic bonding shapes the compound sodium chloride (NaCl). Sodium ions are positive, and chloride ions are negative. Each sodium ion is surrounded on all six sides by chloride ions. Each chloride ion is surrounded on all six sides by sodium ions. A structure with six equal sides is a cube, so sodium and chloride ions form a cube. A cube is one type of crystal.

Ionic compounds tend to be crystals. Remember that a crystal has a regular shape and is made up of parts that repeat in a clear pattern. Since ions bond with other ions on all sides, ionic coupunds have a crystal structure. Most ionic compounds have regular shapes because the ions bond in repeating patterns. NaCl forms cubes, but other ionic compounds can have different shapes. Some have two long sides, two wide sides, or six sides at different angles to each other. Some even have eight or twelve sides.

Mark It Up

Label two sodium ions and two chloride ions in the crystal. Use the correct chemical symbols for these ions.

Why are ionic compounds crystals?

_____

Activity

Crystals
See student text, page 255.

How do covalent bonds help give molecules certain shapes?

When atoms share a pair of electrons, they form molecules with covalent bonds. Atoms in different molecules share pairs of electrons in different ways, so molecules come in many different shapes. For example, some molecules have atoms that bond in a straight line, while other molecules have atoms that bond at different angles.

Some molecules even form long chains of repeating units that link together. These molecules are called **polymers.** A polymer can be a single long chain, or it can have many branches coming off of it.

A molecule made of a long chain can coil, fold in on itself, or wrap around itself. The way molecules bend, fold, and wrap gives them very complex shapes.

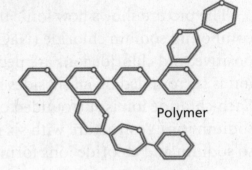

Polymer

Visual Connection
See comparing bonds in student text, page 254.

 **INSTANT REPLAY** What are molecules that form long chains called?

_____

SECTION 8.2	
SUMMARIZE	**VOCABULARY**
1. Which atomic particle is involved in chemical bonding? _____ _____ _____ _____ _____	Write each term next to its definition. **covalent bond** **crystal** **ionic bond** **molecule** 2. Formed when atoms are joined by covalent bonds _____ 3. Formed when one atom gives up an electron and another atom gains the electron _____ 4. Formed of parts that repeat in a clear pattern _____

How do metals bond?

You have read that ionic bonds often form between metals and nonmetals. You have also read that covalent bonds often form between nonmetals. Metals, however, combine with each other using metallic bonds.

Activity

Bonds in Metals
See student text, page 258.

Metallic Bonds

Metals share their electrons with atoms in all directions: above, below, and all around them. **Metallic bonds** are bonds that form because of the equal sharing of electrons. This equal sharing allows electrons to move freely among the atoms in a metal.

 What are metallic bonds?

_____

Explaining the Properties of Metals

Metals conduct* heat and electricity well, and they are easy to shape. These properties are mainly due to metallic bonds.

The picture shows the metal copper. Copper atoms bond by sharing the electrons all around them, allowing the electrons to move easily from atom to atom.

Electric current is the movement of electrical charge. Since electrons have charge and move easily in metals, metals are able to conduct electric current and heat.

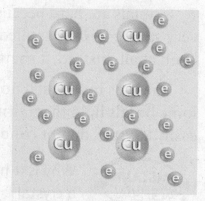

Copper atoms share their electrons freely.

 Why is copper a good conductor of electricity and heat?

_____

*Academic Vocabulary: In science, to **conduct** means to move something from one place to another.

Shaping materials often means breaking and reforming bonds between atoms. Metallic bonds bonds break and reform easily because metals share electrons equally among their atoms. If you pull on a piece of metal, the atoms slide past each other, so it is easy to make metal wire. If you pound on a piece of metal, the atoms spread out easily, so it is easy to shape metal by hitting it.

Copper can be easily shaped.

What are some properties of ionic compounds?

Ionic compounds are usually solid at room temperature. They have high melting points and high boiling points. They are usually hard and brittle, and they do not conduct electric current or heat very well.

Activity

Chemical Bonds
See student text,
pages 262–263.

The properties of ionic compounds are related to the bonds that hold ions together. Ions usually form crystals with very strong bonds that are hard to break. It takes a lot of energy to break the bonds apart, so ionic compounds have high melting and boiling points.

Crystals are hard because strong bonds make crystals rigid. When a very strong force is applied to an ionic compound, the crystal does not bend at all. Instead, it shatters and breaks into many tiny, hard pieces.

The ions in a crystal do not move very much because the strong ionic bonds hold them firmly in place. Since the electrons cannot move easily, crystals do not conduct electricity or heat very well.

Why is it hard to break an ionic compound that is a crystal?

_____

Why do some elements have different forms?

Some elements come in different forms. For example, carbon atoms can form diamond or graphite. Both diamond and graphite have covalent bonds, but the atoms are arranged in different ways.

Diamond is the hardest material in nature. It is pure carbon. Each carbon atom in a diamond forms covalent bonds with four other carbon atoms. These bonds link the carbon atoms in a diamond in all directions, so a diamond is a very strong and hard crystal.

Unlike diamond, graphite is soft and slippery because of the way the atoms bond. Each carbon atom in graphite forms covalent bonds with three other carbon atoms. The carbon atoms are arranged in flat layers that can slide past one another. When you write with a pencil, a thin layer of graphite peels off the pencil point and leaves a black mark on the paper.

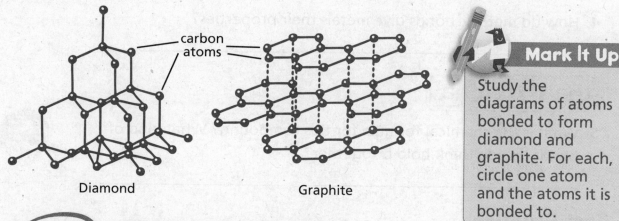

carbon atoms

Diamond

Graphite

Mark It Up

Study the diagrams of atoms bonded to form diamond and graphite. For each, circle one atom and the atoms it is bonded to.

INSTANT REPLAY What makes graphite slippery?

_____

SECTION 8.3	
SUMMARIZE	**VOCABULARY**
1. Why do ionic compounds have high melting points? _____ _____ _____	2. Define metallic bonds. How do metallic bonds help make metals good conductors of heat and electricity? _____ _____ _____

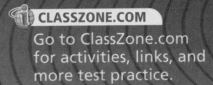

CLASSZONE.COM

Go to ClassZone.com for activities, links, and more test practice.

Vocabulary Answer the questions below.

1 How are covalent, ionic, and metallic bonds similar to one another?

_____

2 How do covalent bonds differ from ionic and metallic bonds?

_____

Reviewing Key Concepts

3 Why is there a bond between ions that have different charges?

_____

4 How do metallic bonds give metals their properties?

_____

the BIG idea

5 What is the chemical formula for this compound? What kind of bonds do you think hold it together?

_____

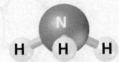

Test Practice

6 What is a molecule?

  A a substance that has only one kind of atom

  B a substance that has two or more different kinds of atoms bonded together

  C a group of atoms held together with covalent bonds

  D a group of atoms held together with ionic bonds

7 The chemical formula for a compound having one barium (Ba) ion and two chloride (Cl) ions is

  A BCl

  B BaCl

  C $BaCl_2$

  D Ba_2Cl_2

9 Chemical Reactions

Getting Ready to Learn

Review Concepts

- Atoms combine to form compounds.
- Atoms gain or lose electrons when they form ionic bonds.
- Atoms share electrons in covalent bonds.

Activity

Reactions
See student text, page 269.

Review Vocabulary

Draw a line to connect each word with its definition.

atom	the measure of the amount of matter an object is made of
chemical change	the smallest particle of an element that has the properties of the element
mass	when one substance turns into another substance due to a reaction with other elements or compounds

Preview Key Vocabulary

Following are some key terms you will see in this chapter. As you read the chapter, note how different terms are related. Use the diagrams to explain the relationship between each pair of terms.

reactant —————— product

endothermic reaction —————— exothermic reaction

Chemical reactions alter arrangements of atoms.

 Student text pages 271–278

What is a chemical reaction?

In Chapter 5, you learned that substances can undergo physical changes. A change in state is an example of a physical change. For example, water changes physically when it boils, but it is still the same substance. The H_2O molecules are the same, so the substance is still water.

Substances can also undergo chemical changes. For example, when an electric current passes through water, the water changes into hydrogen gas (H_2) and oxygen gas (O_2). The process that occurs when one substance changes into another is called a chemical reaction. A **chemical reaction** produces new substances by changing the way in which atoms are arranged.

In the example above, the water molecules separate because the bonds between the hydrogen and oxygen atoms break. New bonds form between hydrogen atoms to make hydrogen gas. New bonds also form between oxygen atoms to make oxygen gas. The water molecules have changed into molecules of hydrogen gas and oxygen gas.

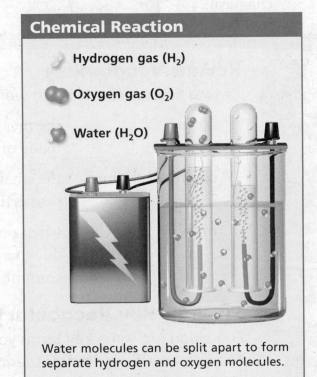

Chemical Reaction

Hydrogen gas (H_2)

Oxygen gas (O_2)

Water (H_2O)

Water molecules can be split apart to form separate hydrogen and oxygen molecules.

 **INSTANT REPLAY** What happens to a substance when it undergoes a chemical reaction?

_____

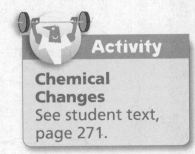 **Activity**

Chemical Changes
See student text, page 271.

What are reactants and products?

A chemical reaction starts with certain substances. The substances present at the beginning of a chemical reaction are called **reactants.**

A chemical reaction ends when other substances have formed. The substances formed by the chemical reaction are called **products.**

In the chemical reaction that occurs when electric current is sent through water, the reactant is water, and the products are hydrogen gas and oxygen gas. The picture below shows the reactants and products in this chemical reaction. The reactants are on the left side of the arrow and the products are on the right side of the arrow.

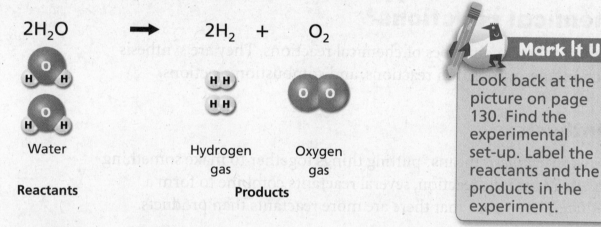

$$2H_2O \rightarrow 2H_2 + O_2$$

Water   Hydrogen gas   Oxygen gas

Reactants   **Products**

Mark It Up

Look back at the picture on page 130. Find the experimental set-up. Label the reactants and the products in the experiment.

 Fill in the blank: The substances present at the beginning of a chemical reaction are called the _____.

What are some signs of a chemical reaction?

The signs of chemical change tell you that a chemical reaction has occurred. Some common signs of a chemical reaction are

- Substances change color.

- A gas is produced.

- A solid substance forms in a liquid. A solid that forms from a chemical reaction is called a **precipitate.**

- The products are a different temperature from the reactants. Some chemical reactions give off heat, and some take in heat.

Sometimes temperature changes from chemical reactions are easy to notice. It is easy to notice that heat is given off when a substance bursts into flames! Other times, temperature changes are hard to notice because the products are only a little warmer or a little cooler than the reactants.

 **INSTANT REPLAY** Name two signs that a chemical reaction has taken place.

_____   _____

What are three types of chemical reactions?

There are three main types of chemical reactions. They are synthesis reactions, decomposition reactions, and combustion reactions.

Synthesis

The word _synthesis_ means "putting things together to make something else." In a synthesis reaction, several reactants combine to form a product. That means that there are more reactants than products.

The picture shows an example of a synthesis reaction. In this reaction, nitrogen gas (N_2) and oxygen gas (O_2) are the reactants. They combine to produce nitrogen dioxide (NO_2). Nitrogen dioxide is in air pollution.

$$N_2 + 2O_2 \longrightarrow 2NO_2$$

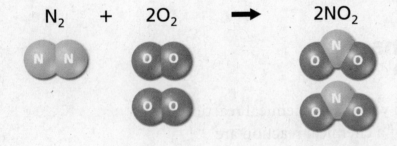

Decomposition

The word *decompose* means "to take apart." In a decomposition reaction, a reactant breaks down into simpler products. The picture shows a decomposition reaction with water molecules (H_2O) as the reactants. They break down into hydrogen gas (H_2) and oxygen gas (O_2). In a decomposition reaction, there are more products than reactants.

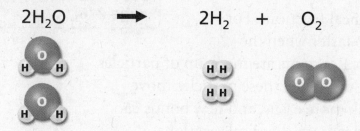

$$2H_2O \rightarrow 2H_2 + O_2$$

Combustion

Combustion means "burning." Something burns when it combines with oxygen and gives off a lot of energy. The energy is seen and felt as fire.

Methane (CH_4) is in natural gas. Many people burn natural gas to heat their homes. Methane combines with oxygen (O_2) in a combustion reaction that produces carbon dioxide (CO_2) and water (H_2O). The picture below shows this reaction.

Mark It Up

Label the reactants and the products in the picture.

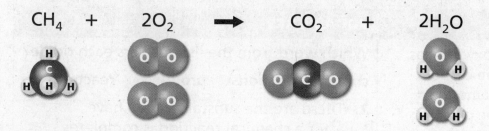

$$CH_4 + 2O_2 \rightarrow CO_2 + 2H_2O$$

INSTANT REPLAY   In a decomposition reaction, what happens to a reactant?

_____

What makes a chemical reaction go faster?

Chemical reactions can go at different speeds. Some happen quickly. For example, a match bursting into flames is a very fast chemical reaction. Others happen slowly. It can take months or years for a piece of iron to rust.

Several things can speed up chemical reactions. For example, most chemical reactions go faster when the temperature of the reactants goes up. Reactants are made up of particles. Particles move faster when they heat up. When these particles move faster, bonds between them can break more easily, and new bonds can form faster. That is why heat often speeds up chemical reactions.

Sometimes adding another substance to the reactants can speed up a chemical reaction. A **catalyst** is a substance that speeds up a reaction but is not changed by the reaction. You have many catalysts in your body. They help you digest your food and help your cells get energy.

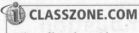

Activity

Chemical Reactions
See student text, page 276.

CLASSZONE.COM

Visualization Observe how changing the concentration of a reactant can change the rate of a reaction.

Name two things that can make a chemical reaction go faster.

_____

_____

SECTION 9.1

SUMMARIZE	VOCABULARY
1. Carbon (C) and oxygen gas (O_2) react to form carbon dioxide (CO_2). Name the reactants and the products in the chemical reaction. What kind of chemical reaction is it?	Which word from the list answers each riddle? **chemical reactions products reactants** 2. These are the substances you have after a chemical reaction is complete. _____ 3. These produce new substances by changing how atoms are arranged. _____ 4. These are the substances you have at the beginning of a chemical reaction. _____

The masses of reactants and products are equal.

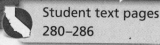

Student text pages 280–286

What is the conservation of mass?

In chemical reactions, atoms are rearranged. Sometimes molecules break apart into atoms, and sometimes atoms come together to form new combinations. Many different kinds of changes can take place, but two changes can never happen.

Activity

Conservation of Mass
See student text, page 281.

1. Atoms are never created.

2. Atoms are never destroyed.

There will always be the same number of atoms at the end of the reaction as at the beginning of the reaction. That is, mass is conserved*. The **law of conservation of mass** states that in a chemical reaction, atoms are neither created nor destroyed. The total mass of the reactants is exactly the same as the total mass of the products, because any atoms present when the reaction starts will also be there when the reaction ends.

Restate the law of conservation of matter in your own words.

_____

What is a chemical equation?

You can describe a chemical reaction in words. You can also describe a chemical reaction with a chemical equation. A chemical equation uses chemical symbols and numbers to show what happens in a reaction.

Carbon combines with oxygen to produce carbon dioxide.

$$C + O_2 \longrightarrow CO_2$$

Academic Vocabulary: Something that is **conserved** is unchanged.

The arrow in a chemical equation points from the reactants to the products. Often the reactants are shown on the left side of the equation and the products are shown on the right side. When the arrow points to the right, you read a chemical equation from left to right, the same way you read a sentence.

Writing a Chemical Equation

To write a chemical equation, you need to answer these questions.

- What are the reactants in the chemical reaction?

- What are the chemical symbols and chemical formulas for the reactants?

- What are the products in the chemical reaction?

- What are the chemical symbols and chemical formulas for the products?

A chemical equation shows the number of different atoms in each reactant and product. Look at the chemical equation below.

$$S \quad + \quad O_2 \quad \longrightarrow \quad SO_2$$

Mark It Up

Label the reactants and the products in this chemical reaction.

The subscript below and to the right of the symbol for oxygen (O) indicates how many atoms of the element are in a molecule. There are two atoms of oxygen in this equation. There are no subscripts next to the symbol for sulfur (S), so there is only one atom of sulfur.

How many atoms of each element are in the product of the chemical reaction above?

Sulfur _____ Oxygen _____

Conservation of Mass in Chemical Equations

Chemical equations are usually written to show that the same atoms that are in the reactants are also in the products. Suppose you count the atoms of each element on one side of the arrow. If you counted the atoms of each element on the other side of the arrow, you should get the same number. These numbers must be equal because no atoms are created or destroyed.

How do you balance a chemical equation?

To be correct, the numbers of the different types of atoms must be the same on both sides of an equation. That means that the equation is balanced. Follow this example below to learn how to balance a chemical equation.

The example describes the reaction of methane (CH_4) and oxygen (O_2). This reaction occurs when you burn natural gas. The products of the reaction are carbon dioxide (CO_2) and water (H_2O). If you simply write down the chemical formulas for the reactants and the products, you get an unbalanced equation.

Unbalanced Equation

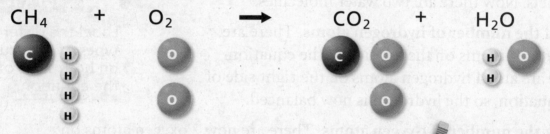

$$CH_4 \quad + \quad O_2 \quad \longrightarrow \quad CO_2 \quad + \quad H_2O$$

This equation is not balanced. To see why, count the number of atoms for each element on both sides.

Carbon There is one carbon (C) atom on each side of the equation. So the carbon is balanced.

Hydrogen The hydrogen (H) on the left side of the equation has a subscript of 4, so there are 4 hydrogen atoms in the reactants. The hydrogen on the right side of the equation has a subscript of 2, so there are only 2 hydrogen atoms in the products. The hydrogen is not balanced.

Oxygen On the left side of the equation, oxygen (O) has a subscript of 2, so there are 2 oxygen atoms in the reactants. On the right side of the equation, oxygen is in both products. One product has 2 oxygen atoms, and the other product has 1 oxygen atom, for a total of 3 oxygen atoms. The oxygen is not balanced.

Mark It Up

Write the numbers of atoms for each element on each side of the equation.

To balance an equation, you might have to add more molecules of the reactants to the left or right sides of the equation. Here is how to balance the equation in our example.

Balanced Equation

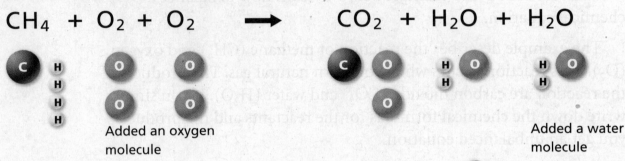

$$CH_4 + O_2 + O_2 \longrightarrow CO_2 + H_2O + H_2O$$

Added an oxygen molecule

Added a water molecule

Balance hydrogen. Add a second water molecule to the products. Now there are two water molecules.

Count the number of hydrogen atoms. There are 4 hydrogen atoms on the left side of the equation. There are also 4 hydrogen atoms on the right side of the equation, so the hydrogen is now balanced.

Mark It Up

Label the different types of molecules on both sides of the equation.

Check the number of oxygen atoms. There are now 2 oxygen atoms on the left side of the equation and 4 oxygen atoms on the right side of the equation.

Balance oxygen. Add a second oxygen molecule to the reactants. Now there are two oxygen molecules.

Count the number of oxygen atoms. There are 4 oxygen atoms on the left side of the equation and 4 oxygen atoms on the right side of the equation. The oxygen is now balanced.

How do you know that this equation is balanced?

_____

Using Coefficients to Balance Equations

A **coefficient** is a number in front of a chemical formula that tells how many molecules take part in the reaction. Instead of writing $H_2O + H_2O$, for example, you can write $2H_2O$. In this formula, the 2 is the coefficient. It means there are two water molecules.

Here is the balanced chemical equation for the reaction of methane and oxygen, with its coefficients.

$$CH_4 \quad + \quad 2O_2 \quad \longrightarrow \quad CO_2 \quad + \quad 2H_2O$$

coefficient   subscript

The equation has a coefficient of 2 in front of the oxygen molecule and a coefficient of 2 in front of the water molecule. There is no coefficient in front of the other molecules, so there is only one of each of these molecules.

To check if a chemical equation is balanced, you need to look at both the coefficients and the subscripts. The oxygen molecule has both a coefficient and a subscript. To figure out how many oxygen atoms there are, multiply the subscript and the coefficient together. The coefficient is 2. The subscript is also 2. This means that there are 2×2, or 4, atoms of oxygen.

When you balance an equation, you can change the coefficients, but you cannot change the subscripts. Changing a subscript would change a molecule into a new substance.

Mark It Up

Underline all of the coefficients in this chemical equation. Circle all of the subscripts.

Visual Connection
See balancing equations with coefficients on page 285 of the student text.

 **INSTANT REPLAY**

What are coefficients in a chemical reaction?

_____

SECTION 9.2	
SUMMARIZE	**VOCABULARY**
1. Is this equation balanced? $$CO \longrightarrow C + O_2$$ Why or why not? _____ _____ _____ _____	Circle the words that make the sentences correct. **2.** The law of conservation of mass states that in a chemical **symbol / reaction,** atoms are neither **created / changed** nor **balanced / destroyed.** **3.** **Subscripts / Coefficients** appear in chemical equations to the right and below chemical symbols. They tell how many atoms are bonded together.

Chemical reactions involve energy changes.

Student text pages
288–293

What energy changes happen in chemical reactions?

In chemical reactions, bonds between atoms can break or form. Breaking bonds takes energy, and forming bonds gives off energy. The amount of energy used or released depends on the atoms in the reactions.

In all chemical reactions, energy is taken in and given off. In some reactions, more energy is taken in than is given off. In other reactions, more energy is given off than is taken in.

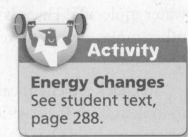

Activity

Energy Changes
See student text, page 288.

Fill in the blanks: Breaking bonds _____ energy. Forming bonds _____ energy.

What happens in an exothermic reaction?

An **exothermic reaction** is a reaction in which energy is given off. It takes energy to break the bonds in the reactants, but more energy is given off when bonds form in a new product.

Burning is an exothermic reaction.

The diagram below shows the burning of methane, an exothermic reaction.

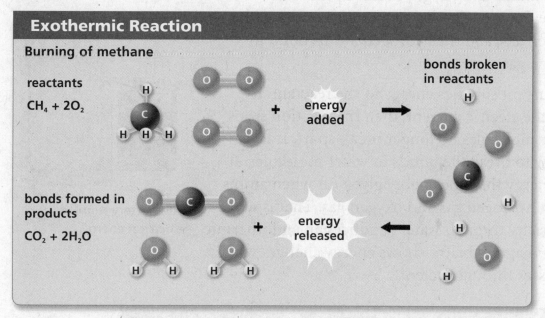

Exothermic Reaction

Burning of methane

reactants
$CH_4 + 2O_2$

bonds formed in products
$CO_2 + 2H_2O$

+ energy added →

bonds broken in reactants

+ energy released ←

When methane burns, it reacts with oxygen to produce carbon dioxide and water. The reaction also gives off heat. The diagram shows that more energy is released than is used to start the reaction. That is why burning methane is an exothermic reaction.

Why is burning methane an exothermic reaction?

_____

What happens in an endothermic reaction?

An **endothermic reaction** is a reaction in which energy is absorbed. Sometimes the energy needed to break the bonds of the reactants is more than the energy released when forming the bonds of the products. This reaction uses more energy than it releases, so it is endothermic.

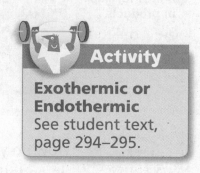

Activity

Exothermic or Endothermic
See student text, page 294–295.

When electric current passes through water, the hydrogen atoms and oxygen atoms in the water molecules break apart. The oxygen atoms bond together to form oxygen gas, and the hydrogen atoms bond to form hydrogen gas.

Electric current supplies energy to the reactant. If you turn off the electric current, then the reaction stops and the water molecules no longer break apart. It takes a lot of energy to break the bonds in water molecules. It takes more energy than the energy given off when atoms bond to form hydrogen gas and oxygen gas. That is why passing electricity through water produces an endothermic reaction. The diagram below shows energy changes when electricity passes through water.

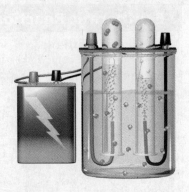

The battery supplies electrical energy.

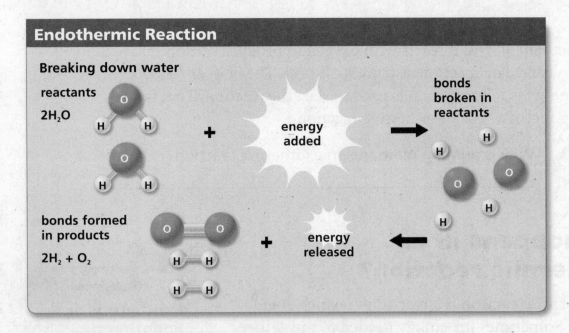

Endothermic Reaction

Breaking down water

reactants

$2H_2O$

+ energy added →

bonds broken in reactants

bonds formed in products

$2H_2 + O_2$

+ energy released ←

How do you know breaking apart water molecules is an endothermic reaction?

_____

How can you compare exothermic and endothermic reactions?

Endothermic reactions and exothermic reactions have opposite energy changes. The general chemical equations below show this.

In an exothermic reaction, energy is given off, so energy can be thought of as one of the products. In an endothermic reaction, energy is absorbed, so energy can be thought of as one of the reactants.

> **CLASSZONE.COM**
>
> **Visualization** View examples of endothermic and exothermic reactions.

Exothermic Reaction

Reactants ➡ Products + Energy

Endothermic Reaction

Reactants + Energy ➡ Products

SECTION 9.3	
SUMMARIZE	**VOCABULARY**
1. Why do chemical reactions have energy changes? (*Hint:* What happens when bonds between atoms are break? What happens when bonds between atoms form?) _____ _____ _____ _____	Fill in the blanks with the correct word. **endothermic** **exothermic** 2. An _____ reaction is a chemical reaction in which more energy is given off than taken in. 3. An _____ reaction is a chemical reaction in which less energy is given off than taken in.

Review

CHAPTER 9

Chemical Reactions

CLASSZONE.COM

Go to ClassZone.com for activities, links, and more test practice.

Vocabulary

Complete the chart by filling in the blanks.

Term	Description
chemical reaction	1
2	occurs when new substances are produced and more energy is taken in than given off
3	occurs when new substances are produced and more energy is given off than taken in

Reviewing Key Concepts

$$2HgO \longrightarrow 2Hg + O_2$$

4 Circle the products in the equation. Underline the reactants.

5 How many Hg atoms are shown in this equation?

____

the BIG idea

6 What does the law of conservation of mass tell you about products and reactants in a chemical equation?

____

Test Practice

7 Chemical equations show summaries of

A chemical reactions
B changes in temperature
C physical changes
D changes of state

8 During a chemical reaction, the total amount of mass present

A decreases
B increases
C may increase or decrease
D does not change

10 Solutions

the **BIG** idea

Forces act in fluids.

Getting Ready to Learn

Review Concepts

- Matter can change from one physical state to another.
- A mixture is a blend of substances that do not react chemically.
- Particles can have electrical charges.

Activity

Acid Test
See student text, page 305.

Review Vocabulary

Fill each blank with the correct word from the list.

ion   **mixture**   **molecule**   **proton**

An atom that has a charge because it has gained or lost an electron is called a(n) _____.

A(n) _____ is a particle in the nucleus of an atom that has a positive charge.

Two or more atoms held together by covalent bonds is a(n) _____.

A(n) _____ is a blend of two or more different things that do not combine chemically.

Preview Key Vocabulary

For each set of terms, explain what they have in common. Then, tell how they are different.

base   **neutral**   **acid**

Similar: _____

Different: _____

concentrated   **dilute**   **saturated**

Similar: _____

Different: _____

Student text pages 307–312

What is a solution?

In Chapter 5, you learned that when substances combine in a mixture, they do not undergo a chemical reaction. You can get the original substances out of the mixture.

A salad is one kind of mixture. You can see all the different kinds of vegetables in a salad. Some parts of the salad might have more tomatoes. Other parts of the salad might have more lettuce pieces. It is easy to see how substances are mixed in a salad.

In other kinds of mixtures, you cannot see the separate parts because they are completely blended. The mixture is the same throughout. This kind of mixture is called a solution. A **solution** is a mixture that is the same throughout.

What is a solution?

_____

Underline the sentence that gives you the definition.

Identifying a Solution

What happens when you stir a spoonful of sand into a glass of water? When you stop stirring, the sand sinks to the bottom of the glass. Sand in water is not a solution because it is not the same throughout. It is just a mixture.

Activity

Mixtures
See student text, page 307.

What happens when you stir a spoonful of sugar into a glass of water? The sugar mixes evenly with the water. When you stop stirring, you cannot see the sugar anymore. The sugar dissolved and spread throughout the water, to make a solution.

Is sand mixed with water a solution? Explain.

_____

Parts of a Solution

Solutions have two parts—the solvent and the solute (SAHL-yoot).

1 The **solvent** is the part of the solution that does the dissolving. It is the substance in the mixture that you have more of.

2 The **solute** is the part of the solution that dissolves to make the solution. It is the substance in the mixture that you have less of.

For example, in a solution of sugar water, water is the solvent and sugar is the solute. Seawater is a solution with water as the solvent and salt as the solute.

 In sugar water, what is the solute? the solvent?

Solute _____   Solvent _____

What are some different kinds of solutions?

In sugar water, the solid sugar dissolves in the liquid water to make a liquid solution. Solutions do not always have solids mixed with liquids. Solids, liquids, and gases can each form solutions. Solutions can be made with the solvent and the solute in the same physical state or in different states.

Activity

Solutions
See student text, page 309.

Solutions with Gases

For example, air is a solution of different gases. The main gas is nitrogen. Nitrogen gas is the solvent. Oxygen and carbon dioxide are solutes dissolved in the nitrogen. Other gases are also dissolved into the nitrogen.

Gases can also dissolve in liquids. A can of soda, such as a soft drink, has carbon dioxide gas dissolved in the liquid. When you open the can, bubbles of this gas come to the surface and make the drink fizzy.

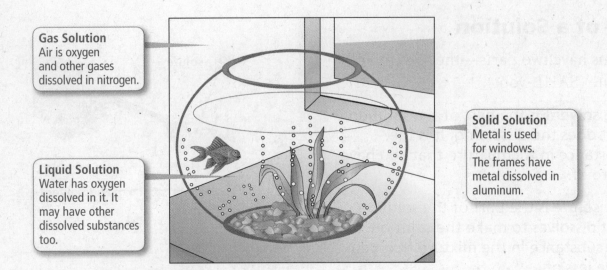

Gas Solution
Air is oxygen and other gases dissolved in nitrogen.

Solid Solution
Metal is used for windows. The frames have metal dissolved in aluminum.

Liquid Solution
Water has oxygen dissolved in it. It may have other dissolved substances too.

Solutions of Solids

Some metals form solid solutions. For example, bronze is a solid solution made of copper and tin. Copper is the main metal and the solvent. Tin is present in a smaller amount and is the solute. To form bronze, you melt tin and copper and mix the two liquid metals together. The tin dissolves in the copper. The solution cools, forming bronze.

Mark It Up

Circle the evidence in the picture that shows that gases are dissolved in the water.

Solutions of Liquids

Liquids can dissolve in liquids. For example, vinegar is a liquid solution made of acetic acid mixed with water. Water is the solvent. Acetic acid makes up a smaller part of the solution and is the solute.

Draw lines to show five pairs of things that can mix together in a solution.

solid	liquid	gas
liquid	gas	solid

How do solvent and solute particles interact?

When something dissolves, it breaks down into small particles. This happens because the solvent and the solute interact. How they interact depends on the type of bonds between the particles in the solute. Particles with ionic bonds dissolve differently than particles with covalent bonds.

How Ionic Compounds Dissolve

Remember that ions are particles with a positive or negative charge. When ions bond with each other, they form an ionic compound.

When an ionic compound dissolves, the ions separate. The positive and negative ions float in the solution and are surrounded by molecules of the solvent, as shown below.

How Covalent Compounds Dissolve

Covalent compounds are atoms that are joined by covalent bonds. Molecules are particles with covalent bonds. Molecules do not break apart when they dissolve. Each solute molecule is surrounded by molecules of the solvent, as shown below.

 Which type of compound dissolves to produce charged particles in a solvent?

_____

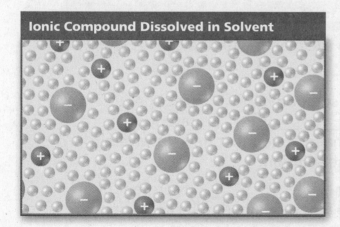

Ionic Compound Dissolved in Solvent

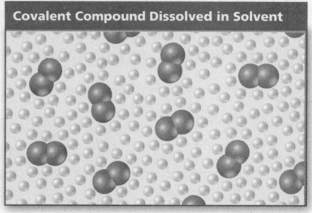

Covalent Compound Dissolved in Solvent

How do solutes change the physical properties of solvents?

Solutes change solvents in important ways. Adding a solute to a liquid lowers its freezing point and raises its boiling point.

Lowering the Freezing Point

The freezing point is the temperature at which a liquid becomes a solid. Dissolving something into a liquid lowers its freezing point. For example, water freezes at $0°C$ ($32°F$), but you can lower the freezing point by dissolving salt in the water. People often spread road salt on icy sidewalks. The saltwater has a lower freezing point than plain water, so it keeps ice from forming on the sidewalk.

Raising the Boiling Point

The boiling point is the temperature at which a liquid becomes a gas. Dissolving something into a liquid raises its boiling point. For example, water boils at $100°C$ ($212°F$), but you can raise the boiling point by dissolving salt in the water. Cars depend on a solution to prevent over-heating. That solution is formed of antifreeze and water.

 How does adding a solute to water change the boiling point of the water?

_____

SECTION 10.1

SUMMARIZE	VOCABULARY
1. How is a solution different from other mixtures? _____ _____ _____ _____ _____	Fill in the blanks with the correct word. **solute** **solvent** 2. A solution has two parts. The _____ is present in the smaller amount. It gets dissolved in the solution. 3. The _____ is present in the greater amount. It causes the other substance to dissolve.

10.2

Key Concept

The amount of solute that dissolves can vary.

 Student text pages 314–320

What is a concentrated solution?

Suppose you want to make a drink by dissolving a fruit punch powder in water. You mix a very small spoonful of powder in one pitcher. This drink has no color and looks like water. You mix several large tablespoons of powder in another pitcher. This drink has some color. You mix two cups full of powder in a third pitcher. This drink has a dark color.

The three pitchers of fruit punch have different amounts of powder mixed in them. The pitchers of fruit punch look and taste different because each has a different concentration. The **concentration** is the amount of solute dissolved in a solvent at a specific temperature.

The fruit punch that looks like water has a low concentration. A solution with a low concentration of solute is **dilute.** The fruit punch that looks very dark has a high concentration. A solution with a high concentration of solute is **concentrated.**

 Define the concentration of a solution.

_____

Underline the sentence that gives you the definition.

How can you change the concentration of a solution?

You can change the concentration of a solution in two ways.

① You can make a solution more dilute by mixing in more solvent.

② You can make a solution more concentrated by mixing in more solute.

Mark It Up

Label the picture that has the most dilute solution. Label the pitcher that has the most concentrated solution.

Adding Solvent or Solute

If you pour yourself some of the fruit drink from the bottom pitcher on page 151, it will not taste good because it is too concentrated. You can change this by adding water. You are making the solution more dilute by mixing in more solvent.

The fruit drink from the top pitcher on page 151 will taste like water. You can change this by adding more powder. You are making the solution more concentrated by adding more solute.

If a solution is dilute, there are just a few particles of solute mixed in with many particles of solvent. If a solution is concentrated, there are many more particles of solute mixed in with the particles of solvent.

Dilute
solvent
solute
Less solute is dissolved in a dilute solution.

Concentrated
More solute is dissolved in a concentrated solution.

Fill in the blank: To make a solution more
_____, you add more solute.

A Limit to the Concentration

There is a limit to how concentrated you can make a solution. Suppose you dissolve two tablespoons of sugar into a glass of iced tea. When you add two more tablespoons, the sugar will still dissolve.

CLASSZONE.COM

Visualization Explore supersaturated solutions and precipitation.

Then you try to add two more tablespoons. The sugar does not all dissolve. You have mixed in all the sugar that will dissolve in iced tea. A **saturated** solution is a solution that has the greatest amount of solute that can dissolve at a given* temperature.

How much of different substance will dissolve in a solvent?

It is easy to dissolve some substances in water. For example, sugar and salt dissolve easily in water. It is difficult to dissolve other things in water. How easy or difficult it is to dissolve a substance in a specific solvent is called the solubility (SAHL–yuh–BIHL-ih-tee) of the substance. The **solubility** of a substance is the amount of the substance that will dissolve in a certain amount of a specific solvent at a given temperature.

Activity

Solubility
See student text, page 317.

For example, ammonia is a household cleaner. A large amount of ammonia will dissolve in water at room temperature. Ammonia has a high solubility in water.

Carbon dioxide is a gas in the air. Only a small amount of carbon dioxide will dissolve in water at room temperature. Carbon dioxide has a low solubility in water.

Oil will not dissolve in hot or cold water. Oil is insoluble in water.

When a large amount of a substance can dissolve in water, the substance has a high

_____ .

*Academic Vocabulary: In science, the word *given* is used to describe a specific instance. It is often used to describe quantities that change, such as temperature or time. For example, when you report a solubility, you must include the temperature at which you took the measurement.

How does temperature affect solubility?

Raising the temperature of a solvent will change how much solute will dissolve in it. How temperature affects solubility depends on whether the solute is a solid or a gas.

Temperature and the Solubility of Solids

Most solids dissolve more quickly in a warm solvent than in a cold solvent. They also dissolve in greater amounts. For example, you can dissolve more sugar in hot tea than in iced tea. We say that solids tend to have a higher solubility at higher temperatures.

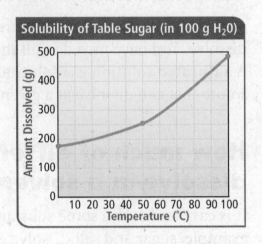

Solubility of Table Sugar (in 100 g H$_2$O)

Amount Dissolved (g) / Temperature (°C)

Can you dissolve more salt in warm water or in cold water?

_____

Temperature and the Solubility of Gases

Gases behave the opposite way of most solids. Gases dissolve less quickly in a warm solvent than in a cold solvent. They also dissolve in smaller amounts. For example, cold water has more oxygen in it than warm water does, because oxygen gas has a higher solubility in cold water than in warm water. That is why many types of fish prefer to live in cold water.

Mark It Up

Circle the part of the chart that shows what happens with a solid solute when temperature goes down.

Which are more soluble when the temperature goes down, gases or solids?

_____

How does pressure affect solubility?

Remember that pressure is force per unit of area. A gas can be under low or high pressure. Gases dissolve in greater amounts when the pressure goes up. In other words, gases have higher solubility with higher pressures and lower solubility with lower pressures.

Pressure and Solubility		
Solute	Increased Pressure	Decreased Pressure
Solid	no effect on solubility	no effect on solubility
Gas	increase in solubility	decrease in solubility

You can see this when you open a can of soda. Soda has carbon dioxide gas dissolved in it. Sealed in the can, the soda is under higher pressure than normal air pressure. When you open the can, you hear a popping sound. That is the pressure being released. The soda is now at normal air pressure. The lower pressure decreases the solubility of the carbon dioxide gas in the soda. That is why you notice bubbles of gas when you drink soda. The bubbles are the carbon dioxide coming out of the solution.

Mark It Up

Circle the part of the chart that shows what happens with a solid solute when the pressure increases.

Pressure does not usually affect the solubility of solids and liquids. Even at high pressure, you cannot dissolve more of a solid in a liquid or more of a liquid in another liquid.

INSTANT REPLAY Why happens to the carbon dioxide gas in soda when you open the can? Use the word *solubility* in your answer.

_____

SECTION 10.2

SUMMARIZE	VOCABULARY
1. What happens to the solubility of a gas when its temperature increases? when its pressure increases? _____ _____ _____ _____ _____	Circle the word that makes each sentence correct. **2.** A solution that has a high concentration of a solute is a **dilute / concentrated** solution. **3.** A solution that has a low concentration of a solute is a **dilute / saturated** solution. **4.** A solution in which no more of a solute can dissolve is said to be **concentrated / saturated**.

Solutions can be acidic, basic, and neutral.

Student text pages
322–329

What is an acid?

An acid is a specific type of solution. Acids are generally solutions in water. You are probably familiar with some kinds of acids. Orange juice and lemon juice are acids. Tomatoes have acid in them. Vinegar is an acid. There is a strong acid in car batteries. When some solids dissolve in water, they show the properties of acids.

Properties of Acids

Only some acids are safe to eat or touch. Foods that contain acids taste sour. The acids that are safe to touch can make your skin tingle or itch. Strong acids will burn your skin.

Oranges, lemons, and tomatoes have acid in them.

Acids produce positively charged hydrogen ions (H^+) when they dissolve in water. A hydrogen ion actually is just a proton. A hydrogen atom is formed of a proton and an electron. When it becomes an ion, the hydrogen atom loses an electron, so all that is left of the hydrogen atom is the positively charged proton.

An **acid** is defined as a substance that produces hydrogen ions— that is, protons—when dissolved in water. The hydrogen ions are free to react with other substances.

INSTANT
REPLAY

What is the definition of an acid?

_____

Underline the sentence where you found the definition.

An Example of an Acid

Hydrogen chloride (HCl) can dissolve in water. The picture shows the results. When hydrogen chloride mixes with water, it splits into chloride ions (Cl^-) and hydrogen ions (H^+). Since hydrogen ions float freely in the water, they can react with other substances. The solution is an acid called hydrochloric acid.

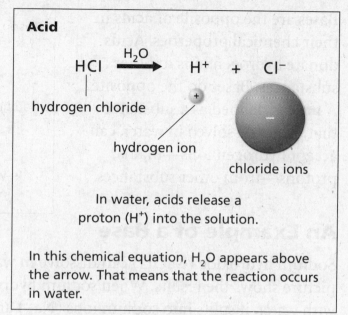

Acid

$$HCl \xrightarrow{H_2O} H^+ + Cl^-$$

hydrogen chloride

hydrogen ion

chloride ions

In water, acids release a proton (H^+) into the solution.

In this chemical equation, H_2O appears above the arrow. That means that the reaction occurs in water.

What is a base?

Like acids, bases are generally a solution in water. You have bases around your home that are used for cleaning. Soap becomes a base when it mixes with water. Shampoo and detergents are bases. Drain cleaners are strong bases. When some solids dissolve in water, they show the properties of bases. Soap, powdered detergents, and drain cleaners are examples.

List three examples of bases.

_____

Properties of Bases

Bases are not as common in foods as acids are. None of the bases you find around the house are safe to eat. If you have washed your face and gotten a bit of soap in your mouth, then you know that bases have a bitter taste. Only some bases are safe to touch. Bases that are safe to touch feel slippery. Like strong acids, strong bases will burn your skin.

Bases are the opposite of acids in their chemical properties. Acids donate hydrogen ions to other substances. Bases do the opposite. A **base** is defined as a substance that, when dissolved in water, can accept hydrogen ions—that is, protons—from other substances.

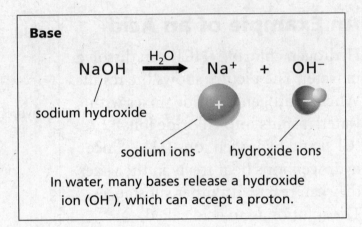

Base

In water, many bases release a hydroxide ion (OH⁻), which can accept a proton.

An Example of a Base

Sodium hydroxide (NaOH) can dissolve in water. The picture shows the results. When sodium hydroxide mixes with water, it splits into sodium ions (Na^+) and hydroxide ions (OH^-). Since the hydroxide ions float freely in the water, they can combine with hydrogen ions from other substances. In other words, hydroxide ions can accept hydrogen ions from other substances. The solution is a base called sodium hydroxide. Many bases produce hydroxide ions.

Mark It Up

Circle the clues in the pictures that tell you that the reaction happens in water.

Bases produce ions that can combine with hydrogen ions. What is the chemical formula of the hydroxide ions that many bases produce? _____

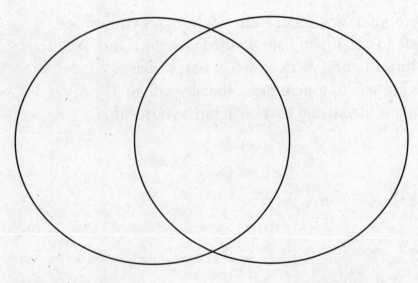

Properties of Acids   Properties of Bases

Vocabulary

In the left oval, list properties of acids. In the right oval, list the properties of bases. In the central part of the diagram, tell what acids and bases have in common.

How can you identify acids and bases?

Acids and bases can react with other substances. In fact, sometimes you can identify acids and bases because of these reactions.

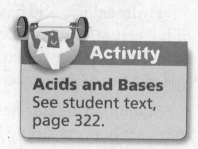

Activity

Acids and Bases
See student text, page 322.

Acids react with many types of metals and produce hydrogen gas. You can see the gas bubbling up from the metal in the picture.

Acids also react with some kinds of rocks. For example, acid reacts with limestone to produce carbon dioxide. The acid also weakens the stone and makes the stone break apart. Many buildings made of limestone, marble, or concrete are crumbling because of acid in rain and snow.

Both acids and bases react with certain substances called acid-base indicators. One of these is litmus. Litmus is a chemical that is soaked into strips of paper. People use the strips of litmus paper to identify acids and bases. The litmus paper turns red if you put a drop of acid on it. It turns blue if you put a drop of a base on it.

Acids react with metals to produce hydrogen gas.

What color does litmus paper turn if you put an acid on it? _____

What color does litmus paper turn if you put a base on it? _____

How can you measure acidity?

You can measure how acidic or basic a solution is. The acidity of a solution depends on how many hydrogen ions (H^+) are dissolved in the water. In other words, acidity depends on the concentration of hydrogen ions in the solution.

Activity

Acids and Bases
See student text, pages 330–331.

Acidity is measured on the **pH** scale. The pH scale generally goes from 0 to 14. Acids have a pH below 7. Bases have a pH above 7. A pH of 7 indicates a neutral solution. A **neutral** substance is neither an acid nor a base. Water is one example of a neutral substance.

Hydrochloric acid has a pH of 0 or lower. This means it is a very strong acid. Lemon juice has a pH of 2. Orange juice has a pH between 3 and 4. Normal rainwater has a pH close to 6. Pure water is neutral. It has a pH of 7.

Sodium hydroxide has a pH of 14 or higher. This means it is a very strong base. Household ammonia has a pH of about 11. Soap has a pH of 10. Seawater has a pH between 8 and 9. Eggs have a pH just under 8.

Mark It Up

Add five examples of substances with different pH to the correct spot on the pH scale.

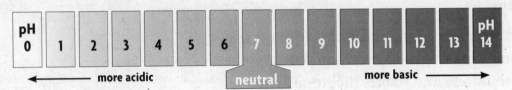

pH 0 | 1 | 2 | 3 | 4 | 5 | 6 | 7 | 8 | 9 | 10 | 11 | 12 | 13 | pH 14

← more acidic   neutral   more basic →

There are different ways of measuring pH. One way is to use strips of paper treated with a universal indicator. This indicator paper can turn 14 different colors. You put a few drops of a substance on the paper, and the paper changes color. The color indicates how acidic or basic the substance is. You match the color to the key to figure out the pH.

Visual Connection
See Common Acids and Bases on student text page 327.

Another way to measure pH is with an electronic meter. You put a probe in the substance you want to test, and the pH is given on the meter.

Which has a higher pH, an acid or a base?

_____

What happens when acids and bases mix?

Acids and bases sometimes combine. For example, hydrochloric acid (HCl) and sodium hydroxide (NaOH) can be mixed. When this happens, a chemical reaction occurs.

$$HCl + NaOH \longrightarrow NaCl + H_2O$$

Hydrochloric acid has free hydrogen ions (H^+). Sodium hydroxide has free hydroxide ions (OH^-). The hydrogen ions and the hydroxide ions combine to form water.

Water is one product of the reaction of hydrochloric acid and sodium hydroxide. The reaction has another product, as well. The sodium ions (Na^+) and the chloride ions (Cl^-) combine to produce table salt (NaCl). Both water and salt are neutral. When an acid combines with a base, the products of the chemical reaction are always neutral.

What is one product of the reaction of an acid and a base?

_____

_____

SECTION 10.3

SUMMARIZE	VOCABULARY
1. Explain the difference between an acid and a base, using the concept of ions.	Write the correct term for each description.
	acid base neutral pH
_____	2. A measure of how acidic or basic a substance is _____
_____	
_____	3. Produces substances that can accept hydrogen ions when dissolved in water _____
_____	
_____	4. Something that is neither acidic nor basic _____
_____	
_____	5. Produces and donates hydrogen ions when dissolved in water
	_____

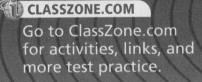
CLASSZONE.COM
Go to ClassZone.com
for activities, links, and
more test practice.

Vocabulary For each word, give its opposite. Explain how the terms differ.

1 acid   Opposite: _____

Difference between the terms: _____

2 concentrated   Opposite: _____

Difference between the terms: _____

3 solvent   Opposite: _____

Difference between the terms: _____

Reviewing Key Concepts

4 How does the boiling point of a liquid change when you dissolve something in it?

_____

5 How can you make a solution more concentrated? How can you make it less concentrated?

_____

the BIG idea

6 Suppose you mix detergent in a bucket of pure water. How does the pH of the liquid change as a result?

_____

Test Practice

7 What makes a solution different from other types of mixtures?

A It is a liquid.

B It is the same throughout.

C Its parts can be seen.

D Its parts can be separated.

8 An unknown substance is found to have a pH of 3. It is

A acidic.

B basic.

C saturated.

D neutral.

11 Chemistry of Living Systems

the **BIG** idea

Carbon and other elements are essential to living things.

Getting Ready to Learn

Review Concepts

- Atoms share electrons when they form covalent bonds.
- Some atoms can form multiple bonds with another atom.
- Chemical reactions alter the arrangement of atoms.

Activity

Polymers
See student text, page 337.

Review Vocabulary

Write the correct term for each description.

catalyst	exothermic reaction	covalent bond	ion

Forms when atoms share a pair of electrons _____

Produces a net release of energy _____

Forms when an atom gains or loses an electron _____

Speeds up chemical reactions _____

Preview Key Vocabulary

Fill in the chart with a description and important properties for each term.

Carbohydrates	Lipids	Proteins	Nucleic Acids

SECTION 11.1

Key Concept

Living things depend on chemical processes.

Student text pages 339–343

What is biochemistry?

You depend on chemistry to stay alive. Because of chemical reactions, you can get energy from food, and your nerves can carry signals. A special branch of chemistry called biochemistry studies living things. The prefix *bio-* means "life." **Biochemistry** is the study of substances and processes in living things.

What elements form living things?

In Chapter 7, you learned that there are more than 100 elements. Living things are made up of about 25 of these elements. The circle graph shows the main elements in the human body. The four most common of these are oxygen, carbon, hydrogen, and nitrogen. They make up 97 percent of your body.

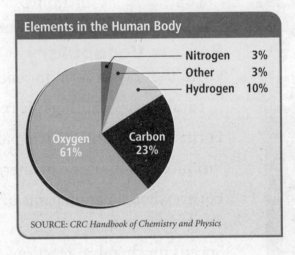

Elements in the Human Body

Nitrogen	3%
Other	3%
Hydrogen	10%

Oxygen 61%

Carbon 23%

SOURCE: *CRC Handbook of Chemistry and Physics*

 List the four most common elements in the human body.

_____   _____

The Six Main Elements

Your body is made of many different molecules and compounds. These molecules and compounds are formed of combinations of elements. Some are small, and many are very large. Six main elements combine to form the molecules and compounds in your body. They are the four elements listed in the graph: oxygen, carbon, hydrogen, and nitrogen. Two other elements, phosphorus and sulfur, are also important. These six elements form thousands of different substances in your body.

- Oxygen
- Carbon
- Hydrogen
- Nitrogen
- Phosphorus
- Sulfur

Other Elements

You need more than a dozen other elements to keep your body running. You need only a very small amount of most of these. Even though the amounts you need are tiny, these elements are still very important. You cannot live without them. Here are some elements you need in tiny amounts.

- Sodium ions (Na^+) and potassium ions (K^+) are necessary for your nerves. They send signals throughout your body.
- Calcium ions (Ca^{2+}) help make your muscles work. They also help you to stop bleeding if you get a cut.
- Calcium (Ca) atoms keep your bones strong.
- Together, fluorine (Fl) and calcium (Ca) atoms keep your teeth strong.

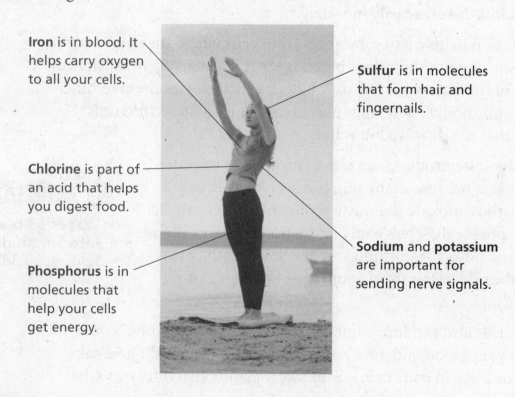

Iron is in blood. It helps carry oxygen to all your cells.

Chlorine is part of an acid that helps you digest food.

Phosphorus is in molecules that help your cells get energy.

Sulfur is in molecules that form hair and fingernails.

Sodium and **potassium** are important for sending nerve signals.

How does your body use sodium?

_____

How does your body use calcium?

_____

Why are water and salt important in your body?

Water is a small molecule with a simple structure. Salt (NaCl) is an ionic compound with a simple structure. Even though water and salt are simple, they are very important in your body. You need the right balance of water and salt to stay healthy.

How Water Helps You

Your body is mostly water. Water is a key to life because many different substances dissolve in water. In your cells, there are many chemical reactions that produce things you need to stay alive. The reactions take place in water because the reactants dissolve easily in water.

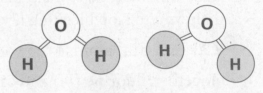

Water Molecules

Water also helps carry substances from cells where they are made to other parts of your body. Your blood is mostly water. Many substances dissolve in the watery part of your blood, which carries them to other parts of your body. There, the substances can easily pass into cells because they are dissolved in water.

Bodily waste products are also made mainly of water. Again, that is because many things dissolve easily in water. Carbon dioxide is a waste product your cells make. Carbon dioxide dissolves easily in the water in your blood. Your blood flows to your lungs. When you breathe out, carbon dioxide passes from your lungs to outside of your body.

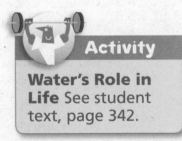

Activity

Water's Role in Life See student text, page 342.

Your cells also produce some salts as waste. They dissolve in the water in your blood and are filtered out by your kidneys. These salts leave your body in your urine. Your sweat glands also filter out salts dissolved into water in the form of sweat.

Fill in the blank: Water is a key to life because many different substances _____ in water.

How Salt Helps You

Salt (NaCl) is an ionic compound. Remember that when ionic compounds dissolve in water, the ions separate into positive ions and negative ions. When salt dissolves, sodium ions (Na^+) and chloride ions (Cl^-) separate.

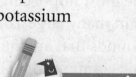

Ions, including sodium ions, have an important role in your body because of their electrical charge. Ions allow electric current to pass through nerve cells. Nerve cells use sodium ions (Na^+) and potassium ions (K^+) to send signals.

Sodium ions are also important in keeping the right amount of water in your body. If your cells have too much water, they burst. If your cells do not have enough water, they die, because key chemical reactions cannot take place without water.

Chloride ions help you digest food. These ions combine with hydrogen ions to make hydrochloric acid. Your stomach makes this acid to help you digest foods.

Mark It Up

Use chemical symbols to label a sodium ion and a chloride ion in the picture.

INSTANT REPLAY   What does your body use to send nerve signals?

_____

SECTION 11.1	
SUMMARIZE	**VOCABULARY**
1. List the six most common elements that make up living things. _____ _____ _____ _____ _____ _____	Circle the word that makes each sentence correct. 2. The study of substances and processes occurring in living things is called **physics / biochemistry.** 3. The solvent in which substances necessary for life are found is **salt / water.** 4. The source of ions important in many life processes is **acid / salt.**

What kinds of compounds have carbon?

Carbon may not be the most common element, but it is the most important element in living things. It is found in many large, complex molecules. Carbon-based compounds that are found in living things are called **organic compounds.** The word *organic* is related to the word *organism,* or living thing.

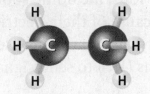

Ethane is an organic compound.

Inorganic compounds are all compounds that are not considered organic. This includes all compounds that have no carbon. Some other simple compounds have carbon but are considered inorganic compounds. For example, diamonds are pure carbon, but they are inorganic compounds.

H—H

H—H

Hydrogen gas is an inorganic compound.

What element is part of all organic compounds? _____

How does carbon form bonds?

Carbon can bond with many different atoms and molecules. It can bond with other carbon atoms, and it can bond with many other elements. Carbon forms covalent bonds. Remember that in a covalent bond, two atoms share a pair of electrons. Each carbon atom can share four pairs of electrons. This means that it can form four covalent bonds. It can form single, double, or triple bonds. This is another reason carbon is an important part of so many molecules.

Forming Single Bonds

Carbon can form four single bonds. It can form these bonds with carbon atoms. For example, every carbon atom in a diamond forms four single bonds with other carbon atoms. Carbon often forms single bonds with hydrogen atoms. For example, in methane, carbon forms four single bonds with hydrogen. In these diagrams, each single bond is shown as a bar.

Single Bond

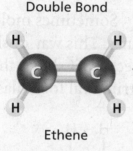
Methane

Forming Double Bonds

Carbon often forms a double bond with another carbon atom. Then it forms single bonds with other atoms, such as hydrogen. For example, in ethene, two carbon atoms form a double bond with each other. In the diagram, the two bars that connect the carbon atoms represent the double bond between them. The carbon atoms also each form two single bonds with hydrogen atoms. Each carbon atom forms a total of four bonds with other atoms.

Double Bond

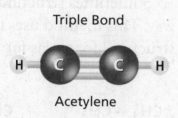
Ethene

Forming Triple Bonds

Carbon can form triple bonds with another carbon atom. Then it forms a single bond with another atom. For example, in acetylene, two carbon atoms form a triple bond with each other. In the diagram, the three bars that connect the carbon atoms represent the triple bond between them. The carbon atoms also each form a single bond with a hydrogen atom.

Triple Bond

Acetylene

In total, how many bonds can one carbon form? _____

Activity

Carbon Bonding
See student text, page 347.

Showing Molecules

Sometimes molecules are shown as models. A circle around an element's chemical symbol represents an atom. Bars show the bonds between atoms.

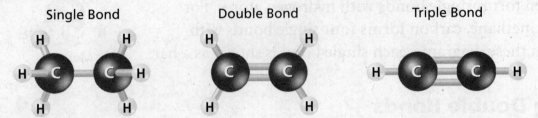

Single Bond   Double Bond   Triple Bond

Sometimes molecules are shown in a simpler way, using letters and lines. This way of showing a molecule is called a structural formula, because it shows the structure of the molecule. Here are the full structural formulas for the three molecules pictured above.

$$H-\overset{\overset{\displaystyle H}{|}}{\underset{\underset{\displaystyle H}{|}}{C}}-\overset{\overset{\displaystyle H}{|}}{\underset{\underset{\displaystyle H}{|}}{C}}-H \qquad \overset{\overset{\displaystyle H}{|}}{\underset{\underset{\displaystyle H}{|}}{C}}=\overset{\overset{\displaystyle H}{|}}{\underset{\underset{\displaystyle H}{|}}{C}} \qquad H-C\equiv C-H$$ **Full Structural Formulas**

Sometimes structural formulas are shown in an even simpler way. This method uses the chemical formulas. Here are the simpler structural formulas for the three molecules pictured above.

$$CH_3-CH_3 \qquad CH_2=CH_2 \qquad CH\equiv CH$$ **Simplified Structural Formulas**

Notice the simpler structural formulas show only the bonds between the carbon atoms. In the leftmost molecule, the carbon atoms are joined by a single bond. In the middle molecule, the carbon atoms are joined by a double bond. In the rightmost molecule, the carbon atoms are joined by a triple bond.

How do we show bonds in a structural formula?

_____

What are large carbon-based molecules like?

Carbon atoms bond with one another. They can form very large molecules. Some large molecules are long chains of atoms, and others are rings of atoms.

CLASSZONE.COM

Simulation Observe and rotate three-dimensional models of carbon-based molecules.

Long-Chain Polymers

Hundreds of carbon atoms can bond together in a chain. The chains can be long and straight. The straight chain in the picture below shows the simpler structural formula of the molecule. Remember, the bonds shown in a simpler structural formula are the bonds between carbon atoms.

$$CH_3 - CH_2 - CH_2 - CH_2 - CH_2 - CH_3$$ Straight Chain

Long chains are not the only kind of chain that carbon atoms can form. Carbon atoms can also link together to form branched chains. In this kind of molecule, branches come off a main chain. There may be one branch, or there may be many branches. The picture shows a molecule with one short branch coming off of the main chain.

$$
\begin{array}{c}
CH_3 \\
| \\
CH_2 \\
| \\
CH_3 - CH - CH_2 - CH_3
\end{array}
$$

Branched Chain

The straight chain has a repeating unit of CH_2. This unit forms four links of the chain. In other molecules, this unit could form more links of the chain. The unit might repeat more than 40 times!

There is a special name for a carbon-based molecule made of repeating units. These molecules are called polymers. A **polymer** is a carbon-based molecule with units that repeat. The straight-chain molecule shown above is a polymer. The branched-chain molecule is also a polymer. Polymers can be very large and can be made of thousands of atoms.

What two kinds of chains can carbon atoms form?

_____ _____

Mark It Up

Circle the repeating units in the straight chain. Circle these same units in the branched chain.

Carbon Rings

Carbon atoms link to one another to form rings. Usually, a carbon ring has five or six carbons. The carbon ring in the picture to the right has six carbon atoms.

Carbon Ring

What are isomers?

There are millions of different carbon-based molecules. One reason for this is that carbon atoms can bond with many different elements. Carbon atoms can also bond with one another. When they bond with one another, they can form straight chains, branched chains, or rings.

Carbon can also form different molecules with the same atoms. These molecules are the same except they have the atoms in different places. Molecules that have the same atoms arranged in different places are called **isomers.** Each isomer below has four carbon atoms and ten hydrogen atoms arranged in different ways.

$$CH_3 - CH_2 - CH_2 - CH_3$$

$$CH_3 - \overset{\displaystyle CH_3}{\overset{|}{CH}} - CH_3$$

Isomers

SECTION 11.2

SUMMARIZE	VOCABULARY
1. Name four reasons why there are so many carbon-based molecules. _____ _____ _____ _____ _____ _____	Which word from the list answers each riddle? **isomers organic compounds polymers** 2. These compounds have the same atoms, but the atoms are in different places. _____ 3. These are carbon-based compounds made up of repeating units. _____ 4. These are complex, carbon-based compounds often found in living things. _____

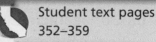
What are the main types of carbon-based molecules in living things?

Four kinds of molecules are important for all living things. They are:

- carbohydrates
- lipids
- proteins
- nucleic acids

All four are organic molecules, so they all are carbon-based. You can read more about each of these important kinds of molecules below.

What are the four kinds of molecules important for all living things?

_____   _____   _____

What are carbohydrates?

Carbohydrates (KAHR-boh-HY-DRATZ) include sugars and starches. They are always formed of the elements carbon, hydrogen, and oxygen. Carbohydrates are the main source of energy for most living things and are found in many foods. Cell walls of plants contain a carbohydrate called cellulose. Cellulose provides support for plants.

Sugars

There are many different kinds of sugars. Many sugars have a ring structure. The pictures show a sugar called glucose. Glucose is a ring with six sides. Five carbon atoms and one oxygen atom form the ring.

Glucose is one kind of sugar. The picture on the right is a simple way of showing a glucose molecule.

Starches

Starches are more complex than sugars. In fact, starches are formed of many sugars linked together. In the diagram below, each hexagon is a molecule of the sugar glucose. The glucose molecules bond together to form a branching chain of starch. Many foods you eat, including bread, potatoes, and noodles, have starch.

Glucose Molecules

Starch

Glucose molecules bond together to form starch.

Using Carbohydrates for Energy

You use glucose for energy. So do most animals and plants. Cells in your body break down glucose. This is an exothermic reaction, so it gives off energy. Your cells use the energy for many different things.

You also get energy from starches, but your body has to break the starch apart. When you digest starchy foods, the starch breaks up into glucose molecules. Your cells use these glucose molecules to get energy.

 What do your cells use glucose for?

_____

Activity

Carbon In Food
See student text, page 352.

What are lipids?

Lipids include fats and oils. Plants and animals use lipids to store energy. Lipids store about twice as much energy as starches do. If you eat a serving of a starch and the same size serving of a lipid, then you will get twice as much energy from the lipid.

 What are lipids? _____
Underline the sentence that gives you the definition.

The Structure of Lipids

Lipids are mainly long chains of carbon and hydrogen atoms. In the diagram below, one end of the chain has oxygen atoms bonded to carbon and hydrogen atoms. Fats and oils are formed of these chains linked together.

$$
\begin{array}{c}
\text{H} \quad \text{H} \quad \text{H} \quad \text{H} \quad \text{H} \quad \text{H} \quad \text{H} \quad \text{H} \quad \text{H} \quad \text{H} \quad \text{H} \qquad\qquad \text{O} \\
| \quad\ | \quad\ | \quad\ | \quad\ | \quad\ | \quad\ | \quad\ | \quad\ | \quad\ | \quad\ | \qquad /\!/ \\
\text{C}\!-\!\text{C}\!-\!\text{C}\!-\!\text{C}\!-\!\text{C}\!-\!\text{C}\!-\!\text{C}\!-\!\text{C}\!-\!\text{C}\!-\!\text{C}\!-\!\text{C}\!-\!\text{C} \\
| \quad\ | \quad\ | \quad\ | \quad\ | \quad\ | \quad\ | \quad\ | \quad\ | \quad\ | \quad\ | \qquad \backslash \\
\text{H} \quad \text{H} \quad \text{H} \quad \text{H} \quad \text{H} \quad \text{H} \quad \text{H} \quad \text{H} \quad \text{H} \quad \text{H} \quad \text{H} \qquad\ \text{HO}
\end{array}
$$

Part of a Lipid Molecule

Lipids in Cell Membranes

Some lipids are important in cell membranes. These lipids are made of carbon, hydrogen, oxygen, and phosphorus. Lipids with phosphorus have long chains with phosphorus attached to the very end. These lipids play an important role in protecting the cell.

What are proteins?

Proteins are large molecules formed of smaller molecules called amino acids. The amino acids are linked together to form a chain. You can think of a protein as a word and amino acids as letters. The meaning of a word depends on which letters form the word. For instance, you use the letters *E, A,* and *T* to form the word *EAT.* Word meaning also depends on the order of the letters. For example, you can rearrange the letters in the word *EAT.* Put the *T* in front, and you get *TEA.*

If a protein is a word, what are the letters that form the word?

_____

Forming Proteins

Proteins are like words. The kind of protein formed depends on the amino acids used and on the order of the amino acids. Changing an amino acid changes the protein. Switching the order of amino acids also changes the protein.

Activity

Organic Molecules
See student text, page 356.

There are twenty amino acids that form hundreds of thousands of proteins. The picture shows some of the different amino acids that link together to form proteins. Amino acids are formed mainly of carbon, hydrogen, and oxygen, but they can also include nitrogen and sulfur.

Linked Amino Acids

tyrosine   lysine   cystine   serine   leucine

Proteins in the Body

The proteins in your muscles are shaped like long coils. They allow your muscles to contract and relax. Other proteins in your body are coils that are curled into a ball. Some examples of these are enzymes. An **enzyme** (EHN-zym) is a catalyst in cells. Remember that catalysts speed up the rate of chemical reactions. Without enzymes, chemical reactions in your body would happen too slowly. Enzymes help you stay alive.

What do enzymes do?

_____

What are nucleic acids?

Nucleic acids (noo-KLEE-ihk AS-ihdz) are large molecules that contain the information that cells need to make proteins. Every cell in your body has nucleic acids. One kind of nucleic acid is DNA. DNA is an acronym* that stands for deoxyribose nucleic acid. DNA has genetic information that your cells need to make new cells.

DNA is shaped like a twisted ladder. The sides of the ladder are made of two kinds of molecules. One is a sugar. This sugar is a ring formed of five carbons. Like all sugars, the sugar in DNA also has hydrogen and oxygen. The other molecule is called a phosphate group. It has the element phosphorus. The rungs of the ladder are called bases. DNA has four different bases that form the code cells used to make proteins.

Activity

Extract and Observe DNA
See student text, pages 360–361.

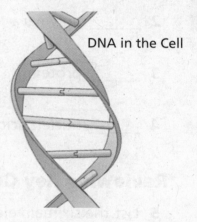

DNA in the Cell

What is a nucleic acid?

_____

*Academic Vocabulary: The letters in an **acronym** each stand for the first letter of another word. In *DNA*, the *D* stands for the sugar "deoxyribose," the *N* stands for "nucleic," and the *A* stands for "acid."

SECTION 11.3

SUMMARIZE	VOCABULARY
Think of the four main types of carbon-based molecules.	Fill in each blank with the correct term from the list.

SUMMARIZE

Think of the four main types of carbon-based molecules.

1. Which two include rings?

_____

_____

_____

2. Which two include long chains?

_____

_____

_____

VOCABULARY

Fill in each blank with the correct term from the list.

> **carbohydrates   enzymes   lipids**
> **proteins   nucleic acids**

3. _____ include fats and oils.

4. You need _____ to speed up chemical reactions in your cells.

5. _____ are formed of amino acids linked together.

6. _____ form and read an important code.

7. Sugars, starches, and cellulose are

_____

Review
11 Chemistry of Living Systems

CLASSZONE.COM

Go to ClassZone.com for activities, links, and more test practice.

Vocabulary Match each word with its definition or description.

1 _____ carbohydrate

2 _____ polymer

3 _____ protein

4 _____ nucleic acid

a. formed of long chains of amino acids

b. encodes information in living things

c. is formed of carbon, hydrogen, and oxygen

d. all are carbon-based and made up of repeating units

Reviewing Key Concepts

5 List the six main elements in living things.

_____

6 Give two properties of carbon that help explain why it combines with so many other atoms and molecules.

_____

the BIG idea

7 What are three things carbohydrates, lipids, proteins, and nucleic acids have in common?

_____

Test Practice

8 Water is essential for life because

A many organic molecules are made completely of water

B many things your cells need dissolve in water

C water cements cell structures in place

D water breaks down to form oxygen

9 If a carbon atom forms a triple bond with another carbon atom, it can also form a

A triple bond with a hydrogen atom

B double bond with an oxygen atom

C single bond with a hydrogen atom

D ring with five other carbon atoms

12 Earth, Moon, and Sun

Getting Ready to Learn

Review Concepts

- The sky seems to turn as Earth rotates.
- The motions of nearby space objects are visible from Earth.
- Light and other radiation carry information about space.

Activity

What Makes the Moon Bright? See student text, page 373.

Review Vocabulary

Draw a line to connect each word with its description.

force	the measure of the amount of matter an object is made of
gravity	the attraction objects have for each other because of their masses
mass	a push or a pull

Preview Key Vocabulary

Following are some key terms you will see in this chapter. As you read the chapter, note how different terms are related. Use the table to explain the relationship between each set of terms.

Terms	Relationship
rotate, axis	
axis, seasons	
solar system, galaxy	

Some space objects are visible to the human eye.

Student text pages
375–380

What is the universe like?

What will you see when you look up at the sky on a clear, dark night? You will see many stars. You might see some planets. You might even see part of the Milky Way. But you will only see a small number of objects compared with all the objects in the entire universe.

Activity

Distance
See student text,
page 375.

The universe is huge. It is bigger than anything we can possibly experience. The number of objects in the universe is very large. These objects are spread throughout space in a pattern. Gravity causes objects in space to be grouped together in different ways. Remember that gravity is the force that objects exert on one another due to their masses.

Arrangement of the Universe

The picture below shows some of the structures* of the universe.

Earth Our planet is Earth. Like all planets, it is round. Earth has a diameter of 13,000 kilometers (8,000 miles). The Moon is about one-fourth the size of Earth. Because of gravity, the Moon orbits, or goes around, Earth. An **orbit** is the path an object in space takes around another object.

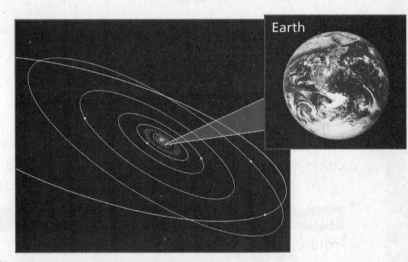

Earth

Earth is the third planet from the Sun in our solar system. The solar system includes planets and many other objects.

What force causes the Moon to orbit Earth? _____

_____

*Academic Vocabulary: The word *structure* refers to the way different parts are arranged to make up a whole.

Solar System Earth orbits the Sun. Compared to Earth, the Sun is very large. It has a diameter about 100 times larger than Earth. The Sun is the center of our solar system. The **solar system** includes the Sun, Earth, other planets, their moons, and many smaller space objects. All of these objects go around the Sun. The solar system extends for billions of miles.

The Sun's gravity keeps the planets in orbit. It also keeps smaller objects in orbit. The Sun's gravity is strong because the Sun has a large mass.

The Milky Way The Sun is a star in the Milky Way galaxy. A **galaxy** is a group of millions or billions of stars. Any individual star you can see is part of the Milky Way. Most of the stars in our galaxy are very far from Earth. We cannot even see them. Others are a little closer. Many are packed together in an arm of our galaxy. We can see a part of the Milky Way as a hazy band of light. On a very dark, clear night, you might see this band of light across the sky.

The stars in a galaxy move around the center of the galaxy. Gravity causes the stars to stay in orbit.

The Universe The Milky Way is just one of billions of galaxies that are spread throughout the universe. The **universe** includes everything. It includes all matter and energy. It includes space, as well.

Milky Way

The Sun and billions of other stars are grouped together in a galaxy. Our galaxy is the Milky Way.

What do Earth and all the planets in the solar system orbit?

_____

Constellations

Constellations are patterns of stars in the sky. Some patterns look a little like the shapes of animals or objects. For example, one well-known constellation looks like a swan. Other constellations are often named after characters in ancient myths.

The stars in constellations often are very far apart, but they look like they are close together when seen from Earth. If you looked at the same group of stars from a different place in space, they might not form the same patterns.

Why do we see planets and stars move across the sky?

Visual Connection
See Constellation Patterns on student text, page 378.

Imagine that you are spinning around in one place. As you turn, the objects in the room appear to move around you. For example, you could see a picture on the wall come into view, but as you continue to turn, you see the picture moving. Eventually, you won't see the picture anymore because it has moved out of your field of view. Similarly, Earth rotates. That means that it spins like a top. Because you are spinning along with Earth, you do not feel the spin. However, as Earth turns, the sky appears to turn in the other direction. This is why the Sun, stars, and other objects appear to move across the sky.

The Apparent Movement of Constellations

We see the Sun rise and set everyday because we turn. Like the Sun, the constellations also seem to move across the sky as we turn. We see some constellations rise and set. These constellations come into view low in the east. As the hours go by, they pass across the sky. Some pass in a high arc. Others pass much lower. Then, they set in the western sky.

Imagine again that you are spinning around. If you look directly above your head, there will be one point that does not seem to move at all. Close to that one point, there will be areas on the ceiling that circle around that point. In the sky, there is one star that does not seem to move at all. That star appears directly above the North Pole. It is called the North Star or Polaris. Because it never seems to move, you can use Polaris to figure out which direction is North. The constellations that appear near Polaris do not rise and set. Instead, they circle around Polaris. You can see them the entire night.

 How do constellations seem to move across the sky?

_____

The Movement of Planets

The word *planet* comes from a Greek word that means "wanderer." You can find planets in the night sky and watch them for a few weeks. Every night, the planets will appear in a slightly different place relative* to the stars. In other words, the planets will be near different stars.

Planets and stars have different paths of motion. The planets move around the Sun. The stars move with the Sun. This is why the planets look as if they are moving differently than the stars are.

The picture shows an example of how Mars moves over two weeks. On September 20, it appears near the center of a constellation called Gemini. Gemini is shown by the white lines connecting some of the stars. Two weeks later, Mars seems to have moved up and to the left.

Sept. 20th 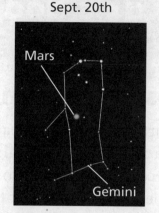   Oct. 4th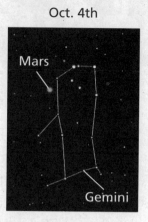

Mars changes position when compared with the stars. In September, it is in the constellation Gemini. In October, it is outside Gemini.

*Academic Vocabulary: The word **relative** is used to compare two different things. The motion of the planets relative to the stars describes the motion of the planets compared to the motion of the stars.

SECTION 12.1

SUMMARIZE	VOCABULARY

1. What keeps the Moon in orbit around Earth?
 	
 _____
	Write the correct term for each description.
	
	    galaxy orbit
	    solar system universe

2. What keeps Earth in orbit around the Sun? _____	4. Everything in space, including all matter and energy _____
3. What keeps the Sun in orbit in the Milky Way? _____	5. A collection of billions of stars held together by gravity _____
	6. The Sun and a collection of planets and other objects held together by gravity _____

12.2 Earth rotates on a tilted axis and orbits the Sun.

Student text pages 381–387

What causes day and night?

As you have read, Earth rotates. This means that Earth spins or turns. It rotates around an imaginary line running through its center from north to south. This imaginary line is called Earth's **axis of rotation.** The north end of the axis is the North Pole. The south end of the axis is the South Pole.

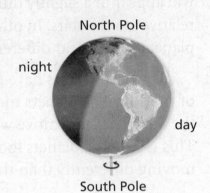

At any time, the Sun lights up half of Earth. The other half of Earth is in darkness. The lit half of Earth has day. The dark half has night.

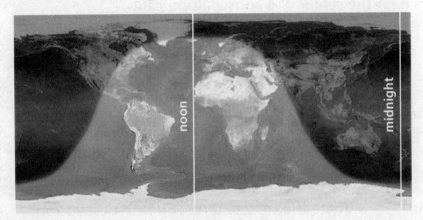

Earth is always rotating. Earth spins once on its axis every 24 hours. This means that the line separating light and darkness is always moving. On one side of Earth, day is becoming night. On the other side of Earth, night is becoming day. In the middle of the lit part, it is noon. In the middle of the dark part, it is midnight. The map above shows these times.

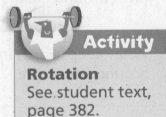
Mark It Up

Draw where you think Earth's axis should be at the top of the globe. Label Earth's axis.

Activity

Rotation
See student text, page 382.

INSTANT REPLAY

How does Earth move to cause day and night?

_____

How do Earth's orbit and tilted axis cause seasons?

Earth does not only rotate. It also moves around the Sun. We say that Earth revolves around the Sun. It takes one year for Earth to revolve once around the Sun. A **revolution** is the motion of one object around another object. As Earth revolves around the Sun, it makes an orbit that is about 300 million kilometers across. The Sun's gravity keeps Earth in its orbit.

Earth's orbit and its rotation do not line up. Earth's rotation is tilted at about a 23° angle from the plane* of Earth's orbit. The picture below shows how Earth's axis is tilted.

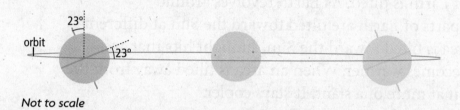

Not to scale

Seasons are patterns of weather changes during a year. They can include changes in the amount of rain, temperature, or sunlight. The amount of change in an area depends on how far it is from the equator. The equator is the imaginary line that goes around the middle of the Earth. Near the equator, temperatures do not change very much during the year. The seasons are similar to each other. Farther from the equator, each season has different temperatures. It is cold in the winter and warm in the summer.

These temperature changes are caused by the tilt of Earth. Because Earth is tilted, the angle of sunlight in a certain place changes as Earth moves around the Sun. The hours of daylight in a certain place also change as Earth moves around the Sun.

Suppose you are far from the equator. What two things related to seasons change because Earth's axis is tilted?

_____   _____

*Academic Vocabulary: A **plane** is a flat surface. For example, imagine that Earth's orbit formed a flat, solid plate. The plane of Earth's orbit would be the surface of that plate.

Tilt and Angle of Sunlight

Imagine that you are shining a flashlight on a wall. When you point the flashlight directly at the wall, the area of light on the wall is small, but very bright. When you point the flashlight at an angle, the light spreads out. It covers more of the wall, but the light is much dimmer.

Similarly, the angle of sunlight affects how much energy is received from the Sun. When sunlight strikes an area from directly overhead, the area gets the most energy. It becomes warm. When sunlight strikes at a slant, the energy spreads out. Places with lower angles of sunlight are cooler because they get less energy.

Activity

Modeling Seasons
See student text, pages 388–389.

Remember that Earth is tilted. As Earth revolves around the Sun, different parts of Earth are tilted toward the Sun at different times. When an area is tilted toward the Sun, sunlight hits that area more directly. It becomes warmer. When an area is tilted away from the Sun, sunlight hits it at more of a slant. It stays cooler.

From May through October, the Northern Hemisphere* is tilted toward the Sun. In these months, the Northern Hemisphere receives sunlight at a steeper angle, so it is warmer. At the same time, the Southern Hemisphere is tilted away from the Sun. Sunlight hits the Southern Hemisphere at a more shallow angle, so it is colder.

From November through April, the seasons are opposite. The Southern Hemisphere is tilted toward the Sun, so the sunlight hits it more directly. This warms the area. At the same time, the Northern Hemisphere is tilted away from the Sun. The Northern Hemisphere is cooler because sunlight hits it at an angle.

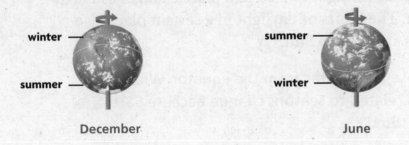

winter — summer — December

summer — winter — June

*Academic Vocabulary: The word **hemisphere** is made of two parts: the root *sphere* and the prefix *hemi-*. A *sphere* is a three dimensional round object. *Hemi-* means "half." Earth's equator divides the Northern Hemisphere from the Southern Hemisphere.

Tilt and Hours of Sunlight

Suppose that you are playing outside. When you first are outside, you do not feel too hot. When you stay out in the sunlight for a long time, you feel warmer and warmer. The same thing happens to Earth. The amount of sunlight an area gets each day changes the weather. Sunlight warms the land. Long hours of sunlight help make summer the warmer time of year. Winter is the opposite. There are fewer hours of sunlight. Things have less time to warm up, so winter is the colder time of year.

Close to the equator, no matter what month it is, there are always about 12 hours of sunlight. The equator is at the middle point of Earth, so the tilt of Earth does not affect how sunlight hits this area very much.

As you move away from the equator, there are large changes in length of daylight, depending on the season. For example, in Sacramento, there are about 15 hours of daylight in the summer. In the winter, there are only about 9 hours of sunlight.

The poles are even more extreme. For several months, there may be nothing but sunlight! From September to March at the South Pole, the Sun does not set at all for about six months. Even at midnight, it shines low in the sky. During the same time at the North Pole, it is constantly dark. The diagram below shows the two extreme seasons at each of the poles.

 Circle the words that make the sentence correct. In December, the Southern Hemisphere is tilted **toward / away** from the Sun. Then, it is **winter / summer.**

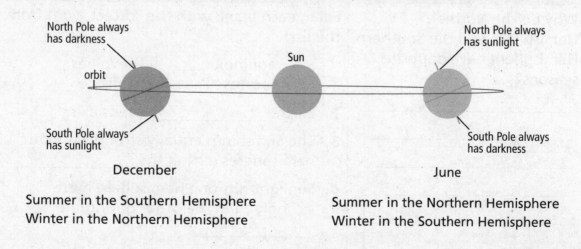

North Pole always has darkness

orbit

Sun

North Pole always has sunlight

South Pole always has sunlight

South Pole always has darkness

December

June

Summer in the Southern Hemisphere
Winter in the Northern Hemisphere

Summer in the Northern Hemisphere
Winter in the Southern Hemisphere

What are equinoxes and solstices?

As you have learned, the tilt of Earth affects how the sunlight hits different areas of Earth depending on where Earth is in its orbit. At times, sunlight hits one hemisphere more strongly than the other. The time when sunlight is at its strongest in one hemisphere and at its weakest in the other is called a **solstice** (SAHL-stihs). The time when the Sun shines equally in each hemisphere is called an **equinox** (EE-kwuh-nahks). This happens twice a year.

When does sunlight hit both hemispheres equally?

_____

Summer, at noon

Winter, at noon

SECTION 12.2

SUMMARIZE	VOCABULARY
1. Why do the Northern Hemisphere and the Southern Hemisphere have opposite seasons?	Fill in each blank with the correct word from the list.

<table>
<tr><td></td><td>equinox   revolves
rotates   solstice</td></tr>
</table>

2. Earth _____ on its axis.

3. The Sun shines equally strongly in both hemispheres during the _____.

4. Sunlight hits one hemisphere more strongly than the other during the _____.

5. Earth _____ around the Sun.

Student text pages
390 395

What is the Moon?

The Moon is a satellite of Earth. A **satellite** is a space object that orbits another space object. The Moon goes around Earth in just over 27 days. As it revolves around Earth, it rotates on its axis. It makes just one rotation each time it goes around Earth. This means that the Moon always keeps the same side toward Earth. We call this side the near side. The half that faces away from the Earth is called the far side. From Earth, we never see the far side of the Moon.

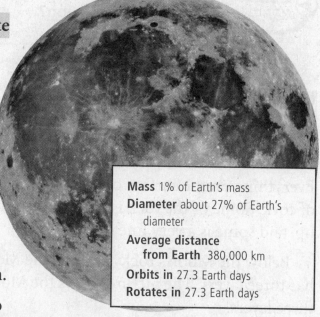

Mass 1% of Earth's mass
Diameter about 27% of Earth's diameter
Average distance from Earth 380,000 km
Orbits in 27.3 Earth days
Rotates in 27.3 Earth days

The Moon is the closest space object to Earth. It is about 380,000 kilometers (240,000 miles) away. That is about 100 times the distance between Los Angeles and New York City.

Why do we call one side of the Moon the far side?

_____

Mark It Up

Label one of the Moon's impact craters.

What does the Moon look like?

Much of the moon is light-colored. These areas are called lunar highlands. The highlands have many round, ridged areas called impact* craters. These craters formed when objects from space hit the Moon.

*Academic Vocabulary: The word *impact* refers to one thing hitting another.

The Moon also has many large, dark areas called maria (MAH-ree -uh). One of these areas is called a **mare** (MAH-ray). Maria formed when hot lava flowed up from inside the Moon and covered some craters. The lava cooled and became a type of rock called basalt.

 What are two types of features that appear on the surface of the Moon?

_____ _____

What is the structure of the Moon?

The Moon has no air, clouds, water, or life. Everything on the surface of the Moon is formed of rock. Some of the rock is solid, some is broken up, and some is a very fine dust.

Below the Moon's rocky surface, the Moon has three layers. The picture shows the Moon's three layers.

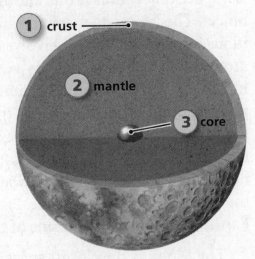

The Structure of the Moon

1 The top layer is the crust. It is the thinnest layer. It is about 70 kilometers (40 miles thick). The rock that makes up the Moon's crust is the least dense part of the Moon.

2 The middle layer is the mantle. The mantle makes up most of the Moon. The rock that forms the mantle is very dense. It includes the elements iron and magnesium.

Activity

Moon Features
See student text, page 393.

3 The innermost layer is the core. The core of the Moon is fairly small. It is about 700 kilometers (400 miles) in diameter. The core of the Moon is made mainly of metals, such as iron.

 Name the three layers of the Moon.

_____ _____ _____

How did the Moon form?

Scientists are not certain exactly how the Moon formed. Here is one idea about it. Many scientists think this idea is likely to be true.

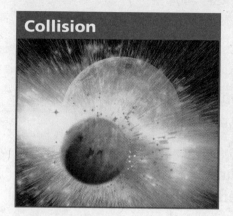

Collision

Early Earth is hit.

Re-Forming

Dust, rock, and metal from the collision are pulled together by gravity. They re-form Earth.

Earth and Moon

The rest of the material is pulled together by gravity. It forms the Moon.

When Earth was quite young, a large space object hit it. Lots of dust, rock, and metal flew into space. Gravity pulled most of the material into a sphere. Much of it clumped together to re-form Earth. The rest of it stayed in orbit around the newly re-formed planet.

Over time, gravity pulled the dust and rock together into clumps. Because of gravity, large clumps pulled more material toward them. Eventually, the clumps formed a single sphere that became the Moon. The Moon orbits Earth as the dust and rock that formed it once did.

SECTION 12.3

SUMMARIZE	VOCABULARY
1. How many times does the Moon rotate on its axis during one trip around Earth? _____ _____ _____	Circle the word that makes each sentence correct. 2. The Moon is Earth's natural **core / satellite**. 3. A flat, dark area of the Moon is called a **mare / basalt**. 4. Objects that hit the Moon caused **the crust / craters** to form on the Moon's surface.

SECTION
12.4
Key Concept
Positions of the Sun and the Moon affect Earth.

Student text pages 397–404

What causes us to see phases of the Moon?

The Moon is the brightest object in the night sky. Although the Moon is bright, it does not give off its own light. Moonlight is really light from the Sun that bounces off the Moon's surface.

At any time, sunlight shines on half of the Moon's surface. The diagram below shows this. The side of the Moon that reflects the Sun's light is white in the diagram. The other side of the Moon is in shadow. It is black in the diagram.

What is the source of the Moon's light?

_____

Phases of the Moon

You probably have noticed that the Moon looks different at different times. When it looks like a full circle, it is called a full moon. When it looks like a crescent, it is called a crescent moon. Sometimes it looks like a half circle. This is called a half moon. Sometimes it looks like a circle with a crescent cut off. Then it is called a gibbous moon.

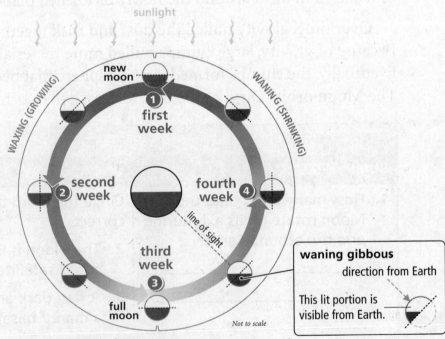

Find the black dashed lines in each picture. Use them to figure out which part of the Moon we can see from Earth.

The pattern of different shapes the Moon seems to take are called the phases of the Moon. The Moon has phases because we see different amounts of the lit side as the Moon orbits Earth. It takes about four weeks for the moon to go through all of its phases. The diagram on page 192 shows what part of the lit side we see. The pictures to the right show how the Moon's appearance changes over four weeks. Compare the diagram with the pictures.

First Week The new moon looks dark because we are facing the unlit side of the Moon. As the Moon moves in its orbit around Earth, sunlight begins to shine on the side of the Moon facing us. At first, it lights up only a small part of the near side. We see a crescent moon. From one night to the next, the crescent gets bigger. We say that the Moon is waxing, or growing.

Second Week As the Moon continues in its orbit around Earth, the portion of the lit side that we see gets bigger. Half of the face of the Moon shines in the sky. As time passes, more than half of the near side of the moon is bright. We call it a waxing gibbous.

Third Week The Moon has come halfway through its orbit. The near side of the Moon is fully lit by the Sun. We call it a full moon. From now on, the lit part of the Moon that we can see will get smaller. We say the Moon is waning. It is a waning gibbous.

Fourth Week The Moon is three-quarters of the way through its orbit around Earth. Half of the side facing Earth is lit up. As the week goes by, the Moon continues to wane. It wanes until it is the thinnest crescent. The cycle begins again with the new moon.

The Moon is beginning its cycle. Write the phases in the correct order.

_____

_____

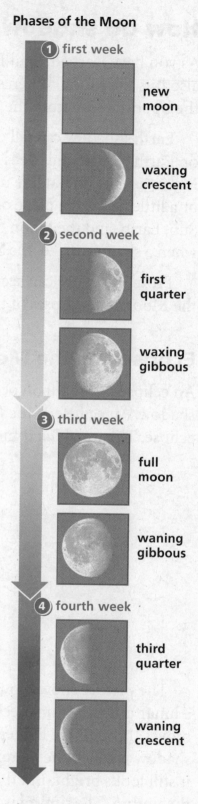

Phases of the Moon

1 first week — new moon
waxing crescent

2 second week — first quarter
waxing gibbous

3 third week — full moon
waning gibbous

4 fourth week — third quarter
waning crescent

How do shadows cause eclipses?

As you have learned, light from the Sun hits Earth. Light from the Sun also hits the Moon. When sunlight hits something, a shadow forms on the opposite side from the Sun.

Earth's shadow can fall on the Moon. The Moon's shadow can fall on Earth. Usually this does not happen, because the Sun, Earth, and the Moon usually do not line up exactly. Usually, the Moon is a little above or a little below the plane of Earth and the Sun. Sometimes, however, the Sun, Earth, and the Moon do line up in a straight line. An eclipse occurs when a shadow makes the Sun or the Moon appear to grow dark.

From Earth, we can see two kinds of eclipses. They are eclipses of the Moon and eclipses of the Sun.

Eclipses of the Moon

An eclipse of the Moon occurs when the Moon moves through Earth's shadow. An eclipse of the Moon has another name. It is called a lunar eclipse. The word *lunar* means "related to the Moon."

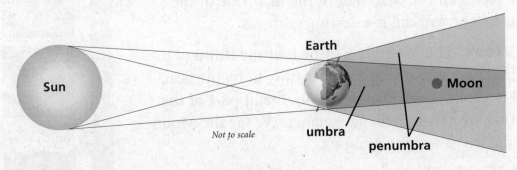

Sun

Earth

Moon

Not to scale

umbra

penumbra

Lunar Eclipse

The picture shows how the Sun, Earth, and the Moon line up during a lunar eclipse. A lunar eclipse happens during a full moon. The Moon moves through the lighter part of Earth's shadow. This part of the shadow is called the **penumbra.** When the Moon is in the penumbra, it still looks bright. But the Moon gets much darker when it moves into the umbra. The **umbra** is the dark part of Earth's shadow.

Why does the Moon become darker during a lunar eclipse?

It can take over an hour for the Moon to pass through the umbra. During this time, Earth's shadow seems to creep across the Moon. You can still see the Moon, but it is not bright. It often looks dark orange or red.

Eclipses of the Sun

An eclipse of the Sun occurs when the Moon casts a shadow on Earth. This blocks the sunlight from part of Earth. An eclipse of the Sun is called a solar eclipse. The word *solar* means "related to the Sun."

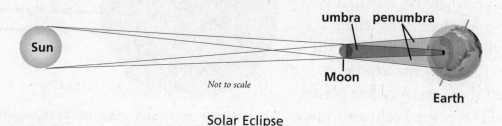

Solar Eclipse

The picture shows how the Sun, the Earth, and the Moon line up during a solar eclipse. Before a solar eclipse occurs, it is daylight. But the Moon is moving in its orbit. It moves to a position directly between the Sun and Earth. You cannot see the Moon because only the side away from Earth is lit up. It is a new moon.

If you are in the umbra of the Moon's shadow, you will see a total eclipse of the Sun. At the beginning, you will see the Moon's shadow just as it starts to cross in front of the Sun. The Moon blocks out the Sun's light. The edge of the Sun seems to disappear. Slowly, the Moon blocks more and more of the Sun. During the middle of the eclipse, the Moon blocks the disk of the Sun completely. The sky gets quite dark. You can even see stars. Then, slowly, the Moon moves away from the disk of the Sun. The Sun grows larger like the waxing moon. When the Moon moves away completely, daylight returns.

Where is the Moon during a solar eclipse?

_____

Where We Can See Solar Eclipses

In a total eclipse of the Sun, the Moon completely covers the disk of the Sun. You will see a total eclipse if you are in the path of the Moon's umbra. If you are in the penumbra of the moon's shadow, something slightly different happens. Then you will see the Moon cover only part of the Sun. This is called a partial solar eclipse.

The map shows that the Moon's shadow moves across only part of Earth. This means that a solar eclipse is not visible everywhere on Earth. It is visible only from the locations where the Moon's shadow falls. Notice that the umbra falls across a very narrow band. This means that there are very few places where you could see a total eclipse of the Sun. The penumbra of the Moon falls across a larger area. So there are many more places where you could see a partial eclipse of the Sun.

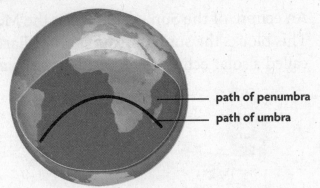

path of penumbra
path of umbra

Path of the Moon's Shadow Across Earth

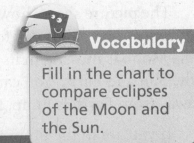

Vocabulary

Fill in the chart to compare eclipses of the Moon and the Sun.

Type of eclipse	What is the cause?	What does it look like?
Lunar		
Solar		

How does the Moon affect Earth's oceans?

You know that gravity is the force of two masses pulling on each other. Earth pulls on the Moon and the Moon pulls on Earth. This force keeps the Moon in orbit around Earth. The Moon's gravity has another important effect on Earth. The Moon's gravity pulls on Earth's oceans. This pull causes tides.

Tides are the rising and falling of the water level at a beach. As the tide comes in, the waves creep higher and higher onto the shore. The water level rises slowly. It takes about six hours for the water to go from its lowest point to its highest point. This is called high tide. Then the water level starts to drop. It goes down for six hours until the waves reach their lowest point. This is low tide. There are two high tides and two low tides every day.

> **Visual Connection**
> See Causes of Tides on student text, page 404.

 What causes tides on Earth?

_____

SECTION 12.4	
SUMMARIZE	**VOCABULARY**
Suppose that the Moon passes between Earth and the Sun.	Draw a line to connect each term with the phrase it best matches.
1. If the Moon passes directly between these two bodies, what happens?	3. umbra the light part of a shadow
_____	4. penumbra when a shadow makes the Sun or the Moon appear to grow dark
2. If the Moon is above the plane of Earth, what happens?	5. eclipse the dark part of a shadow
_____	

🌐 **CLASSZONE.COM**

Go to ClassZone.com for activities, links, and more test practice.

Vocabulary Complete the chart by filling in the blanks.

Term	Description
Axis of rotation	1
2	The path in space an object takes around another object
3	An event when a space object casts a shadow on another space object.

Reviewing Key Concepts

4 In which galaxy are the stars you see at night?

_____

5 Why is the same side of the Moon always visible to us on Earth?

_____

the BIG idea

6 Describe how the orbit of the Moon relates to its phases.

_____

_____

Test Practice

7 A picture shows the South Pole in sunlight. When could the picture have been taken?

A May
B June
C August
D December

8 Earth is in a line directly between the Moon and the Sun. Which of these will you see?

A a lunar eclipse
B a total solar eclipse
C a partial solar eclipse
D a gibbous moon

the BIG idea

Planets and other objects form a system around our Sun.

Getting Ready to Learn

Review Concepts

- The planets we see are much closer than the stars in constellations.
- The Sun, the planets, and smaller bodies make up the solar system.

Activity

How Big Is Jupiter?
See student text, page 411.

Review Vocabulary

Write the word on the line that answers each question.

orbit   **solar system**   **gravity**   **methane**

What is the Sun and the planets and other bodies that orbit around it? _____

What is a compound made up of carbon and hydrogen? _____

What is the path one space object takes around another space object? _____

Preview Key Vocabulary

Following are some key terms you will see in this chapter. Compare the paired terms. As you read, write down two similarities and two differences you note between the objects.

Pairs of Terms	Similarities	Differences
terrestrial planet gas giant		
asteroid comet		
meteor meteorite		

SECTION
13.1

Key Concept
Planets orbit the Sun at different distances.

Student text pages
413–417

Where are the planets in our solar system?

Mercury

If you know where to look, you can see planets in the night sky. The five planets you can see look like bright stars. The planets that are visible without a telescope are Mercury, Venus, Mars, Jupiter, and Saturn. Venus is the brightest planet because it is closest to Earth. Venus appears low in the sky around sunrise or sunset. Jupiter is also very bright. Although it is farther from Earth than Venus or Mars, it is very large. Mercury is hard to see because it is so close to the Sun.

Venus

Earth

Although these five planets look like stars, they are not stars. They do not give off light of their own. You can see the planets only because light from the Sun bounces off them. Like the Moon, the planets all reflect light from the Sun. Asteroids, moons, and other smaller space objects also reflect the Sun's light.

Mars

asteroids

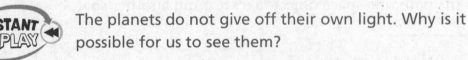

INSTANT REPLAY The planets do not give off their own light. Why is it possible for us to see them?

_____

Jupiter

Sizes in the Solar System

The pictures show the relative sizes of the planets. Jupiter is the largest planet. Its diameter is about ten times that of Earth. Saturn is also very large. But the largest object in the solar system is the Sun. The diameter of the Sun is about 100 times that of Earth.

Activity

Distances
See student text, page 416.

Distances in the Solar System

The solar system is huge. Giving distances in the solar system in kilometers or miles would be difficult. Each number would have many zeroes at the end. Astronomers have come up with a special unit of measurement for the solar system. It is called the astronomical unit. One **astronomical unit** is the average distance between Earth and the Sun. Its abbreviation is AU. An AU is about 150 million kilometers.

Mercury and Venus are less than 1 AU from the Sun. Mars is about 2 AUs. Jupiter is about 5 AUs. Pluto can be as far away as 50 AUs from the Sun.

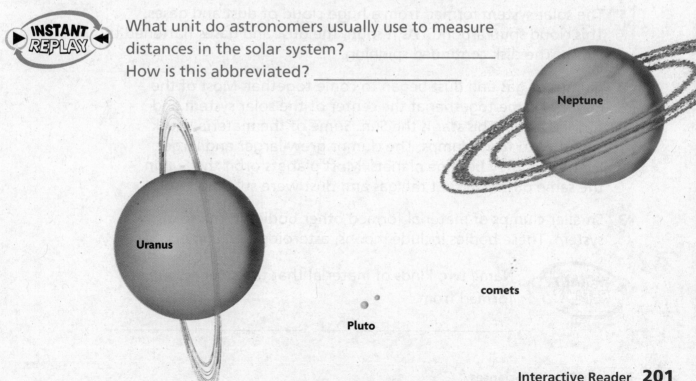

Saturn

Neptune

Uranus

Pluto

comets

▶ **INSTANT REPLAY** ◀ What unit do astronomers usually use to measure distances in the solar system? _____ How is this abbreviated? _____

What do orbits around the Sun look like?

The Sun is the most massive object in the solar system. In fact, if you measured the mass of the entire solar system, the Sun would make up more than 99% of the mass. The Sun has a very strong gravitational force. The planets, comets, and asteroids all orbit around it.

Planets orbit the Sun in a path that is close to a circle. The path is actually an ellipse. An **ellipse** has the shape of a flattened circle. Some ellipses are very long and thin. Others are close to round. A circle is actually a special type of ellipse that is perfectly round.

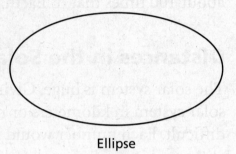

Ellipse

The orbits of most of the planets are ellipses that are almost circles. The orbits of many comets are longer, flatter ellipses.

What is the general shape of the orbits of objects in the solar system?

_____

How did the solar system form?

The pictures on page 203 show the main steps in the formation of the solar system.

1) The solar system formed from a huge cloud of dust and gases. This cloud spun around. As it spun, the dust and gases flattened to a disk. The disk continued spinning.

2) Clumps of gas and dust began to come together. Most of the material came together at the center of the solar system and formed a star. This star is the Sun. Some of the material stuck together to form clumps. The clumps grew larger and larger. Eventually they became planets. Most planets orbit the Sun in the same direction that the gas and dust were swirling.

3) Smaller clumps of material formed other bodies in the solar system. These bodies include moons, asteroids, and comets.

Name two kinds of material that the solar system formed from.

_____

Cloud	Disk	Solar System
Part of a huge cloud of material collapsed into a flattened disk.	The Sun formed at the center of the disk. Other objects formed from the whirling material of the disk.	Larger clumps of material become planets. The planets attract other objects to orbit them. They are moons. The solar system has formed.

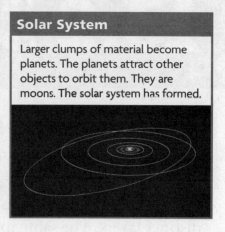

How does gravity affect the shape of objects in the solar system?

You can tell some things about the mass of an object by looking at its shape. An object with a lot of mass is usually a round shape. Gravity has pulled this mass strongly from all directions toward the very center. This produces a round shape. That is why planets and large moons are spheres.

Other space objects have less mass. Gravity is not strong enough to pull in all the uneven lumps. That is why most asteroids, meteors, and comets have lumpy shapes.

Visual Connection
See Objects in the Solar System on student text, page 414.

How does gravity help give the planets a round shape?

_____

SECTION 13.1	
SUMMARIZE	**VOCABULARY**
1. Planets do not produce their own light. Why can we see them? _____ 2. Why do planets have a round shape? _____	Write the correct term for each description. **astronomical unit ellipse gravity** 3. the shape of a planet's orbit _____ 4. causes the planets, stars, and the solar system to form _____ 5. the average distance from Earth to the Sun _____

Student text pages
419–426

What are terrestrial planets?

The four planets closest to the Sun are Mercury, Venus, Earth, and Mars. They are called the **terrestrial planets.** They are grouped together because they have important similarities. They all have three distinct layers. The same forces have shaped their surfaces, which are very rocky. They all formed in similar ways.

How the Terrestrial Planets Formed

You have read about dust and gas clumping together to form the planets. This was not a gentle process. The clumps got big and hard. When they came together, the collisions gave the clumps energy. Some of the energy was in the form of heat. The heat from many collisions melted the four young planets closest to the Sun.

As the terrestrial planets melted, they changed. The material the planets were made of separated into three layers.

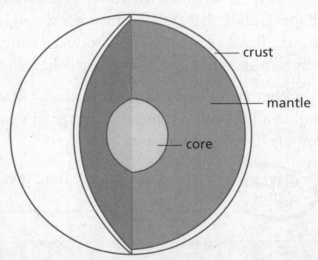

Layers of a Terrestrial Planet

crust

mantle

core

1. Most of the dense elements were metals that sank. They mixed together at the center of each planet to form the core.

2. The less dense material formed the mantle. The mantle makes up most of the planet.

3. The least dense elements formed the thin, outside layer. This is the crust.

Mark It Up

Circle the label of the layer that is made mostly of metals.

Which layer of the terrestrial planets has the most dense elements?

_____

Forces that Shape Terrestrial Planets

There are four main processes that shape the surfaces of the terrestrial planets.

Tectonics As you have read, the mantle is the layer beneath a planet's crust. The mantle is hot and can flow. The flowing mantle can change the planet's crust. It can make parts of the crust move or wrinkle. It can force parts of the crust to stretch or to twist.

The mantle can make a planet's crust wrinkle. This is an example of tectonics.

Tectonics is the way that the crust changes due to the movement of the mantle. Whenever the mantle causes the crust to change, processes of tectonics are at work.

Volcanism There is hot, melted rock under the surface of Earth and other planets. This melted rock can come out onto the surface of a planet. The hole the hot rock escapes through is called a volcano. When the rock reaches the surface, it is called lava. Volcanoes can shape a planet's surface in important ways. Volcanoes can form tall mountains, or they can send out lava that forms wide, flat plains. Volcanoes are found on Earth, Venus, and Mars.

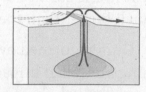

Hot rock moves from inside a planet out onto its surface. This is volcanism.

Volcanism is the way that the crust changes when hot rock from inside the planet comes to the surface. Whenever hot melted rock from the inside of a planet comes out onto the surface, the process of volcanism is at work.

Name two ways that volcanoes can shape a planet's surface.

_____   _____

Weathering and Erosion Wind can wear away rock. Water and some gases can wear away rock. Heating and cooling can crack rock. Then the rock breaks into smaller pieces. Any process that breaks rock into small pieces is called weathering.

Activity

Surfaces
See student text, page 419.

Small pieces of rock can be carried away by wind or water. They can tumble downhill, pulled by the force of gravity. Any process that moves small bits of rock is called erosion. Weathering and erosion shape the surfaces of planets. They create slopes, canyons, and dunes.

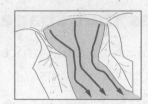

Weathering breaks down rock. Erosion moves it. Both processes help create features on a planet's surface.

Impact Cratering A small space object can hit a planet with great force. This causes an explosion and forms a crater. A crater is a round dent in the surface of a planet. Often a crater is much bigger than the object that made it.

Craters formed by something hitting another thing are called impact craters. Impact cratering can change the surface of a planet. On Earth, most of the craters have been erased by tectonics, volcanism, and weathering. When a planet still has a lot of craters, then the other processes have not changed the surface for a long time.

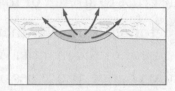

A small space object hits a planet and leaves a crater. This process changes a planet's surface.

List the four main processes that shape the surfaces of rocky planets.

_____ _____ _____ _____

What is Mercury like?

Mercury is the planet closest to the Sun. It is a small planet. A day on Mercury is three months long. During the long day, the part of the planet's surface that faces the Sun gets very, very hot. In contrast, during the three-month-long night, the back side of the planet gets very cold.

Long ago, volcanoes formed large flat plains on Mercury. These are similar to the feature called a mare on the Moon. Mercury has long, high cliffs, formed by tectonic forces wrinkling the crust. Today, Mercury's surface is covered with craters. Because of this, we know that the volcanoes are no longer active.

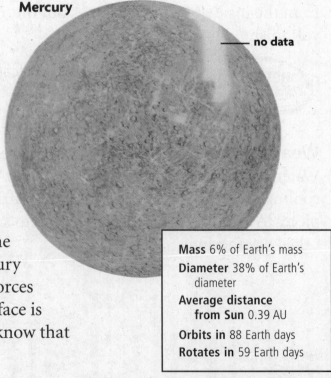

Mercury

— no data

Mass 6% of Earth's mass
Diameter 38% of Earth's diameter
Average distance from Sun 0.39 AU
Orbits in 88 Earth days
Rotates in 59 Earth days

What is Venus like?

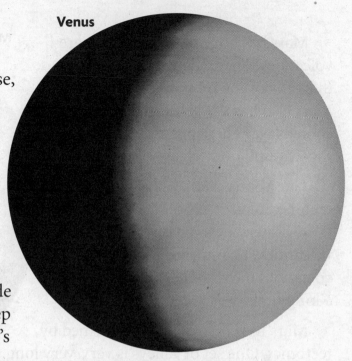

Venus

Venus is close to Earth in size. Otherwise, it is very different from our planet. Like Mercury, Venus has days and nights that are months long. But on Venus the days and nights are both very hot. That is because Venus is covered with a thick layer of clouds that hold in the heat.

Venus has many volcanoes that are mountains. It also has many plains made by cooled lava. It has high cliffs and deep cracks formed by tectonic forces. Venus's thick clouds prevent many space objects from reaching the surface, so there are few craters.

Mass 82% of Earth's mass	**Orbits in** 225 Earth days
Diameter 95% of Earth's diameter	**Rotates in** 243 Earth days
Average distance from Sun 0.72 AU	

Which feature of Venus holds in heat and may prevent space objects from reaching the surface of the planet?

What is Mars like?

Mars is about half the size of Earth. It has polar ice caps, as Earth does. But Mars's polar ice caps are not made of water. They are made of carbon dioxide. Mars probably once had water on its surface, but now it might be frozen in the ground. Mars looks red because it has rocks and dust made of iron and oxygen. Iron and oxygen combine to form rust.

Mars has two small moons. They might have been asteroids near Mars. The gravity of Mars might have pulled the asteroids away from their path around the Sun. It might have pulled the asteroids into orbit around Mars.

Mars has huge mountains that are volcanoes. These mountains are taller than any of the mountains on Earth. Mars also has flat plains made by cooled lava. These plains are like those found on Mercury and Venus.

Like Venus, Mars has impact craters that are very old. Some of these craters are even on Mars's volcanoes. That means that the volcanoes have not been active for a long time.

Mars has cliffs and valleys formed by tectonics. One set of valleys is very, very long. If the valleys were here on Earth, they would stretch across the United States.

Mars has strong winds. They help break down rock on Mars's surface. They carry bits of rock across the planet. Mars has sand dunes. It also has violent dust storms. Sometimes these storms cover most of the planet.

Mars

Mass 11% of Earth's mass	
Diameter 53% of Earth's diameter	
Average distance from Sun 1.5 AU	
Orbits in 1.9 Earth years	
Rotates in 25 hours	

 What two landforms does Mars have that are bigger than any on Earth?

_____ _____

SECTION 13.2	
SUMMARIZE	**VOCABULARY**

1. List the terrestrial planets in order from the planet closest to the Sun to the planet farthest from the Sun.
 	
  a. _____ **b.** _____
 	
  c. _____ **d.** _____
 	
2. List the terrestrial planets in order from smallest to largest.
 	
  a. _____ **b.** _____
 	
  c. _____ **d.** _____
	Answer the questions related to the key terms.
	
	3. Name two things the **terrestrial planets** all have in common.
	
	_____
	
	4. How are **tectonics** and **volcanism** similar?
	
	_____
	
	5. How are **tectonics** and **volcanism** different?
	
	_____

SECTION
13.3

Key Concept
The outer solar system has four giant planets.

Student text pages
428–433

What are gas giants?

The four planets beyond Mars are Jupiter, Saturn, Uranus (YUR-uh-nuhs), and Neptune. These planets are very large. They are made up mainly of gases. That is why they are called **gas giants.**

You know that Earth's air is made up of gases. Some of these gases, including hydrogen, form the gas giant planets.

The Structure of a Gas Giant

Gas giant planets have a very deep atmosphere. At the outer edge, the atmosphere is thin and cold. The closer you get to the center of the planet, the atmosphere becomes denser and hotter. Under the thin and cold edge, there is a layer of clouds. Further down, the atmosphere becomes dense enough that it is a liquid. At the very center, it is so hot and dense that it is probably solid. The diagram below shows the interior of Jupiter, one of the gas giants. You can see that the outer layer is mostly made of hydrogen gas. The middle layer is liquid, and there is a solid core.

As you near the center of a gas giant, what happens to the density? to the temperature?

_____   _____

Jupiter

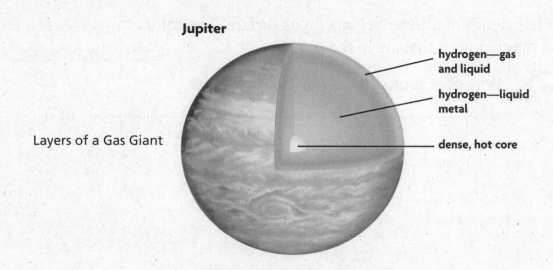

Layers of a Gas Giant

hydrogen—gas and liquid

hydrogen—liquid metal

dense, hot core

What is Jupiter like?

Jupiter is the largest planet in the solar system. It has a larger mass than all of the other planets put together. It takes Jupiter 12 Earth years to complete its path around the Sun. Jupiter spins quickly on its axis. It makes one rotation in less than 10 hours.

Jupiter

Mass 318 Earth masses	
Diameter 11 Earth diameters	
Average distance from Sun 5.2 AU	
Orbits in 12 Earth years	
Rotates in 9.9 hours	

Jupiter's fast spin causes strong winds. This winds lead to large, violent storms. The large oval on the lower right side of the planet is an example. This feature is a large storm called the Great Red Spot. It has been raging for more than 100 years.

Jupiter has clouds of different colors on its surface. The colors depend on the chemicals that are in the cloud.

Why does Jupiter have very strong winds?

_____

_____

What is Saturn like?

Like Jupiter, Saturn is very large. But it is not as dense as Jupiter. Saturn has less gravitational pull than Jupiter, so the gases spread out more.

Saturn's most striking feature is its rings. A planet's **rings** are wide, flat zones of small particles that orbit around the planet. They circle the middle of the planet. In other words, they are in orbit at the planet's equator. All four gas giants have rings around their equators.

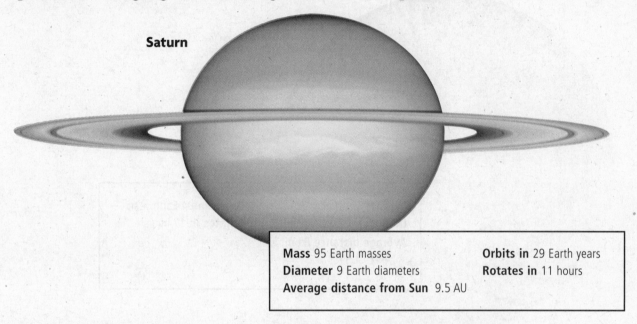

Saturn

Mass 95 Earth masses	**Orbits in** 29 Earth years
Diameter 9 Earth diameters	**Rotates in** 11 hours
Average distance from Sun 9.5 AU	

Saturn's rings are made of chunks of ice. These chunks can be as large as a building. Saturn's rings are also very wide. They are almost as wide as the distance between Earth and the Moon. You can see Saturn's rings with a telescope. The other gas giant planets also have rings. They are not as easy to see. Their ring systems are not as wide as Saturn's rings. They circle each planet at the planet's equator.

What are a planet's rings?

_____

Activity

Giant Planets
See student text, page 431.

What is Uranus like?

Uranus is the seventh planet from the Sun. Its gases are heavier than those of Jupiter and Saturn. It doesn't have as much hydrogen and helium. It has more ammonia, methane, and water. This makes Uranus denser than Jupiter and Saturn. The methane gives Uranus its blue-green color. Its surface does not change much.

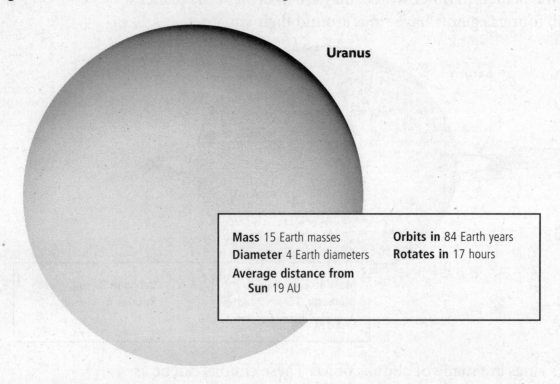

Uranus

Mass 15 Earth masses	**Orbits in** 84 Earth years
Diameter 4 Earth diameters	**Rotates in** 17 hours
Average distance from Sun 19 AU	

Uranus seems to spin on its side. Its axis of rotation is almost in the same plane as its orbit. Early in Uranus's history, the planet might have had a big collision. This might have knocked the planet on its side.

Uranus has rings that orbit around the equator. The extreme tilt of Uranus's axis means that the rings are at almost right angles to the planet's orbit.

During the summer in each hemisphere, one pole points directly toward the Sun. Almost the entire hemisphere is bathed in sunlight for the whole season. Since it takes Uranus 84 Earth years to revolve around the Sun, a season is decades long.

Compared with the other planets, how does Uranus spin?

What is Neptune like?

Like Uranus, the main gas forming the outer layers of Neptune is methane. This gas gives Neptune its deep blue color. Neptune has white clouds high in its atmosphere. It has dark blue storms. The storms move or break up, so Neptune's surface changes over time. Neptune has rings. It has a moon that goes around in the opposite direction from the way Neptune spins. This may mean that Neptune had a collision in its past.

Neptune

Mass 17 Earth masses
Diameter 4 Earth diameters
Average distance
  from Sun 30 AU
Orbits in 164 Earth years
Rotates in 16 hours

What are two similarities and one difference between Uranus and Neptune?

Similarities: _____

_____

Difference: _____

SECTION 13.3

SUMMARIZE	VOCABULARY
1. List the gas giants in order from the planet closest to the Sun to the planet farthest from the Sun. a. _____ b. _____ c. _____ d. _____ **2.** List the gas giants in order from smallest to largest. a. _____ b. _____ c. _____ d. _____	Answer the question related to the key terms. **3.** Why is **gas giants** a good name for the four planets beyond Mars? _____ _____ _____ _____ _____ _____ _____ _____

Student text pages
434–439

What are small objects in the outer solar system like?

The solar system has many objects besides the Sun and the planets. These objects tend to be smaller than planets, but some are quite large. What these space bodies are like depends on where they formed. What they are like also depends on their mass.

Place of Formation

Different places in the solar system are at different temperatures. Even before the Sun formed, the center of the solar system was warmer than the far edges. After the Sun formed, the center of the solar system stayed very warm. The edges of the solar system continued to be cold.

Space bodies that formed closer to the center of the solar system are made mainly of rock and metal. Bodies that formed far from the center of the solar system are made mainly of ice. The ice is not just frozen water. It includes frozen ammonia and frozen carbon dioxide. Bits of rock, metal, and dust are also mixed in the ice.

Circle the word that makes each sentence correct: A space body that formed closer to the center of the solar system is made mainly of **rock / ice**. A space body that formed far from the center of the solar system is made mainly of **ice / metal**.

Mass

Space bodies with a small mass do not have a strong force of gravity. Gravity cannot pull them into a round shape. Instead, these space bodies are lumpy. Their shapes are irregular. Space bodies with a large mass have a stronger force of gravity. Gravity pulls these objects into a round shape. They become spheres.

What are some space bodies beyond Neptune like?

Neptune is the gas giant that is farthest from the Sun. Many smaller space bodies are farther away than Neptune. These objects are made of ice and rock. Most are irregular in shape, but some are round.

Astronomers are just learning about many of these space bodies. They are smaller than planets like Earth and Mars. They are hard to study because they are so small and so far away. But people have known about Pluto since 1930.

Pluto

Pluto is smaller than Earth's Moon. It is round. It probably has a crust, mantle, and core. It has a thin atmosphere. Pluto even has its own moon named Charon. Charon has a mass of about one-seventh that of Pluto. That is large for a moon. We don't know what Pluto looks like. At this time, no spacecraft has flown close to its surface.

Pluto

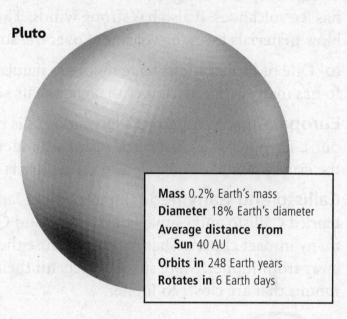

Mass 0.2% Earth's mass
Diameter 18% Earth's diameter
Average distance from
    Sun 40 AU
Orbits in 248 Earth years
Rotates in 6 Earth days

Pluto's Orbit

Pluto's orbit is at an angle compared with the orbits of the planets in the solar system. Also, Pluto's orbit is not as circular. It is a longer ellipse, so Pluto's distance from the Sun changes a lot during its orbit. Sometimes Pluto is less than 30 AU from the Sun. Then it is closer to the Sun than Neptune is. Other times it is almost 50 AU from the Sun.

Pluto's Orbit

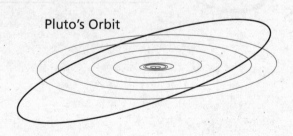

What are two ways that Pluto's orbit differs from the orbits of the planets?

_____   _____

What are the moons of gas giants like?

Each of the gas giant planets has a system of moons*. Some of the moons are large. In fact, six of them are larger than Pluto. Here is some information about these large moons.

Titan Saturn's largest moon is named Titan. Titan has a thick atmosphere that is mostly nitrogen gas. Titan's atmosphere makes it hard to see features on the surface of this moon.

Triton Neptune's largest moon is named Triton. Triton has ice volcanoes. It also has strong winds. The winds blow materials from the volcanoes over the surface.

Io One of Jupiter's four large moons is named Io (EYE-oh). Io has many active volcanoes that change its surface.

Europa Another of Jupiter's large moons is named Europa (yu- ROH-puh). Europa has a crust made of frozen water. The mantle has pushed the crust up in places. It has also caused parts of the crust to crack.

Callisto and Ganymede Jupiter's other large moons are named Callisto and Ganymede. Callisto and Ganymede have many impact craters. That may be because their orbits are far away from Jupiter. More space objects hit them than hit the moons that are closer to Jupiter.

Activity

Exploring Impact Craters See student text, pages 440–441.

Visual Connection See Some Moons of Gas Giants on student text, page 436.

INSTANT REPLAY Name four large moons that orbit Jupiter.

_____ _____ _____ _____

*Academic Vocabulary: Earth's natural satellite is named the Moon. But the word *moon* is used to refer to the natural satellites of other planets. Many moons have been given specific names. Charon, Titan, and Callisto are examples.

The rest of the moons around the gas giants are smaller than Pluto. Some of them are 1600 kilometers (1000 miles) wide. Others are only a few kilometers wide. The smallest moons have irregular shapes.

The gas giants might have captured some of the smaller moons. These large planets all have a strong force of gravity. Gravity could have pulled some of the smaller moons into orbit when they came too close to the planet.

 **INSTANT REPLAY** How might a small moon have come into orbit around a gas giant?

_____

What are asteroids?

Small, solid, rocky bodies in orbit fairly close to the Sun are called **asteroids.** Many of the asteroids are in a large area between Mars and Jupiter called the asteroid belt. There are more than 10,000 asteroids spread throughout this area. They are so far apart that spacecraft from Earth have flown through the asteroid belt.

The asteroids in the asteroid belt have little mass even when they are all added together. If all the asteroids could be put together in one place, they would have less mass than the Moon.

The largest asteroids are close to 1000 kilometers (600 miles) in diameter. The smallest asteroids have a diameter of less than 1 kilometer (0.6 miles). Only the largest asteroids are round. They are the only ones with a strong enough force of gravity to pull all their mass into a sphere. Some of the largest asteroids may have a crust, mantle, and core. They may even have an atmosphere.

Most asteroids are small and have irregular shapes. Many have surfaces that are covered with impact craters. Even the smaller asteroids can be hit by other space objects every once in a while.

Mark It Up

Label two impact craters in the asteroid shown above.

 **INSTANT REPLAY** What are asteroids?

_____

What is a comet?

A **comet** is a small, icy object in orbit around the Sun. While asteroids formed close to the center of the solar system, comets formed far from the center. Remember that the parts of the solar system that are far from the Sun have always been very cold. That is why comets are icy. They are mostly frozen gases with only a little rock and metal in them.

Visual Connection
See Comets on student text, page 438.

Comets have orbits that are different from those of planets and asteroids. Planets and asteroids orbit the Sun in a plane. Comets orbit the Sun at a steep angle compared with the orbits of planets and asteroids. The picture shows the orbit of a famous comet called Halley's comet.

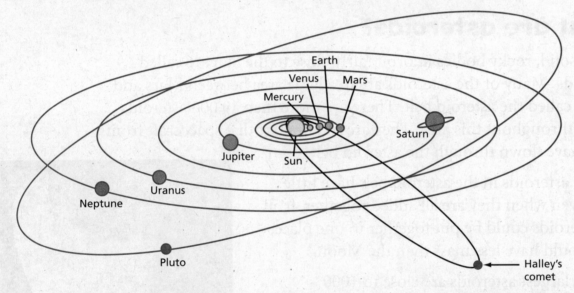

Sun and planets not to scale

Planets and asteroids have orbits that are close to circles. Comets have orbits that are very long ellipses. At one end of a comet's orbit, it comes very close to the Sun. At the other end of its orbit, the comet is very far from the Sun.

When a comet comes close to the Sun, it warms up. Some of its ice melts and evaporates. Gases stream off the comet. The gases carry dust particles with them. This gives the comet a long tail. Sunlight reflects off of the tail. If the comet is close to Earth, you might be able to see the comet without a telescope.

What is a comet?

_____

What are meteors and meteorites?

There are particles of dust in space. As Earth travels in its orbit, sometimes these particles enter Earth's atmosphere. The particles are going at high speeds. They quickly burn up. As they burn, they produce a brief streak of light called a **meteor.**

A meteor shower occurs when Earth's path crosses the old path of a comet's tail. During a meteor shower, you can see many meteors every hour. In contrast, on a night with no meteor shower, you can see only a few meteors.

Most meteors are the size of a speck of dust. Every now and then, larger objects enter Earth's atmosphere. Any object larger than 10 grams will not burn up completely in the atmosphere. Instead, it will fall to Earth. A space object that falls to Earth is called a **meteorite.** Most meteorites come from the asteroid belt. A few meteorites are pieces from the Moon or from Mars.

What is a meteor?

_____

SECTION 13.4	
SUMMARIZE	**VOCABULARY**
1. List two ways that Pluto is different from the six large moons of the gas giant planets. _____ _____ _____ _____	Match the terms with their definitions. 2. asteroid a. a space object that reaches the surface of Earth 3. comet b. an icy body with a long elliptical orbit that brings it close to the Sun 4. meteorite c. a rocky body orbiting fairly close to the Sun

Review
CHAPTER
13 Our Solar System

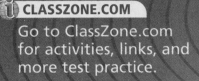

CLASSZONE.COM
Go to ClassZone.com
for activities, links, and
more test practice.

Vocabulary Complete the chart by filling in the blanks.

Term	Description
astronomical unit	1
2	planets close to the Sun with a rocky surface
3	planets far from the Sun that are very large and have a deep atmosphere

Reviewing Key Concepts

4 Why do some space bodies have irregular shapes?

_____

5 Which gas makes up most of the mass of Uranus and Neptune?

_____

the BIG idea

6 Ice is less dense than rock. Rock is less dense than metal. Circle the object that is the least dense. Explain.

Mercury   a moon of Mars   a moon of Uranus

_____

Test Practice

7 What do all four gas giants have that terrestrial planets do not have?

A atmospheres
B solid surfaces
C rings
D moons

8 Which of these, by definition, has to reach the surface of Earth?

A an asteroid
B a comet
C a meteor
D a meteorite

CHAPTER
14 Stars, Galaxies, and the Universe

the **BIG** idea

Our Sun is one of billions of stars in one of billions of galaxies in the universe.

Getting Ready to Learn

Review Concepts

- Our solar system is in the Milky Way.
- A galaxy is a group of millions or billions of stars.

Activity

How Can Stars Differ? See student text, page 451.

Review Vocabulary

Match each word with its definition or description.

solar system   **galaxy**   **universe**

_____ **a.** a star and the various bodies, including planets, that orbit the star

_____ **b.** all space, matter, and energy that exist

_____ **c.** a group of millions or billions of stars held together by gravity

Preview Key Vocabulary

Following are some key terms you will see in this chapter. When you reach each one, write its definition. Then sketch a picture in the space provided to help you remember the term and the definition.

Term	Definition	Sketch
fusion		
light-year		
main sequence		

Student text pages
453–457

Why is the Sun important to us?

The Sun is our source of light and heat. It is the main source of energy for
Earth. The Sun is the largest thing in our solar system. If the Sun were the
size of a basketball, then Earth would be about the size of a small pebble.

The Sun is a star. It is the star that is closest to us. We have learned a
lot about stars by studying the Sun. We have learned that stars are made
mostly of hydrogen. We have learned about their structure and how
they produce energy.

What is the largest thing in our solar system?

_____

What are the layers of the Sun?

The Sun is made mainly of hydrogen. The Sun is densest at its center. This
is where the Sun produces its energy. The energy flows out from the center
of the Sun. It passes through the layers of the Sun. Then it passes through
the Sun's atmosphere. It passes into space to the distant regions of the
solar system.

The Layers of the Sun

The Sun's energy travels from the core, through the Sun's six layers, and out into space.

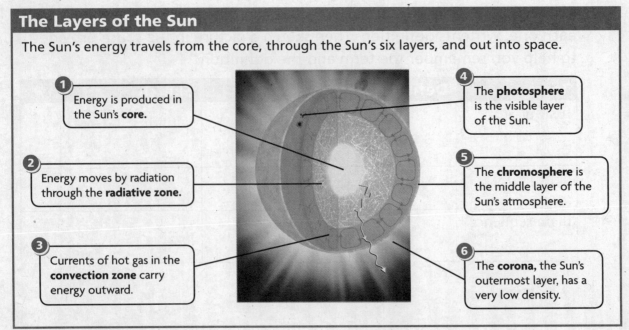

1 Energy is produced in the Sun's **core**.

2 Energy moves by radiation through the **radiative zone**.

3 Currents of hot gas in the **convection zone** carry energy outward.

4 The **photosphere** is the visible layer of the Sun.

5 The **chromosphere** is the middle layer of the Sun's atmosphere.

6 The **corona**, the Sun's outermost layer, has a very low density.

Inside the Sun

The Sun has three main layers.

Core The center of the Sun is called the core. The core of the Sun is made of very hot, dense gas. It gets as hot as 15 million degrees Celsius! The heat and pressure affect the hydrogen atoms. They collide with each other with great force. When this happens, they can combine to form helium.

The process of two atoms combining to form another element is called **fusion.** In the Sun, hydrogen atoms fuse to form helium atoms. Fusion does not just form a new element. It also releases a lot of energy. This energy travels outward from the core.

Radiative Zone This is the middle layer of the Sun. The radiative zone is hot. The pressure is high. But the heat and pressure are not as high as they are in the core. Fusion does not take place in the radiative zone. Energy from the Sun's core travels through the radiative zone by radiation.

Convection Zone This is the layer just below the Sun's atmosphere. Energy moves through this layer by convection. **Convection** is the transfer of energy from one place to another by the motion of gases or liquids. Remember that gases and liquids are fluids. Hot fluids rise. Cool fluids sink. Rising fluids carry heat energy from the radiative zone to the Sun's atmosphere.

How does the Sun produce energy? _____

In which layer is the energy produced? _____

The Sun's Atmosphere

The Sun's an atmosphere has three layers.

Photosphere This is the layer of the Sun that you can see. That is because energy escapes this layer as visible light. There is a lot of energy. So the light is very bright.

Chromosphere This is a thin layer in the middle of the Sun's atmosphere. It gives off pink light.

Activity

Solar Atmosphere
See student text, page 453.

Corona The corona is the outermost layer of the Sun's atmosphere. It is not very dense. It extends out from the Sun for several million kilometers. The corona is not very bright. It is only visible during a solar eclipse.

Visual Connection
See Solar Features in student text, page 456.

What are some features of the Sun?

The Sun rotates on its axis. Scientists realized this by watching dark markings on the photosphere called **sunspots.** Sometimes the Sun has a lot of sunspots. Other times, it has very few sunspots.

Gases sometimes burst out from the photosphere. This happens near sunspots. A jet of gas can flow away from the Sun. This is called a flare. A loop of gas can form. This is called a prominence (PRAHM-uh-nunhs).

Flares and prominences send charged particles into space. These particles form the solar wind. The **solar wind** can harm satellites orbiting Earth. Earth's magnetic field keeps most of the particles away from Earth. Particles from the Sun that do enter Earth's atmosphere can produce beautiful, glowing lights called the auroras (uh-RAWR-uhz). People see auroras mainly in far northern or far southern regions of Earth.

Mark It Up

Draw what you think a solar flare and a prominence look like on the surface of the Sun.

SECTION 14.1

SUMMARIZE	VOCABULARY

1. List the layers of the Sun in order from the innermost layer to the outermost part of the atmosphere.
 	
 _____
 _____
 _____
 _____
 _____
	Write the correct term for each description.
	
	     convection fusion
	     solar wind sunspot
	
	 2. a dark mark on the Sun _____
	
	 3. how energy moves because of the motion of fluids _____
	
	 4. how charged particles move from the Sun out into space _____
	
	 5. atoms of one element combine to form another element, releasing energy
	 _____

14.2 Stars change over their life cycles.

Student text pages
460–466

How do we measure distances in space?

Stars are huge, glowing balls of gas. Many stars are about the same size as the Sun. Some stars are much larger than the Sun, and others are much smaller. The Sun is the only star that is visible as more than a point of light in our sky. That is because we are much closer to the Sun than we are to other stars.

The distances between stars are tremendous. If these distances are measured in kilometers or astronomical units, the numbers have many zeroes at the end. It is hard to work with such numbers. To solve this problem, astronomers have a different unit for measuring distances between stars. The unit is called the light-year. A **light-year** is the distance light travels in one year. That distance is 9.5 trillion kilometers or 6 trillion miles.

The Sun is only a very small fraction of a light-year away. The next closest star is 4 light-years away.

What unit is used to measure distances between stars?

_____

What is parallax?

Astronomers have different ways to measure distances in space. One way to measure distances is with parallax.

Parallax is the apparent shift in the position of an object when it is viewed from a different location. You can understand how parallax works by following these steps. Hold an object about arm's length away from your face. Cover one eye and look at the object. Then cover the other eye and look at the object. Notice that the object seems to shift position against the background when you switch eyes. That is because you are viewing the object first from one angle and then from another angle. That is how parallax works, as well.

Activity

Parallax
See student text, page 461.

To use parallax, astronomers photograph a star against a background of other stars. They photograph the star when Earth is in a particular place in its orbit around the Sun. Then they photograph the star again six months later. Then Earth is in the opposite place in its orbit. They compare the two photographs of the star. They see how the star has shifted its position against the background. They use this information to figure out the distance to the star.

How do stars vary in color and temperature?

On a clear night, if you look at the stars, you will see that the stars are not all exactly the same color. Most stars are white. Some stars are red, and other stars are blue. You might be able to detect orange stars or stars that look slightly yellow.

Activity

Temperature, Brightness, and Color
See student text, pages 458–459.

Why are stars different colors? Stars differ in color because they differ in temperature. Objects in your everyday life also change color when they change temperature. Think about the metal coils in a toaster. When the toaster is off, the coils are cold. They are probably a black or dark gray color. When you first turn on the toaster, the coils begin to glow. They have a dull red color. As the coils heat up more, they become bright orange. If the coils could get even hotter, they would turn yellow. If they could get hotter still, they would turn white. The color of the coils tells you how hot they are.

The same thing is true of stars. The color of a star tells how hot the star's surface is. Stars that are relatively cool are red. The hottest stars are blue. Stars of average temperature are yellow or white. The chart gives the temperatures of stars of different colors.

Star Colors and Temperatures

Class	Color	Surface Temperature (°C)
O	blue-white	above 25,000
B	blue-white	10,000–25,000
A	white	7500–10,000
F	yellow-white	6000–7500
G	yellow	5000–6000
K	orange	3500–5000
M	red	below 3500

INSTANT REPLAY

What does a star's color tell you about the star?

_____

Visual Connection
See Color and Temperature on student text, page 463.

How do stars vary in size?

Most stars are huge. To get an idea of how big stars are, think about the Sun. The Sun is an average-sized star. It is about 100 times larger than Earth. A trip in a jet plane around Earth takes two full days. The same trip around the Sun would take more than seven months!

Some stars are much larger than the Sun. Giant stars are 10 to 100 times larger than the Sun. They tend to be blue or red. Supergiant stars are 100 to 1000 times larger than the Sun.

Giant and supergiant stars are usually brighter than average-sized stars. Large stars look bright even if they are far away. For example, the star named Betelgeuse (BEET-uhl-JOOZ) is one of the brightest stars in the night sky. It is 522 light-years away. Betelgeuse looks so bright even at a great distance is because it is so large. It is a red supergiant. It is about 600 times bigger than the Sun. The enormous surface of Betelgeuse glows with light, making the star very bright.

Some stars are much smaller than the Sun. White dwarf stars are about one one-hundredth the size of the Sun. They are not much larger than Earth. Because they are small, they give off less light than larger stars do. White dwarf stars tend to be dim. To see a white dwarf, you need a telescope.

Giant star 10–100 times the Sun's diameter; can be red, blue, yellow, or white in color

Supergiant star 100–1000 times the Sun's diameter; can be red, blue, or yellow in color

White dwarf 1/100 the Sun's diameter

A star the size of the Sun Diameter = 1.4 million kilometers (900,000 miles)

 Circle the correct answers: The Sun is a **small / medium / large** star. Dwarf stars are **100 / 1000** times smaller than the Sun.

How do stars change over time?

Stars are not alive, but they go through stages. These stages are like the stages in a life cycle.

Stars form inside a cloud of dust and gas in space. A cloud of dust and gas in space is called a **nebula** (NEHB-yuh-huh). Gravity acts on the nebula. It pulls the dust and gas close together. The matter becomes dense and forms a sphere.

Inside the sphere, particles of matter hit each other. They get hotter and hotter. Gravity pulls the matter closer together. The sphere gets denser and denser. If the matter gets hot and dense enough, fusion occurs and the sphere has become a star. The stages a star goes through after it forms depends on the mass of the star.

Life Cycle of a Lower-Mass Star

Lower-mass stars are about the size of the Sun. Stars this size can spend billions of years in one stage of the star life cycle. This stage is called the main sequence. The **main sequence** is the stage when stars produce energy through the fusion of hydrogen atoms into helium atoms. When a star runs out of hydrogen, the main sequence stage is over.

When a lower-mass star runs out of hydrogen, it expands. It becomes a giant star. In a giant star, helium atoms fuse to produce carbon. This is called helium fusion. Helium fusion gives off lots of energy in the form of light and heat.

In time, the giant uses all its fuel. It sheds its outer layers. All that remains is a small, white core. This is a white dwarf. Fusion does not occur in a white dwarf. A white dwarf will continue to glow for billions of years.

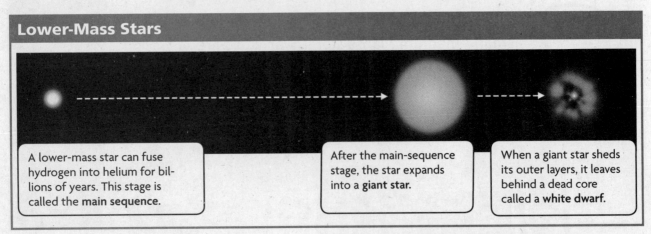

Lower-Mass Stars

A lower-mass star can fuse hydrogen into helium for billions of years. This stage is called the **main sequence**.

After the main-sequence stage, the star expands into a **giant star**.

When a giant star sheds its outer layers, it leaves behind a dead core called a **white dwarf**.

Life Cycle of a Higher-Mass Star

Higher-mass stars are at least eight times the size of the Sun. Higher-mass stars have a shorter life cycle than lower-mass stars do. Higher-mass stars use their fuel very quickly. They do not spend billions of years in the main sequence stage. Instead, they spend only millions of years in this stage.

When a higher-mass star uses all of its hydrogen, it expands. It becomes a supergiant. Helium fusion goes on in the core of a supergiant star. But fusion does not stop with carbon, as it does in the core of a giant star. Instead, heavier and heavier elements are produced. Fusions stops when the core is made up of the element iron. When fusion stops, the core collapses due to the pull of gravity. Then something dramatic happens. The star explodes. The explosion of a supergiant star is called a **supernova.**

Mark It Up

Mark on the diagram the kind of element that makes up the core of the red supergiant when the star ends that stage.

 **INSTANT REPLAY** Which kind of star spends longer in the main sequence stage? Circle the correct answer:
higher-mass stars   lower-mass stars

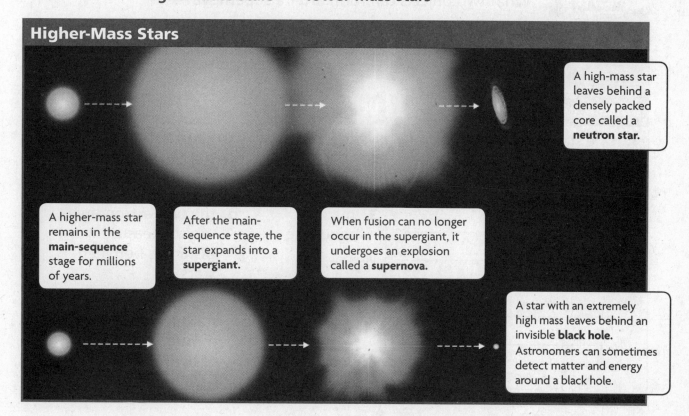

Higher-Mass Stars

A higher-mass star remains in the **main-sequence** stage for millions of years.

After the main-sequence stage, the star expands into a **supergiant.**

When fusion can no longer occur in the supergiant, it undergoes an explosion called a **supernova.**

A high-mass star leaves behind a densely packed core called a **neutron star.**

A star with an extremely high mass leaves behind an invisible **black hole.** Astronomers can sometimes detect matter and energy around a black hole.

A supernova sends elements into space. In time, this material may form a new star or planet.

After a supernova, the collapsed core of the supergiant remains behind. The form the core takes depends on its mass. Some cores become neutron stars. Others become black holes.

If the mass of the remaining core is less than three times the mass of the Sun, the core will become a neutron star. A neutron star is much smaller than Earth. It is only about 20 kilometers (12 miles) across. A neutron star does not produce much light. Instead, it sends out beams of x-rays or radio waves. Astronomers can detect these waves with special telescopes.

If the mass of the core is more than three times the mass of the Sun, the core will become a black hole. The gravity of a black hole is so strong that no light escapes from it. No other kind of radiation escapes either. A black hole does not send out x-rays. It does not send out radio waves. Astronomers locate a black hole by watching how matter acts near the black hole.

 **What two objects can form after a supernova?**

_____   _____

SECTION 14.2	
SUMMARIZE	**VOCABULARY**
1. One star is red. Another star is yellow. Another star is blue. What does the color difference tell about these stars? _____ _____ _____ _____ _____	Match the terms with their definitions. **2.** light-year **a.** a cloud of gas and dust in space **3.** main sequence **b.** the unit astronomers use to measure distances between stars **4.** nebula **c.** the stage in which a star produces energy through the fusion of hydrogen into helium

Student text pages
468–471

What is our galaxy like?

Remember that a galaxy is a group of millions or billions of stars held together by gravity. Our galaxy is called the Milky Way. The Milky Way has hundreds of billions of stars. It also has large areas of gas and dust.

The Milky Way is a disk with an oval bulge at the center. Both the disk and the bulge are filled with stars. The picture shows a side view of the Milky Way. The Milky Way's disk is more than 100,000 light-years across. Remember that a light-year is the distance light travels in one year. The Milky Way is extremely large.

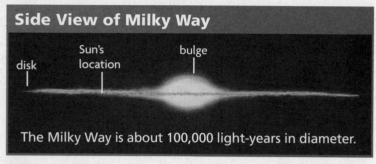

Side View of Milky Way

disk | Sun's location | bulge

The Milky Way is about 100,000 light-years in diameter.

The Sun is in the disk of the Milky Way. It is about halfway between the center of the bulge and the edge of the disk. Find the Sun's location in the picture. It is about 26,000 light-years from the Sun to the center of the bulge.

Since the Sun is in the disk of the Milky Way, the solar system is in the disk, too. When we look at the night sky, we can see part of our galaxy edge-on. This part of the galaxy looks like a hazy band of white light. It is the light of many stars that are far away and in the disk of the Milky Way. We cannot see the bulge of the Milky Way. Our view is blocked by thick clouds of dust and gas.

The stars in the Milky Way revolve around the center of the galaxy. They are moving at high speeds. The galaxy is so large that it takes a long time for a star to complete its orbit. For example, the Sun takes 250 million years to go around the galaxy one time.

Mark It Up

Mark the distance from the Sun to the center of the bulge of the Milky Way galaxy.

Activity

The Milky Way See student text, page 468.

Why does the Milky Way look hazy to us?

_____

What are the different kinds of galaxies?

Some galaxies are very large. Large galaxies have more than a trillion stars. Some are much smaller. Small galaxies have about one hundred million stars. The shapes of galaxies also vary. There are three main shapes of large galaxies.

Spiral Galaxies A spiral is a smooth, open curve. A **spiral galaxy** has arms that curve away from the central section of the galaxy. The spiral arms are made up of gas, dust, and stars.

There are many spiral galaxies. The Milky Way is one. Like the Milky Way, all spiral galaxies have a disk with a central bulge. The spiral arms are part of the disk. They have many young, bright stars. The rest of the disk and the bulge are formed mainly of old stars.

Spiral Galaxy

 What kind of galaxy is the Milky Way?

_____

Elliptical Galaxies You have learned that an ellipse is a flattened circle. An **elliptical galaxy** is shaped like an ellipse. But elliptical galaxies are not flat. They are three-dimensional. So an elliptical galaxy can be shaped like an egg. Or it can be almost perfectly round and shaped like a sphere. An elliptical galaxy has very little dust and gas in it. All of the stars in an elliptical galaxy are old stars.

Activity

Galaxy Shapes
See student text, page 469.

Elliptical Galaxy

Irregular Galaxies Objects with an irregular shape may have bumps in one place and indents in another. They do not have any particular shape. An **irregular galaxy** does not have a definite shape. Irregular galaxies are usually smaller than spiral galaxies and elliptical galaxies. They have many fewer stars. Irregular galaxies are less common than spiral galaxies and elliptical galaxies.

 What is an irregular galaxy?

_____

_____

_____

Irregular Galaxy

Vocabulary

In each oval write the name of the three kinds of galaxies. Under the name, note three facts about each kind of galaxy.

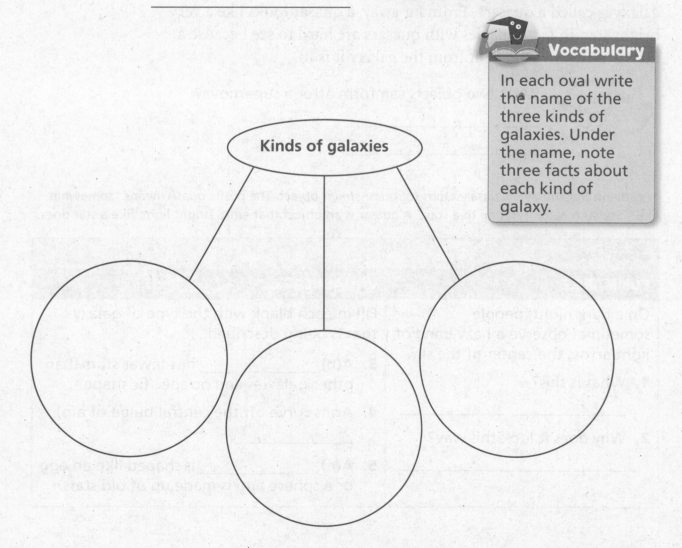

Kinds of galaxies

What is at the center of a galaxy?

A large galaxy may have a black hole at its center. Remember that a black hole is an object with very strong gravity. The gravity is so strong that light cannot escape from it. Neither can any other kind of radiation.

A black hole at the center of a galaxy has much more mass than a black hole left behind by a dead star. Astronomers call these black holes supermassive black holes. The mass of a supermassive black hole can be millions or billions of times the mass of the Sun. For example, there is a supermassive black hole at the center of the Milky Way. This black hole has a mass that is three million times that of the Sun.

Black holes are invisible, but they can be detected. They pull on gases from stars near them. Astronomers can detect gas being pulled away from stars and swirling into a black hole.

Some galaxies have a very bright center. The bright center of a galaxy is called a quasar*. From far away, a quasar looks like a very bright star. In fact, galaxies with quasars are hard to see because a quasar outshines the light from the galaxy it is in.

> **INSTANT REPLAY** What two objects can form after a supernova?
>
> _____
>
> _____

*Academic Vocabulary: **Quasar** stands for *quasi-stellar object*. The prefix *quasi-* means "somewhat like." *Stellar* means "relating to a star." A quasar is an object that emits bright light, like a star does.

SECTION 14.3	
SUMMARIZE	**VOCABULARY**
On a dark night, people sometimes observe a hazy band of light across the center of the sky. **1.** What is this? _____ **2.** Why does it look this way? _____	Fill in each blank with the type of galaxy that is being described. **3.** A(n) _____ has fewer stars than other galaxies and no specific shape. **4.** Arms curve off the central bulge of a(n) _____. **5.** A(n) _____ is shaped like an egg or a sphere and is made up of old stars.

SECTION
14.4

Key Concept
The universe is expanding.

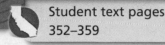
Student text pages
352–359

What is in the universe?

You have learned that the universe is everything. It includes all the matter, all the energy, and all the space there is. The universe is almost too big to imagine. It has about 100 billion galaxies.

Galaxies are found together in groups called superclusters. Between the groups of galaxies are large areas of space. These areas are almost completely empty of matter.

Although the universe is very large, the chemical elements are the same everywhere. The same physical processes are at work, too.

List three types of things that make up the universe.

_____   _____   _____

How do we learn about the universe?

Remember that a light-year is the distance light travels in one year. The Milky Way is 100,000 light-years across. Galaxies in our supercluster are far away. The Andromeda Galaxy is one of the galaxies closest to us. It is 2 million light-years away.

The great distances of the universe give astronomers a tool to learn about the past. To understand how, think about light. When you see a dog jump outside your window, you see light bouncing off the dog. Since you are fairly close to the dog, it takes the light only a tiny fraction of a second to reach your eyes. You can say that you see the dog jump at the same moment that he actually jumps.

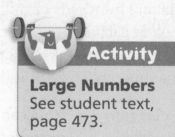

Activity

Large Numbers
See student text, page 473.

Now think about the Sun. The Sun is 150 million kilometers from Earth. It takes light from the Sun 8 minutes to reach Earth. If the Sun suddenly stopped giving off light, it would take 8 minutes for Earth to go dark.

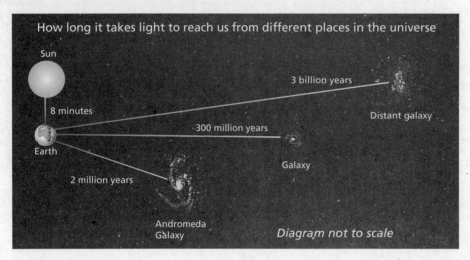

How long it takes light to reach us from different places in the universe

Sun

8 minutes

Earth

2 million years

Andromeda Galaxy

300 million years

Galaxy

3 billion years

Distant galaxy

Diagram not to scale

Now think about galaxies beyond the Milky Way. The Andromeda Galaxy is 2 million light-years away. That means it takes 2 million years for the light from that galaxy to reach us. What astronomers see today is the Andromeda Galaxy as it was 2 million years ago. This means that looking out into space is the same as looking back in time! The most distant objects in space give us views of the earliest times in the development of the universe.

Astronomers can look at galaxies that are different distances from us. They can look at galaxies that are several million light-years away. They can look at galaxies that are hundreds of millions light-years away. They can look at galaxies that are even a few billion light-years away. Each view is like a photograph of the universe taken at a different stage in its history.

Activity

Galaxies
See student text, page 476.

How can scientists see what the universe was like at different stages of development?

_____

How did the universe begin?

Scientists think that all the matter, energy, and space in the universe were once packed into a tiny spot. Suddenly, the universe began to expand. The matter started moving outward in all directions. The moment that the universe started expanding is called the **big bang.** Scientists think that the big bang happened about 14 billion years ago. The universe has been expanding ever since.

 What is the big bang?

_____

What is some evidence of the big bang?

Scientists came up with the idea of the big bang once they learned that the universe is expanding. They discovered the expansion by studying how galaxies move.

Galaxies Move Away from Each Other

Next time you hear an ambulance siren, listen to it closely. You will probably hear the pitch of the siren change as it passes you. When the ambulance is coming toward you, the pitch sounds high. After the ambulance passes you, the pitch sounds much lower. The changing pitch of the siren is an example of the Doppler effect. The **Doppler effect** is a change in the observed wavelength of a wave. The change occurs because either the source of the wave or the observer is moving.

In the example above, the ambulance siren is the source of sound waves. The ambulance is moving toward you. You observe that the siren sounds high because the sound waves are closer together. The wavelengths of the sound waves are getting shorter. Then the ambulance passes you. You observe the sound of the siren getting lower because the sound waves are getting stretched out. The wavelengths of the sound waves are getting longer.

The Doppler effect also occurs with light. If a galaxy is moving toward us, its light appears to be bluer than we would expect. That is because the wavelengths of the light waves are getting shorter. If a galaxy is moving away from us, its light appears to be redder than we would expect. That is because the wavelengths of the light waves are getting longer.

In the early 1900s, astronomers built new, stronger telescopes. They started to be able to identify galaxies. They saw that the light from most galaxies was redder than they had expected. They realized that this was due to the Doppler effect. That means that the galaxies are moving away from us. That is strong evidence that the universe is expanding.

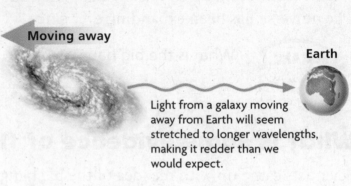

Moving away

Earth

Light from a galaxy moving away from Earth will seem stretched to longer wavelengths, making it redder than we would expect.

Observing galaxies moving away from us

Is the light from distant galaxies bluer or redder than expected? What does the color shift mean?

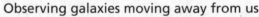

Galaxies Move at Different Rates

The astronomers from the early 1900s learned that distant galaxies are moving away from us faster than closer galaxies are. This showed that the universe is expanding.

To help you understand why scientists concluded that the universe is expanding, think of the universe as a ball of bread dough. The bread dough has raisins in it. The raisin-bread dough is set out to rise.

Imagine you are a raisin in the dough. As the dough rises, the other raisins in the dough seem to move away from you. The expanding dough puts distance between all of the raisins. But raisins that are far from you seem to move farther away, at a faster rate. That is because there is more dough between you and the more distant raisins.

Now compare the raisin-bread dough to the universe. The raisins are like galaxies. The universe expands, like the dough. Like the raisins, the galaxies that are far apart seem to move away from each other faster than the galaxies that are close together.

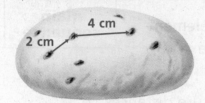
As the dough rises, the raisins are pushed farther apart from each other. The more distance there is between raisins, the faster and farther they move apart.

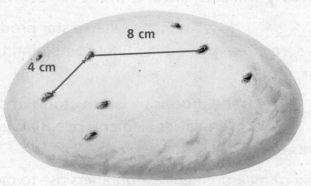

Before dough rises

After dough rises

There is other evidence that the universe is expanding. This evidence comes from studying microwaves from space. It comes from physics experiments with small particles and from computer models. All of this evidence helps us gain an understanding of the universe and how it formed.

INSTANT REPLAY Which galaxies are moving away from each other the fastest, the galaxies that are close to one another or the galaxies that are far from one another?

_____

SECTION 14.3	
SUMMARIZE	**VOCABULARY**
1. If a star 100 light-years from Earth is seen to be expanding into a giant star, how long ago did this event take place? Explain. _____ _____ _____ _____ _____	Circle the phrase that makes each sentence correct. 2. The big bang is **the way we know that / the moment in time when** the universe started to expand. 3. The Doppler effect shows us that most galaxies are moving **toward / away** from us. 4. Due to the Doppler effect, most galaxies look **redder / bluer** than we would expect them to look.

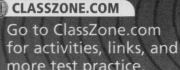

Vocabulary Fill each blank with the correct word from the list.

1 The _____ is the stage when a star produces most of its energy from hydrogen atoms combining to produce helium.

2 _____ is the process by which atoms of an element combine to form a heavier element, releasing large amounts of energy.

3 The unit of measurement astronomers use to measure distances to stars and to galaxies is called a _____.

> fusion
>
> light-year
>
> main sequence

Reviewing Key Concepts

4 How does the Sun produce energy?

_____

5 Why don't astronomers use astronomical units to measure distances between stars?

_____

6 What keeps stars in orbit around the center of the galaxy?

_____

the BIG idea

7 How is the Universe changing now?

_____

Test Practice

8 Which of the following colors indicates the hottest star?

   A red
   B yellow
   C blue
   D white

9 What type of galaxy is the Milky Way?

   A elliptical galaxy
   B spiral galaxy
   C irregular galaxy
   D quasar galaxy

Glossary

A

acceleration
The rate at which velocity changes over time. (p. 10)

aceleración La razón a la cual la velocidad cambia con respecto al tiempo.

acid
A substance that can donate a proton to another substance and has a pH below 7. (p. 156)

ácido Una sustancia que puede donar un protón a otra sustancia y que tiene un pH menor a 7.

adaptation
A characteristic, a behavior, or any inherited trait that makes a species able to survive and reproduce in a particular environment.

adaptación Una característica, un comportamiento o cualquier rasgo heredado que permite a una especie sobrevivir o reproducirse en un medio ambiente determinado.

air resistance
The fluid friction due to air. (p. 46)

resistencia del aire La fricción fluida debida al aire.

asteroid
A small, solid, rocky body that orbits the Sun. Most asteroids orbit in a region between Mars and Jupiter called the asteroid belt. (p. 217)

asteroide Un pequeño cuerpo sólido y rocoso que orbita alrededor del Sol. La mayoría de los asteroides orbitan en una región entre Marte y Júpiter denominada cinturón de asteroides.

astronomical unit AU
Earth's average distance from the Sun, which is approximately 150 million kilometers (93 million mi). (p. 201)

unidad astronómica ua La distancia promedio de la Tierra al Sol, la cual es de aproximadamente 150 millones de kilómetros (93 millones de millas).

atmosphere (AT-muh-SFEER)
The outer layer of gases of a large body in space, such as a planet or star; the mixture of gases that surrounds the solid Earth; one of the four parts of the Earth system.

atmósfera La capa externa de gases de un gran cuerpo que se encuentra en el espacio, como un planeta o una estrella; la mezcla de gases que rodea la Tierra sólida; una de las cuatro partes del sistema terrestre.

atom
The smallest particle of an element that has the chemical properties of that element. (p. 64)

átomo La partícula más pequeña de un elemento que tiene las propiedades químicas de ese elemento.

atomic mass
The average mass of the atoms of an element. (p. 103)

masa atómica La masa promedio de los átomos de un elemento.

atomic mass number
The total number of protons and neutrons in an atom's nucleus. (p. 99)

número de masa atómica El número total de protones y neutrones que hay en el núcleo de un átomo.

atomic number
The number of protons in the nucleus of an atom. (p. 98)

número atómico El número de protones en el núcleo de un átomo.

axis of rotation
An imaginary line about which a turning body, such as Earth, rotates. (p. 184)

eje de rotación Una línea imaginaria alrededor de la cual gira un cuerpo, como lo hace la Tierra.

B

base
A substance that can accept a proton from another substance and has a pH above 7. (p. 158)

base Una sustancia que puede aceptar un protón de otra sustancia y que tiene un pH superior a 7.

big bang
According to scientific theory, the moment in time when the universe started and began to expand. (p. 237)

la gran explosión De acuerdo a la teoría científica, el momento en el tiempo en el cual el universo empezó a expandirse.

biochemistry
The study of the substances and processes occurring in living organisms. (p. 164)

bioquímica El estudio de sustancias y procesos que ocurren en organismos vivos.

black hole
The final stage of an extremely massive star, which is invisible because its gravity prevents any form of radiation from escaping.

hoyo negro La etapa final de una estrella de enorme masa, la cual es invisible porque su gravedad evita que cualquier tipo de radiación escape.

boiling
A process by which a substance changes from its liquid state to its gas state. The liquid is heated to a specific temperature at which bubbles of vapor form within the liquid. (p. 91)

ebullición Un proceso mediante el cual una sustancia cambia de su estado líquido a su estado gaseoso se calienta el líquido a una determinada temperatura a la cual se forman burbujas de vapor dentro del líquido.

boiling point
The temperature at which a substance changes from its liquid state to its gas state through boiling. (p. 91)

punto de ebullición La temperatura a la cual una sustancia cambia de su estado líquido a su estado gaseoso mediante ebullición.

bond energy
The amount of energy in a chemical bond between atoms.

energía de enlace La cantidad de energía que hay en un enlace químico entre átomos.

buoyant force
The upward force on objects in a fluid; often called buoyancy. (p. 58)

fuerza flotante La fuerza hacia arriba que ejerce un fluido sobre un objeto inmerso en él, a menudo llamada flotación.

C

carbohydrate (KAHR-boh-HY-drayt)
A type of molecule made up of subunits of sugars and used for energy and structure. (p. 173)

carbohidrato Un tipo de molécula compuesta de unidades de azúcares y usada como fuente de energía y como material estructural.

catalyst
A substance that increases the rate of a chemical reaction but is not consumed in the reaction. (p. 134)

catalizador Una sustancia que aumenta el ritmo de la velocidad de una reacción química pero que no es consumida en la reacción.

cell
The smallest unit that is able to perform the basic functions of life.

célula La unidad más pequeña capaz de realizar las funciones básicas de la vida.

centripetal force (sehn-TRIHP-ih-tuhl)
Any force that keeps an object moving in a circle. (p. 27)

fuerza centrípeta Cualquier fuerza que mantiene a un objeto moviéndose en forma circular.

chemical bond
A force that holds atoms together. (p. 114)

enlace químico Fuerza que mantiene unidos entre sí los átomos.

chemical change
A change of one substance into another substance. (p. 76)

cambio químico La transformación de una sustancia a otra sustancia.

chemical formula
An expression that shows the number and types of atoms joined in a compound. (p. 116)

fórmula química Una expresión que muestra el número y los tipos de átomos unidos en un compuesto.

chemical property
A characteristic of a substance that describes how it can form a new substance. (p. 76)

propiedad química Una característica de una sus-tancia que describe como puede formar una nueva sustancia.

chemical reaction

The process by which chemical changes occur. In a chemical reaction, atoms are rearranged, and chemical bonds are broken and formed. (p. 130)

reacción química El proceso mediante el cual ocurren cambios químicos. En una reacción química, los átomos se reorganizan y los enlaces químicos se rompen y se vuelven a formar.

coefficient

The number before a chemical formula that indicates how many molecules are involved in a chemical reaction. (p. 138)

coeficiente El número anterior a una fórmula química que indica cuántas moléculas están involucradas en una reacción química.

comet

A body that produces a coma of gas and dust; a small, icy body that orbits the Sun. (p. 218)

cometa Un cuerpo que produce una coma de gas y polvo; un cuerpo pequeño y helado que se mueve en órbita alrededor del Sol.

compound

A substance made up of two or more different types of atoms bonded together. (p. 67)

compuesto Una sustancia formada por dos o más diferentes tipos de átomos enlazados.

compression

The process of pushing the particles of a material closer together. (p. 41)

compresión El proceso de empujar partículas materiales más cerca unos de otros.

concentrated

Having a high concentration of solute. (p. 151)

concentrado Se dice de lo que tiene una alta proporción de soluto.

concentration

The amount of solute dissolved in a solvent at a given temperature. (p. 151)

concentración La cantidad de soluto disuelta en un solvente a una temperature determinada.

condensation

The process by which a gas becomes a liquid. (p. 93)

condensación El proceso mediante el cual un gas se convierte en un líquido.

constellation

A group of stars that form a pattern in the sky. (p. 181)

constelación Un grupo de estrellas que forman un patrón en el cielo.

convection

The transfer of energy from place to place by the motion of heated gas or liquid; in Earth's mantle, convection is thought to transfer energy by the motion of solid rock, which when under great heat and pressure can move like a liquid. (p. 223)

convección La transferencia de energía de un lugar a otro por el movimiento de un líquido o gas calentado; se piensa que en el manto terrestre la convección transfiere energía mediante el movimiento de roca sólida, la cual puede moverse como un líquido cuando está muy caliente y bajo alta presión.

corona

The outer layer of the Sun's atmosphere.

corona La capa exterior de la atmósfera del Sol.

covalent bond

A pair of electrons shared by two atoms. (p. 121)

enlace covalente Un par de electrones compartidos por dos átomos.

crystal

A solid substance in which the atoms are arranged in an orderly, repeating, three-dimensional pattern. (p. 66)

cristal Una sustancia sólida en la cual los átomos están organizados en un patrón tridimensional y ordenado que se repite.

cycle

n. A series of events or actions that repeat themselves regularly; a physical and/or chemical process in which one material continually changes locations and/or forms. Examples include the water cycle, the carbon cycle, and the rock cycle.

v. To move through a repeating series of events or actions.

ciclo *s.* Una serie de eventos o acciones que se repiten regularmente; un proceso físico y/o químico en el cual un material cambia continuamente de lugar y/o forma. Ejemplos: el ciclo del agua, el ciclo del carbono y el ciclo de las rocas.

D

data

Information gathered by observation or experimentation that can be used in calculating or reasoning. *Data* is a plural word; the singular is *datum*.

datos Información reunida mediante observación o experimentación y que se puede usar para calcular o para razonar.

density

A property of matter representing the mass per unit volume. (p. 53)

densidad Una propiedad de la materia que representa la masa por unidad de volumen.

dilute

adj. Having a low concentration of solute. (p. 151)

v. To add solvent in order to decrease the concentration of a solution.

diluido *adj.* Que tiene una baja concentración de soluto.

diluir *v.* Agregar solvente para disminuir la concentración de una solución.

Doppler effect

A change in the observed frequency of a wave, occurring when the source of the wave or the observer is moving. Changes in the frequency of light are often measured by observing changes in wavelength, whereas changes in the frequency of sound are often detected as changes in pitch. (p. 237)

efecto Doppler Un cambio en la frecuencia observada de una onda que ocurre cuando la fuente de la onda o el observador están en movimiento. Los cambios en la frecuencia de la luz a menudo se miden observando los cambios en la longitud de onda, mientras que los cambios en la frecuencia del sonido a menudo se detectan como cambios en el tono.

E

eclipse

An event during which one object in space casts a shadow onto another. On Earth, a lunar eclipse occurs when the Moon moves through Earth's shadow, and a solar eclipse occurs when the Moon's shadow crosses Earth.

eclipse Un evento durante el cual un objeto en el espacio proyecta una sombra sobre otro. En la Tierra, un eclipse lunar ocurre cuando la Luna se mueve a través de la sombra de la Tierra, y un eclipse solar ocurre cuando la sombra de la Luna cruza la Tierra.

elastic force

The force in an object that resists stretching or pressing. (p. 39)

fuerza elástica La fuerza en un objeto que resiste el estiraje o la presión.

electrical conductivity

A measure of how easily electric current passes through a particular substance. (p. 111)

conductividad eléctrica La capacidad de un medio de permitir el paso de la corriente eléctrica a su través.

electromagnetic radiation

Energy that travels across distances as certain types of waves. Types of electromagnetic radiation are radio waves, microwaves, infrared radiation, visible light, ultraviolet radiation, x-rays, and gamma rays.

radiación electromagnética Energía que se transmite a través de la distancia por medio de ciertos tipos de ondas, tales como ondas de radio, microondas, luz infrarroja, luz visible, radiación ultravioleta, rayos X y rayos gamma.

electron

A negatively charged particle located outside an atom's nucleus. An electron is about 2000 times smaller than either a proton or a neutron. (p. 96)

electrón Una partícula con carga negativa localizada fuera del núcleo de un átomo. Un electrón es como aproximadamente 2000 veces más pequeño que un protón o un neutrón.

element

A substance that cannot be broken down into a simpler substance by ordinary chemical changes. An element consists of atoms of only one type. (p. 67)

elemento Una sustancia que no puede descomponerse en otra sustancia más simple por medio de cambios químicos normales. Un elemento consta de átomos de un solo tipo.

ellipse

An oval or flattened circle. (p. 202)

elipse Un óvalo o círculo aplanado.

elliptical galaxy

A galaxy that is shaped like a sphere or a flattened sphere. (p. 232)

galaxia elíptica Galaxia que tiene forma de esfera o esfera aplanada.

endothermic reaction

A chemical reaction that absorbs energy. (p. 141)

reacción endotérmica Una reacción química que absorbe energía.

energy

The ability to do work or to cause a change. For example, the energy of a moving bowling ball knocks over pins; energy from food allows animals to move and to grow; and energy from the Sun heats Earth's surface and atmosphere, which causes air to move.

energía La capacidad para trabajar o causar un cambio. Por ejemplo, la energía de una bola de boliche en movimiento tumba los pinos; la energía proveniente de su alimento permite a los animales moverse y crecer; la energía del Sol calienta la superficie y la atmósfera de la Tierra, lo que ocasiona que el aire se mueva.

environment

Everything that surrounds a living thing. An environment is made up of both living and nonliving factors.

medio ambiente Todo lo que rodea a un organismo vivo. Un medio ambiente está compuesto de factores vivos y factores sin vida.

enzyme

A type of protein that is a catalyst for chemical reactions in living things. (p. 176)

enzima Un tipo de proteína que es un catalizador de reacciones químicas en organismos vivos.

equinox (EE-kwuh-NAHKS)

In an orbit, a position and time in which sunlight shines equally on the Northern Hemisphere and the Southern Hemisphere; a time of year when daylight and darkness are nearly equal for most of Earth. (p. 188)

equinoccio En una órbita, la posición y el tiempo en los cuales la luz del Sol incide de la misma manera en el Hemisferio Norte y en el Hemisferio Sur; una época del año en la cual la luz del día y la oscuridad son casi iguales para la mayor parte de la Tierra.

evaporation

A process by which a substance changes from its liquid state to its gas state by random particle movement. Evaporation usually occurs at the surface of a liquid over a wide range of temperatures. (p. 92)

evaporación Un proceso mediante el cual una sustancia cambia de su estado líquido a su estado gaseoso por medio del movimiento aleatorio de las partículas. La evaporación normalmente ocurre en la superficie de un líquido en una amplia gama de temperaturas.

exothermic reaction

A chemical reaction that releases energy. (p. 140)

reacción exotérmica Una reacción química que libera energía.

experiment

An organized procedure to study something under controlled conditions.

experimento Un procedimiento organizado para estudiar algo bajo condiciones controladas.

extinction

The permanent disappearance of a species.

extinción La desaparición permanente de una especie.

F

fluid

A substance that can flow easily, such as a gas or a liquid. (p. 47)

fluido Una sustancia que fluye fácilmente, como por ejemplo un gas o un líquido.

force

A push or a pull; something that changes the motion of an object. (p. 18)

fuerza Un empuje o un jalón; algo que cambia el movimiento de un objeto.

freezing

The process by which a substance changes from its liquid state into its solid state. (p. 90)

congelación El proceso mediante el cual una sustancia cambia de su estado líquido a su estado sólido.

freezing point

The temperature at which a substance changes from its liquid state to its solid state through freezing. (p. 90)

punto de congelación La temperatura a la cual una sustancia cambia de su estado líquido a su estado sólido mediante congelación.

friction

A force that resists the motion between two surfaces in contact. (p. 43)

fricción Una fuerza que resiste el movimiento entre dos superficies en contacto.

fusion

A process in which particles of an element collide and combine to form a heavier element, such as the fusion of hydrogen into helium that occurs in the Sun's core. (p. 223)

fusión Un proceso en el cual las partículas de un elemento chocan y se combinan para formar un elemento más pesado, como la fusión de hidrógeno en helio que ocurre en el núcleo del Sol.

G

galaxy

Millions or billions of stars held together in a group by their own gravity. (p. 181)

galaxia Millones o miles de millones de estrellas unidas en un grupo por su propia gravedad.

gas

Matter with no definite volume and no definite shape. The molecules in a gas are very far apart, and the amount of space between them can change easily. (p. 83)

gas Materia sin volumen definido ni forma definida. Las moléculas en un gas están muy separadas unas de otras, y la cantidad de espacio entre ellas puede cambiar fácilmente.

gas giant

A large planet that consists mostly of gases in a dense form. The four large planets in the outer solar system—Jupiter, Saturn, Uranus, and Neptune—are gas giants. (p. 209)

gigante de gas Un planeta grande compuesto principalmente de gases en forma densa. Los cuatro planetas grandes en el sistema solar exterior—Júpiter, Saturno, Urano y Neptuno—son gigantes de gas.

geosphere (JEE-uh-SFEER)

All the features on Earth's surface—continents, islands, and seafloor—and everything below the surface—the inner and outer core and the mantle; one of the four parts of the Earth system.

geosfera Todas las características de la superficie de la Tierra, es decir, continentes, islas y el fondo marino, y de todo bajo la superficie, es decir, el núcleo externo e interno y el manto; una de las cuatro partes del sistema de la Tierra.

gravity

The force that objects exert on each other because of their mass. (p. 34)

gravedad La fuerza que los objetos ejercen entre sí debido a su masa.

group

A vertical column in the periodic table of the elements. Elements in a group have similar properties. (p. 104)

grupo Una columna vertical en la tabla periódica de los elementos. Los elementos en un grupo tienen propiedades similares.

H

half-life

The amount of time it takes for half of the nuclei of a radioactive isotope to decay into atoms of another element.

vida media La cantidad de tiempo necesario para que se desintegren la mitad de los átomos de una muestra.

horizontal

Parallel to the horizon; level.

horizontal Paralelo al horizonte; nivelado.

hydrosphere (HY-druh-SFEER)

All water on Earth—in the atmosphere and in the oceans, lakes, glaciers, rivers, streams, and underground reservoirs; one of the four parts of the Earth system.

hidrosfera Toda el agua de la Tierra: en la atmósfera y en los océanos, lagos, glaciares, ríos, arroyos y depósitos subterráneos; una de las cuatro partes del sistema de la Tierra.

hypothesis

A tentative explanation for an observation or phenomenon. A hypothesis is used to make testable predictions.

hipótesis Una explicación provisional de una observación o de un fenómeno. Una hipótesis se usa para hacer predicciones que se pueden probar.

I, J

inertia (ih-NUR-shuh)

The resistance of an object to a change in the speed or the direction of its motion. (p. 23)

inercia La resistencia de un objeto al cambio de la velocidad o de la dirección de su movimiento.

inorganic compound

A compound that is not considered organic. All compounds that do not contain carbon are inorganic, as are some types of carbon-containing compounds. (p. 168)

compuesto inorgánico Un compuesto que no se considera orgánico. Todos los compuestos que no contienen carbono son inorgánicos, al igual que algunos tipos de compuestos que contienen carbono.

ion

An atom or group of atoms that has a positive or negative electric charge. (p. 100)

ión Un átomo o un grupo de átomos que tiene una carga eléctrica positiva o negativa.

ionic bond

The electrical attraction between a negative ion and a positive ion. (p. 121)

enlace iónico La atracción eléctrica entre un ión negativo y un ión positivo.

ionic compound

A substance held together by ionic bonds. (p. 121)

compuesto iónico Sustancia que se mantiene unida por enlaces iónicos.

irregular galaxy

A galaxy that does not have a well-defined shape. (p. 233)

galaxia irregular Galaxia que no tiene una forma bien definida.

isomer
Any of two or more compounds that contain the same atoms but that have different structures. (p. 172)

isómero Cualquiera de dos o más compuestos que contienen los mismos átomos pero que tienen estructuras diferentes.

isotope
An atom of one element that has a different number of neutrons than another atom of the same element. (p. 99)

isótopo Un átomo de un elemento que tiene un número diferente de neutrones que otro átomo del mismo elemento.

K

kinetic energy (kuh-NEHT-ihk)
The energy of motion. A moving object has the most kinetic energy at the point where it moves the fastest. (p. 84)

energía cinética La energía de movimiento. Un objeto en movimiento tiene la mayor energía cinética en el punto en donde se mueve más rápidamente.

kinetic theory of matter (kuh-NEHT-ihk)
A theory stating that all matter is made of particles in motion. (p. 84)

teoría cinética de la materia Una teoría que establece que toda materia está compuesta de partículas en movimiento.

L

law
In science, a rule or principle describing a physical relationship that always works in the same way under the same conditions. The law of conservation of energy is an example.

ley En las ciencias, una regla o un principio que describe una relación física que siempre funciona de la misma manera bajo las mismas condiciones. La ley de la conservación de la energía es un ejemplo.

law of conservation of energy
A law stating that no matter how energy is transferred or transformed, it continues to exist in one form or another.

ley de la conservación de la energía Una ley que establece que no importa cómo se transfiere o transforma la energía, toda la energía sigue presente en alguna forma u otra.

law of conservation of mass
A law stating that atoms are not created or destroyed in a chemical reaction. (p. 135)

ley de la conservación de la masa Una ley que establece que los átomos ni se crean ni se destruyen en una reacción química.

light-year
The distance light travels in one year, which is about 9.5 trillion kilometers (6 trillion mi). (p. 225)

año luz La distancia que viaja la luz en un año, la cual es de casi 9.5 billones de kilómetros (6 billones de millas).

lipid
A type of molecule made up of subunits of fatty acids. Lipids are found in the fats, oils, and waxes used for structure and to store energy. (p. 174)

lípido Un tipo de molécula compuesta de unidades de ácidos grasos. Los lípidos se encuentran en las grasas, los aceites y las ceras usadas como materiales estructurales y para almacenar energía.

liquid
Matter that has a definite volume but does not have a definite shape. The molecules in a liquid are close together but not bound to one another. (p. 82)

líquido Materia que tiene un volumen definido pero no tiene una forma definida. Las moléculas en un líquido están cerca unas de otras pero no están ligadas.

M

main sequence
The stage in which stars produce energy through the fusion of hydrogen into helium. (p. 228)

secuencia principal La etapa en la cual las estrellas producen energía mediante la fusión de hidrógeno en helio.

mare (MAH-ray)
A large, dark plain of solidified lava on the Moon. The plural form of *mare* is *maria* (MAH-ree-uh). (p. 190)

mare Una planicie grande y oscura de lava solidificada en la Luna. El plural de *mare* es *maría*.

mass
A measure of how much matter an object is made of.

masa Una medida de la cantidad de materia de la que está compuesto un objeto.

matter

Anything that has mass and volume. Matter exists ordinarily as a solid, a liquid, or a gas.

materia Todo lo que tiene masa y volumen. Generalmente la materia existe como sólido, líquido o gas.

melting

The process by which a substance changes from its solid state to its liquid state. (p. 89)

fusión El proceso mediante el cual una sustancia cambia de su estado sólido a su estado líquido.

melting point

The temperature at which a substance changes from its solid state to its liquid state through melting. (p. 90)

punto de fusión La temperatura a la cual una sustancia cambia de su estado sólido a su estado líquido mediante fusión.

metal

An element that tends to be shiny, easily shaped, and a good conductor of electricity and heat. (p. 105)

metal Un elemento que tiende a ser brilloso, fácilmente deformable moldeado y buen conductor de electricidad y calor.

metallic bond

A certain type of bond in which nuclei float in a sea of electrons. (p. 125)

enlace metálico Cierto tipo de enlace en el cual los núcleos flotan en un mar de electrones.

metalloid

An element that has properties of both metals and nonmetals. (p. 108)

metaloide Un elemento que tiene propiedades de los metales así como de los no metales.

meteor

A brief streak of light produced by a small particle entering Earth's atmosphere at a high speed. (p. 219)

meteoro Un breve rayo luminoso producido por una partícula pequeña que entra a la atmósfera de la Tierra a una alta velocidad.

meteorite

A small object from outer space that passes through Earth's atmosphere and reaches the surface. (p. 219)

meteorito Un pequeño objeto del espacio exterior que pasa a través de la atmósfera de la Tierra y llega a la superficie.

meter m

The international standard unit of length, about 39.37 inches.

metro La unidad estándar internacional de longitud, aproximadamente 39.37 pulgadas.

mixture

A combination of two or more substances that do not combine chemically but remain the same individual substances. Mixtures can be separated by physical means. (p. 69)

mezcla Una combinación de dos o más sustancias que no se combinan químicamente sino que permanecen como sustancias individuales. Las mezclas se pueden separar por medios físicos.

molecule

A group of atoms that are held together by covalent bonds so that they move as a single unit. (pp. 65, 121)

molécula Un grupo de átomos que están unidos mediante enlaces covalentes de tal manera que se mueven como una sola unidad.

motion

A change of position over time. (p. 4)

movimiento Un cambio de posición a través deltiempo.

N

nebula (NEHB-yuh-luh)

A cloud of gas and dust in space. Stars form in nebulae. (p. 228)

nebulosa Una nube de gas y polvo en el espacio. Las estrellas se forman en las nebulosas.

net force

The overall force acting on an object when all of the forces acting on it are combined. (p. 19)

fuerza neta La fuerza resultante que actúa sobre un objeto cuando todas las fuerzas que actúan sobre él son combinadas.

neutral

Describing a solution that is neither an acid nor a base. A neutral solution has a pH of 7. (p. 159)

neutro Que describe una solución que no es un ácido ni una base. Una solución neutra tiene un pH de 7.

neutron

A particle that has no electric charge and is located in an atom's nucleus. (p. 96)

neutrón Una partícula que no tiene carga eléctrica y que se encuentra en el núcleo de un átomo.

neutron star

A dense core that may be left behind after a higher-mass star explodes in a supernova.

estrella de neutrones Un núcleo denso que puede resultar después de que una estrella de mayor masa explota en una supernova.

Newton's first law

A scientific law stating that objects at rest remain at rest, and objects in motion remain in motion with the same velocity, unless acted on by an unbalanced force.

primera ley de Newton Una ley científica que esta blece que los objetos en reposo permanecen en reposo, y que los objetos en movimiento permanecen en movimiento con la misma velocidad, a menos que actúe sobre ellos una fuerza no balanceada.

Newton's second law

A scientific law stating that the acceleration of an object increases with increased force and decreases with increased mass.

segunda ley de Newton Una ley científica que esta-blece que la aceleración de un objeto aumenta al incrementar la fuerza que actúa sobre él y disminuye al incrementar su masa.

Newton's third law

A scientific law stating that every time one object exerts a force on another object, the second object exerts a force that is equal in size and opposite in direction back on the first object.

tercera ley de Newton Una ley científica que esta-blece que cada vez que un objeto ejerce una fuerza sobre otro objeto, el segundo objeto ejerce una fuerza de la misma magnitud y en dirección opuesta sobre el primer objeto.

nonmetal

An element that is not a metal and has properties gener-ally opposite to those of a metal. (p. 107)

no metal Un elemento que no es un metal y que tiene propiedades generalmente opuestas a las de los metales.

nucleic acid (noo-KLEE-ihk)

A type of molecule, made up of subunits of nucleotides, that is part of the genetic material of a cell and is needed to make proteins. DNA and RNA are nucleic acids. (p. 177)

ácido nucleico Un tipo de molécula, compuesto de unidades de nucleótidos, que es parte del material genético de una célula y se necesita para producir proteínas. El ADN y el ARN son ácidos nucleicos.

nucleus

The central region of an atom, where most of the atom's mass is found in protons and neutrons. (p. 96)

núcleo La región central de un átomo donde se encuentra la mayor parte de la masa del átomo en forma de protones y neutrones.

O

orbit

n. The path of an object in space as it moves around another object due to gravity; for example, the Moon moves in an orbit around Earth. (pp. 38, 180)

v. To revolve around, or move in an orbit; for example, the Moon orbits Earth.

órbita *s.* La trayectoria de un objeto en el espacio a medida que se mueve alrededor de otro objeto debido a la gravedad; por ejemplo, la Luna se mueve en una órbita alrededor de la Tierra.

orbitar *v.* Girar alrededor de algo, o moverse en una órbita; por ejemplo, la Luna orbita la Tierra.

organic compound

A compound that is based on carbon. (p. 168)

compuesto orgánico Un compuesto basado en el carbono.

P

parallax

The apparent shift in the position of an object when viewed from different locations. (p. 225)

paralaje El cambio aparente en la posición de un objeto cuando se observa desde diferentes puntos.

particle

A very small piece of matter, such as an atom, molecule, or ion.

partícula Una cantidad muy pequeña de materia, como un átomo, una molécula o un ión.

pascal Pa

The unit used to measure pressure. One pascal is the pressure exerted by one newton of force on an area of one square meter, or one N/m^2.

pascal La unidad utilizada para medir presión. Un pascal es la presión ejercida por un newton de fuerza sobre un área de un metro cuadrado, o un N/m^2.

penumbra
A region of lighter shadow that may surround an umbra; for example, the spreading cone of lighter shadow cast by a space object. (p. 194)

penumbra Una región de sombra más tenue que puede rodear a una umbra; por ejemplo, la sombra más tenue cónica proyectada por un objeto espacial.

period
A horizontal row in the periodic table of the elements. Elements in a period have varying properties. (p. 104)

período Un renglón horizontal en la tabla periódica de los elementos. Los elementos en un período tienen distintas propiedades.

periodic table
A table of the elements, arranged by atomic number, that shows the patterns in their properties. (p. 102)

tabla periódica Una tabla de los elementos, organizada en base a número atómico, que muestra los patrones en sus propiedades.

pH
The concentration of hydrogen ions in a solution; a measurement of acidity. (p. 159)

pH La concentración de iones de hidrógeno en una solución;, una medida de acidez.

physical change
A change in a substance that does not change the substance into a different one. (p. 74)

cambio físico Un cambio en una sustancia que no transforma la sustancia a otra sustancia.

physical property
A characteristic of a substance that can be observed without changing the identity of the substance. (p. 72)

propiedad física Una característica de una sustancia que se puede observar sin cambiar la identidad de la sustancia.

polar covalent bond
The unequal sharing of electrons between two atoms that gives rise to negative and positive regions of electric charge.

enlace polar covalente El compartir electrones desigualmente entre dos átomos y que lleva a la formación de regiones de carga eléctrica positiva y regiones de carga eléctrica negativa.

polymer
A very large carbon-based molecule made of smaller, repeating units. (pp. 66, 124, 171)

polímero Una molécula muy grande basada en el carbono compuesta de unidades más pequeñas que se repiten.

position
An object's location. (p. 2)

posición La ubicación de un objeto.

precipitate
n. A solid substance that forms as a result of a reaction between chemicals in two liquids. (p. 131)

v. To come out of solution.

precipitado *s.* Una sustancia sólida que se forma como resultado de la reacción entre sustancias químicas en dos líquidos.

precipitar *v.* Salir de solución.

pressure
A measure of how much force is acting on a certain area; how concentrated a force is. Pressure is equal to the force divided by area. (p. 55)

presión Una medida de cuánta fuerza actúa sobre cierta área; el nivel de concentración de la fuerza. La presión es igual a la fuerza dividida entre el área.

product
A substance formed by a chemical reaction. A product is made by the rearrangement of atoms and bonds in reactants. (p. 131)

producto Una sustancia formada por una reacción química. Un producto se hace mediante la reorganización de los átomos y los enlaces en los reactivos.

protein
One of many types of molecules made up of chains of amino acid subunits. Proteins control the chemical activity of a cell and support growth and repair. (p. 175)

proteína Uno de muchos tipos de moléculas formadas por cadenas de aminoácidos. Las proteínas controlan la actividad química de una célula y sustentan el crecimiento y la reparación.

proton
A positively charged particle located in an atom's nucleus. (p. 96)

protón Una partícula con cargada positivamente localizada en el núcleo de un átomo.

quasar
The very bright center of a distant galaxy.

quásar El centro muy brillante de una galaxia distante.

R

radiation (RAY-dee-AY-shuhn)
Energy that travels across distances in the form of electromagnetic waves.

> **radiación** Energía que viaja a través de la distancia en forma de ondas electromagnéticas.

radioactivity
The process by which the nucleus of an atom of an element releases energy and particles. (p. 109)

> **radioactividad** El proceso mediante el cual el núcleo de un átomo de un elemento libera energía y partículas.

reactant
A substance that is present at the beginning of a chemical reaction and is changed into a new substance. (p. 131)

> **reactivo** Una sustancia que está presente en el comienzo de una reacción química y que se convierte en una nueva sustancia.

reactive
Likely to undergo a chemical change. (p. 105)

> **reactivo** Que es probable que sufra un cambio químico.

reference point
A location with which another location is compared. (p. 2)

> **punto de referencia** Una ubicación con la cual se compara otra ubicación.

revolution
The motion of one body around another, such as Earth in its orbit around the Sun; the time it takes an object to go around once. (p. 185)

> **revolución** El movimiento de un cuerpo alrededor de otro, como la Tierra en su órbita alrededor del Sol; el tiempo que le toma a un objeto dar la vuelta una vez.

ring
In astronomy, a wide, flat zone of small particles that orbit around a planet's equator. (p. 211)

> **anillo** En astronomía, una zona ancha y plana de pequeñas partículas que orbitan alrededor del ecuador de un planeta.

S

satellite
An object that orbits a more massive object. (p. 189)

> **satélite** Un objecto que orbita un objecto de mayor masa.

saturated
Containing the maximum amount of a solute that can be dissolved in a particular solvent at a given temperature and pressure. (p. 153)

> **saturado** Que contiene la máxima cantidad de soluto que se puede disolver en un solvente en particular a determinada temperatura y presión.

season
One part of a pattern of temperature changes and other weather trends over the course of a year. Astronomical seasons are defined and caused by the position of Earth's axis relative to the direction of sunlight. (p. 185)

> **estación** Una parte de un patrón de cambios de temperatura y otras tendencias meteorológicas en el curso de un año. Las estaciones astronómicas se definen y son causadas por la posición del eje de la Tierra en relación a la dirección de la luz del Sol.

second s
A unit of time equal to one-sixtieth of a minute.

> **segundo** Una unidad de tiempo igual a una sesentava parte de un minuto.

solar system
The Sun and its family of orbiting planets, moons, and other objects. (p. 181)

> **sistema solar** El Sol y su familia de planetas, lunas y otros objetos en órbita.

solar wind
A stream of electrically charged particles that flows out in all directions from the Sun's corona. (p. 224)

> **viento solar** Una corriente de partículas eléctricamente cargadas que fluye hacia fuera de la corona del Sol en todas las direcciones.

solid
Matter that has a definite shape and a definite volume. The molecules in a solid are in fixed positions and are close together. (p. 82)

> **sólido** La materia que tiene una forma definida y un volumen definido. Las moléculas en un sólido están en posiciones fijas y cercanas unas a otras.

solstice (SAHL-stihs)

In an orbit, a position and time during which one hemisphere gets its maximum area of sunlight, while the other hemisphere gets its minimum amount; the time of year when days are either longest or shortest, and the angle of sunlight reaches its maximum or minimum. (p. 188)

solsticio En una órbita, la posición y el tiempo durante los cuales un hemisferio obtiene su área máxima de luz del Sol, mientras que el otro hemisferio obtiene su cantidad mínima; la época del año en la cual los días son los más largos o los más cortos y el ángulo de la luz del Sol alcanza su máximo o su mínimo.

solubility

The amount of solute that dissolves in a certain amount of a solvent at a given temperature and pressure to produce a saturated solution. (p. 153)

solubilidad La cantidad de soluto que se disuelve en cierta cantidad de solvente a determinada temperatura y presión para producir una solución saturada.

solute

In a solution, a substance that is dissolved in a solvent. (p. 147)

soluto En una solución, una sustancia que se disuelve en un solvente.

solution

A mixture of two or more substances that is identical throughout; a homogeneous mixture. (p. 146)

solución Una mezcla de dos o más sustancias que es idéntica en su totalidad; una mezcla homogénea.

solvent

In a solution, the substance that dissolves a solute and makes up the largest percentage of a solution. (p. 147)

solvente En una solución, la sustancia que disuelve un soluto y que compone el porcentaje mayor de la una solución.

species

A group of living things that are so closely related that they can breed with one another and produce offspring that can breed as well.

especie Un grupo de organismos que están tan estrechamente relacionados que pueden aparearse entre sí y producir crías que también pueden aparearse.

speed

A measure of how fast something moves through a particular distance over a definite time period. Speed is distance divided by time. (p. 5)

rapidez Una medida del desplazamiento de un objeto a lo largo de una distancia específica en un período de tiempo definido. La rapidez es la distancia dividida entre el tiempo.

spiral galaxy

A galaxy that has a central bulge of stars and bands of stars that extend out in a curved pattern. (p. 232)

galaxia espiral Galaxia que tiene una concentración central de estrellas y bandas de estrellas que se prolongan siguiendo un patrón curvo.

states of matter

The different forms in which matter can exist. Three familiar states are solid, liquid, and gas. (p. 80)

estados de la materia Las diferentes formas en las cuales puede existir la materia. Los tres estados conocidos son sólido, líquido y gas.

sublimation

The process by which a substance changes directly from its solid state to its gas state without becoming a liquid first.

sublimación El proceso mediante el cual una sustancia cambia directamente de su estado sólido a su estado gaseoso sin convertirse primero en líquido.

subscript

A number written slightly below and to the right of a chemical symbol that shows how many atoms of an element are in a compound.

subíndice Un número que se escribe en la parte inferior a la derecha de un símbolo químico y que muestra cuantos átomos de un elemento están en un compuesto.

substance

Matter of a particular type. Elements, compounds, and mixtures are all substances.

sustancia La materia de cierto tipo. Los elementos, los compuestos y las mezclas son sustancias.

sunspot

A darker spot on the photosphere of the Sun. A sunspot appears dark because it is cooler than the surrounding area. (p. 224)

mancha solar Una mancha oscura en la fotosfera del Sol. Una mancha solar se ve oscura porque es más fría que el área que la rodea.

supernova

The explosion that occurs when a high-mass star is no longer able to produce energy by fusion. (p. 229)

supernova La explosión producida cuando una estrella de alta masa ya no puede producir energía por fusión.

suspension

A mixture in which the different parts are identifiable as separate substances; a heterogeneous mixture.

suspensión Una mezcla en la cual las diferentes partes son identificables como sustancias distintas; una mezcla heterogénea.

system

A group of objects or phenomena that interact. A system can be as simple as a rope, a pulley, and a mass. It also can be as complex as the interaction of energy and matter in the four parts of the Earth system.

sistema Un grupo de objetos o fenómenos que interactúan. Un sistema puede ser algo tan sencillo como una cuerda, una polea y una masa. También puede ser algo tan complejo como la interacción de la energía y la materia en las cuatro partes del sistema de la Tierra.

T

technology

The use of scientific knowledge to solve problems or engineer new products, tools, or processes.

tecnología El uso de conocimientos científicos para resolver problemas o para diseñar nuevos productos, herramientas o procesos.

tectonics (tehk-TAHN-ihks)

The processes in which the motion of hot material under a crust changes the crust of a space body. Earth has a specific type of tectonics called plate tectonics. (p. 205)

tectónica Los procesos en los cuales el movimiento del material caliente bajo una corteza cambia la corteza de un cuerpo espacial. La Tierra tiene un tipo específico de tectónica denominado tectónica de placas.

temperature

A measure of the average amount of kinetic energy of the particles in an object. (p. 86)

temperatura Una medida de la cantidad promedio de energía cinética de las partículas en un objeto.

tension

The force that stretches an object. Tension also refers to the force transmitted through a stretched object. (p. 40)

tensión La fuerza que estira un objeto. La tensión se refiere también a la fuerza transmitida a través de un objeto estirado.

terrestrial planet

Earth or a planet similar to Earth that has a rocky surface. The four planets in the inner solar system—Mercury, Venus, Earth, and Mars—are terrestrial planets. (p. 204)

planeta terrestre La Tierra o un planeta parecido a la Tierra que tiene una superficie rocosa. Los cuatro planetas en el sistema solar interior—Mercurio, Venus, la Tierra y Marte—son planetas terrestres.

theory

In science, a set of widely accepted explanations of observations and phenomena. A theory is a well-tested explanation that is consistent with all available evidence.

teoría En las ciencias, un conjunto de explicaciones de observaciones y fenómenos que es ampliamente aceptado. Una teoría es una explicación bien probada que es consecuente con la evidencia disponible.

thermal conductivity

A measure of how easily thermal energy is transferred through a particular substance. (p. 111)

conductividad térmica La capacidad de los materiales para dejar pasar el calor.

thermometer

A device for measuring temperature. (p. 86)

termómetro Un aparato para medir la temperatura.

U

umbra

The dark, central region of a shadow, such as the cone of complete shadow cast by an object. (p. 194)

umbra La región central y oscura de una sombra, como la sombra completa cónica proyectada por un objeto.

universe

Space and all the matter and energy in it. (p. 181)

universo El espacio y toda la materia y energía que hay dentro de él.

V

variable

Any factor that can change in a controlled experiment, observation, or model.

variable Cualquier factor que puede cambiar en un experimento controlado, en una observación o en un modelo.

vector

A quantity that has both size and direction. (p. 9)

vector Una cantidad que tiene magnitud y dirección.

velocity

A speed in a specific direction. (p. 9)

velocidad Una rapidez en una dirección específica.

vertical

Straight up or down from a level surface.

vertical Que está dispuesto hacia arriba o hacia abajo de una superficie nivelada.

volcanism

The process of molten material moving from a space body's hot interior onto its surface. (p. 205)

vulcanismo El proceso del movimiento de material fundido del interior caliente de un cuerpo espacial a su superficie.

volume

An amount of three-dimensional space, often used to describe the space that an object takes up. (p. 50)

volumen Una cantidad de espacio tridimensional; a menudo se usa este término para describir el espacio que ocupa un objeto.

W, X, Y, Z

wavelength

The distance from one wave crest to the next crest; the distance from any part of one wave to the identical part of the next wave.

longitud de onda La distancia de una cresta de onda a la siguiente cresta; la distancia de cualquier parte de una onda a la parte idéntica de la siguiente onda.

weight

The force of gravity on an object. (p. 37)

peso La fuerza de la gravedad sobre un objeto.

The Periodic Table of the Elements

Key (example cell):
- Atomic Number: 1
- Symbol: H
- Name: Hydrogen
- Atomic Mass: 1.008

Legend:
- Metal
- Metalloid
- Nonmetal

1	2	3	4	5	6	7	8	9	10	11	12	13	14	15	16	17	18
1 H Hydrogen 1.008																	2 He Helium 4.003
3 Li Lithium 6.941	4 Be Beryllium 9.012											5 B Boron 10.811	6 C Carbon 12.011	7 N Nitrogen 14.007	8 O Oxygen 15.999	9 F Fluorine 18.998	10 Ne Neon 20.180
11 Na Sodium 22.990	12 Mg Magnesium 24.305											13 Al Aluminum 26.982	14 Si Silicon 28.086	15 P Phosphorus 30.974	16 S Sulfur 32.066	17 Cl Chlorine 35.453	18 Ar Argon 39.948
19 K Potassium 39.098	20 Ca Calcium 40.078	21 Sc Scandium 44.956	22 Ti Titanium 47.87	23 V Vanadium 50.942	24 Cr Chromium 51.996	25 Mn Manganese 54.938	26 Fe Iron 55.845	27 Co Cobalt 58.933	28 Ni Nickel 58.69	29 Cu Copper 63.546	30 Zn Zinc 65.39	31 Ga Gallium 69.723	32 Ge Germanium 72.61	33 As Arsenic 74.922	34 Se Selenium 78.96	35 Br Bromine 79.904	36 Kr Krypton 83.80
37 Rb Rubidium 85.468	38 Sr Strontium 87.62	39 Y Yttrium 88.906	40 Zr Zirconium 91.224	41 Nb Niobium 92.906	42 Mo Molybdenum 95.94	43 Tc Technetium (98)	44 Ru Ruthenium 101.07	45 Rh Rhodium 102.906	46 Pd Palladium 106.42	47 Ag Silver 107.868	48 Cd Cadmium 112.4	49 In Indium 114.818	50 Sn Tin 118.710	51 Sb Antimony 121.760	52 Te Tellurium 127.60	53 I Iodine 126.904	54 Xe Xenon 131.29
55 Cs Cesium 132.905	56 Ba Barium 137.327	57 La Lanthanum 138.906	72 Hf Hafnium 178.49	73 Ta Tantalum 180.95	74 W Tungsten 183.84	75 Re Rhenium 186.207	76 Os Osmium 190.23	77 Ir Iridium 192.217	78 Pt Platinum 195.078	79 Au Gold 196.967	80 Hg Mercury 200.59	81 Tl Thallium 204.383	82 Pb Lead 207.2	83 Bi Bismuth 208.980	84 Po Polonium (209)	85 At Astatine (210)	86 Rn Radon (222)
87 Fr Francium (223)	88 Ra Radium (226)	89 Ac Actinium (227)	104 Rf Rutherfordium (261)	105 Db Dubnium (262)	106 Sg Seaborgium (266)	107 Bh Bohrium (264)	108 Hs Hassium (269)	109 Mt Meitnerium (268)	110 Ds Darmstadtium (271)	111 Rg Roentgenium (272)	112 Uub Ununbium (277)						

Lanthanide series:

58 Ce Cerium 140.116	59 Pr Praseodymium 140.908	60 Nd Neodymium 144.24	61 Pm Promethium (145)	62 Sm Samarium 150.36	63 Eu Europium 151.964	64 Gd Gadolinium 157.25	65 Tb Terbium 158.925	66 Dy Dysprosium 162.50	67 Ho Holmium 164.930	68 Er Erbium 167.26	69 Tm Thulium 168.934	70 Yb Ytterbium 173.04	71 Lu Lutetium 174.967

Actinide series:

90 Th Thorium 232.038	91 Pa Protactinium 231.036	92 U Uranium 238.029	93 Np Neptunium (237)	94 Pu Plutonium (244)	95 Am Americium (243)	96 Cm Curium (247)	97 Bk Berkelium (247)	98 Cf Californium (251)	99 Es Einsteinium (252)	100 Fm Fermium (257)	101 Md Mendelevium (258)	102 No Nobelium (259)	103 Lr Lawrencium (262)

Periodic Table

Acknowledgments

Photography

cov, title page © Siegfried Layda/Getty Images; 28 © Getty Images; 37 Earth NASA; moon © Getty Images; 52 © Marilyn Barbone, 2006. Used under license from Shutterstock, Inc.; 55 both © Getty Images; 56 © Daniel Gustavsson, 2006. Used under license from Shutterstock, Inc.; 57 both © Robert F. Balazik, 2006. Used under license from Shutterstock, Inc.; 59 © Getty Images; 70 © Artville: Fast Food; 72 © Getty Images; 82 © Artville/Royalty-Free; 85 © Getty Images; 092 © Stockbyte; 146 © Artville; 156 all © Stockbyte; 165 © Ingram Publishing/Superstock; 180 NASA/Johnson Space Center; 184 both © 2003 The Living Earth Inc.; 189 NASA/Lunar and Planetary Institute; 193 NASA; 206 U. S. Geological Survey ; 207 NASA; 208 NASA Johnson Space Center; 210 NASA/JPL/Caltech; 211 NASA/Hubble Heritage Team (STScl/AURA); 212 © Calvin J. Hamilton; 213, 214 NASA/JPL/Caltech; 215 NASA/Hubble Space Telescope; 217 NASA/JPL/Caltech; 232, 233 David Malin Images/Anglo-Australian Observatory.

Photographs by Sharon Hoogstraten 5, 24, 25, 30, 41, 44, 45, 50, 52, 58, 61, 86, 118, 147, 152, 159, 160

Illustrations

Map by MapQuest.com, Inc. 3
Illustrations by Ampersand Design Group 81, 140
Illustrations by Stephen Baum 191, 222, 228, 229, 231
Illustration by Peter Bull 186
Illustration by Steve Cowden 188
Illustrations by David A. Hardy 180, 200, 201, 203, 209
Illustration by Ian Jackson 157
Illustration by KO Studios 177
Illustrations by Stephen Durke 51, 65, 67, 96, 100, 101, 119, 121-123, 127, 128, 130-133, 141, 142, 149, 167-170, 176, 183
Illustration by Rob Wood/Wood Ronsaville Harlin 190